BEYOND UHURA

UHURA

BEYOND UHURA

STAR TREK® AND OTHER MEMORIES

NICHELLE NICHOLS

BOXTREE

First published in paperback in the UK 1995 by
Boxtree Limited,
Broadwall House,
21 Broadwall,
London, SE1 9PL

First published in hardback in the UK 1995 by
Boxtree Limited

First published in the USA 1994 by
G.P. Putnam's Sons,
200 Madison Avenue, New York, NY 10016

ISBN: 0 7522 0787 3

10 9 8 7 6 5 4 3 2 1

Printed in Finland by WSOY

A CIP Catalogue record for this book is available from the British Library.

ACKNOWLEDGMENTS

This recording of my life experiences was both cathartic and traumatic. I am so thankful to so many for so much it would be impossible to give all their due. However, I especially want to thank the following for their loving inspiration!

I cannot say enough about Patty Romanowski, who unfailingly aided me in bringing this book to fruition with her caring, her understanding, her unerring guidance, her sisterhood, and her extraordinary talent.

My editor, George Coleman, who gently held my hand and guided me during my first journey through the literary maze; my dear friend and legal counsel, Doug Conway, whose initiative and enthusiasm provided the impetus for starting this project, and whose expertise and persistent pursuit brought me to the attention of the publishing world; my literary agents, Russell Galen and Shawna McCarthy, who believed.

Samuel and Lishia Nichols, who gave me life and values and strength; Kyle Johnson, the jewel of my existence, who has kept me going through every stage of my life, and without whom none of this would have mattered; my two beautiful sisters, Marian and Diane, who proofread the drafts, provided vital family and historical inputs, and guided my recording of our history to assure the family tree would not be askew; my other loving siblings, Ruth, Billie, Frank, Sammy, and Tommy, who provided photos, memories, and encouragement.

My dear friends Barnaby Davidson, Lillian Lehman, Faith Lee, Shannon O'Brien, Allen Crowe, Judy Pace Flood, Bruce Weber, Hy Sieger, Richard Arnold, and Florence Butler, who have always given me loving support and generous assistance in my myriad of journeys; Bunny Meechan, whose patience and tolerance of the antics of aR-Way Productions are deeply appreciated, and whose martini wisdom I share and treasure; Vicki Johnson-Campbell, whose friendship and expertise has been ever constant.

My Kwanza Sisters, all of whom I love and who make this world a better place.

Whoopi Goldberg and Dr. Mae Jemison, who have inspired me as much as I inspired them.

Gene Roddenberry, who provided me a place in entertainment history; the crew of the *Enterprise,* who gave life to the lore; and my fans throughout the world, whose love and devotion have been a mainstay in my life.

And finally and ultimately to my friend and partner, Jim Meechan, who rescued me from a life without music and performance, who writes the music that makes me sing once more, who in sixteen years has never forgotten a damned word I ever told him—which made this book possible.

This book is dedicated to
Samuel and Lishia Nichols

Kyle Johnson

Jim Meechan

PROLOGUE

As I sat on the stage and looked out at the hundreds of mourners who filled the Hall of Liberty at Forest Lawn Cemetery, I couldn't help but think that this was exactly how Gene would have wanted it. No coffin, no prayers, no candles.

A devoted humanist, Gene Roddenberry ascribed to the belief that the future rested in our mortal hands, that our answers were to be found among ourselves, here on Earth or beyond. It was only fitting then that Gene should be eulogized by friends who shared his vision, rather than a representative of organized religion, which Gene had long rejected in favor of a philosophy of reason. Gene was many things in his life, but never a hypocrite. In contrast to most services, Gene's memorial was truly a celebration marked by poignant remembrances and laughter, a tribute to the man who had changed and illuminated so many lives. No one ever denied he would be deeply and sadly missed, but certainly, the knowledge that he would remain with us, through the influence of his dreams and the legacy of his creation, comforted each of us.

Every now and then I glanced at the portrait of him that rested on an easel, and, as always, found myself drawn to his eyes. If one wanted proof that the eyes are the windows to the soul, one needed only to look into Gene's. Luminous and blue, they blazed with his insatiable passion for life. Through many struggles, both personal and professional, Gene never looked away. And although his sights were always set on the future, Gene was a man of the moment who believed The Future Is Now. To be with Gene was to be reminded that you were truly, fully alive. I recalled his unflagging energy, his devotion, and his courage as I sang the two songs his wife, Majel, had requested: Paul McCartney's "Yesterday" and my own tribute to him, "Gene," which I co-wrote with Jim Meechan.

The pianist struck the final chords and I somehow finished the lyrics. As I made my way back to my chair, I found it hard to believe Gene was dead. I'd last seen him only a week and a half before. He was sitting in his wheelchair, smiling, looking at a beautiful plaque I'd had made for him. It bore the inscription "To the Great Bird of the Galaxy," and a gold-plated compact disc of the album on which I'd recorded the song "Gene." He regarded it carefully, then asked me to read the lyrics, which were printed on parchment paper, and I began:

"Gene"

Gene, you future visionary.
Gene, you gave me tears and laughter
Gene, you shined the starlight on my dreams.

Gene, a daring flying hero
Gene, you always soar with eagles
Gene, your universe was meant to be.

Gene, Great Bird of my galaxy,
You gave me wings
And you set me free . . .
You dreamed our spatial family.

Gene, your boyish grin's deceiving
Gene, it isn't easy being
Gene, I'm sure you know just what I mean.

Gene, Great Bird of my galaxy,
You gave me wings
And you set me free . . .
You dreamed our Star Trek family.

Gene, you showed us galaxies afar,
You tied our hopes to every star,
We're lucky you are who you are . . .

Our loving . . . Gene.

As I read, I glanced up and saw tears roll unashamedly down his beautiful face. A great lump welled in my throat, and I knew then I was losing this great man whom I had loved for so many years.

Gene wanted to have a picture taken of us with the plaque, but his assistant, Ernie Over, wisely declined. Gene did not look well, and while, on one hand, I understood their concern, I was very disappointed.

I had made this appointment with Gene the previous Friday. I knew he had been suffering from a combination of chronic health problems for several years, including a stroke in 1989 that weakened his right side. The weekend before our meeting, Gene suffered a setback, but Majel had assured me that despite his poor condition, Gene was very much looking forward to seeing me. She said she was sorry that she could not be home when I arrived, though Ernie and Gene's nurse would be there. Over the past several weeks, I'd heard that Gene was not doing well, and, in fact, his assistant had delicately cautioned me to try not to be too shocked by his appearance.

I braced myself. But when I was shown into Gene's den and saw him dressed in light-gray slacks and a light-blue shirt that brought out the blue in his beautiful eyes, I thought he looked wonderful. I don't think I've ever seen him when he didn't strike me as being the same old Gene. His warm, courageous, sometimes flinty spirit always shone, even through his declining health and the plethora of medications it demanded.

He seemed especially touched that I'd brought him a song. Gene always understood and encouraged my love of music; it was ironic, then, that once I came aboard his *Star Trek*, that part of my career was temporarily eclipsed by the character he and I created, Lieutenant Uhura. (Even though Gene made sure that she sang several times on the show, audiences assumed it was someone else's voice dubbed in.) Though we are forever bound through his futuristic creation, that is not where our story began. Nor where it would end.

After a few moments of talking, it became clear that while Gene was in most ways himself, it required all his energy and concentration to sustain that illusion for me. We spoke of personal things we had talked about many, many times before, yet this time Gene seemed to be communicating to me a sense of urgency, as if he needed me to understand that every word he said that day had a new, special meaning.

He held my hand and said, "Nichelle, you know I always loved you. Remember what I told you: Someday you'll tell our story."

I hugged him tightly and wished him well. And then we said goodbye. Gene had been ill for quite a while by then, and though I knew that he was just as likely to live several more years as not, the minute I got back in my car, I broke down in tears. Try as I might, there was no denying that Gene felt his time had come, and he was prepared to surrender to death, not in defeat but acceptance. Later that day he attended a private screening of *Star Trek VI: The Undiscovered Country;* two days later, on Thursday, October 24, he died of a blood clot at his doctor's office. Majel was there beside him, as she had been for so many years.

I took my seat on the hall's stage, with the five eulogists: Whoopi Goldberg, Patrick Stewart, Christopher Knopf, E. Jack Neuman, and Ray Bradbury. Whoopi and Patrick appeared in Gene's second *Star Trek* series, *The Next Generation;* Knopf, Neuman, and Bradbury were fellow writers and good friends. I was the only member of the original series' cast, although several, including George Takei, Walter Koenig, Leonard Nimoy and his wife, Susan, and Grace Lee Whitney, were there to pay their respects.

I was determined not to break down the way I did when I got the call that Gene was gone. That was eight days ago, and, honestly, I didn't think I had any tears left. Sitting next to me, Whoopi took my hand and held me together throughout the service by whispering funny comments to me. At one point when I felt I would break down for sure, she leaned over, pointed to the wide-brimmed black velour hat I wore, and said, "Hold on, girl, you're wearin' that hat!" I suppressed a chuckle and smiled appreciatively. With her help, I made it through the service.

In her eulogy, Whoopi remarked that twenty-five years before she was a "kid from the projects" who saw in *Star Trek*'s Lieutenant Uhura "the only vision [of] Black people in the future." Twenty-five years ago, I was the young actress who played Uhura. Like all of Gene's characters, Uhura embodied humankind's highest values and lived according to principles that he was certain would one day guide all human endeavor. In *Star Trek* Gene created a work of fiction through which he communicated a timely, yet timeless message about humankind's power to shape its future. But most important, he gave that vision to the world: to writers, to enlarge upon; to directors, to dramatize; to actors, to personify and make real; and to audiences, to enjoy, cherish, and incorporate into their own hopes for the future and for humanity.

The man I met in 1963 was not yet the Great Bird of the Galaxy or the father of the Starship *Enterprise.* He was a television writer and producer who was seeking a vehicle for his progressive—some would say provocative—ideals about equality, freedom, and personal accountability. Unlike some people, Gene did not express these thoughts because they were considered "correct" or in vogue, and, in truth, at that time they were not. As he explained in an interview published in *The Humanist* just a few months before he died, "Understand that *Star Trek* is more than just my political philosophy. It is my social philosophy, my racial philosophy, my overview on life and the human condition." You could no more separate who Gene was from what he thought and believed than you could take a slice out of the sky. They were one. That was Gene.

Many people found Gene's tenacious intensity discomforting or intimidating; I did not. Perhaps that is because I grew up in a racially integrated family that was shaped over three generations by the same so-called "futuristic" concepts of racial equality and reason that Gene put forth in *Star Trek.* At various points in time, my parents and grandparents risked their lives for what they believed was right. In countless ways, great and small, they lived their lives in service of dreams and principles most others of their time said were foolish, impossible, or simply wrong. Like Gene and his Starfleet progeny, they were pioneers on a new frontier, going where few had gone before. When I first told Gene my family's story, he listened with rapt attention. I know he felt they were his kindred spirits, too. And they were. While only my mother lived to "meet" Lieutenant Uhura, I know that my white grandfather and my Black grandmother would have recognized her immediately and never once questioned that she, or any of their descendants, would claim their rightful position in the future.

Fittingly, the service ended with a eulogy from Patrick Stewart, who portrayed Captain Picard in the second series. Gene had created the brash, daring Captain Kirk and the highly logical Mr. Spock as his own alter egos over two decades before. It was telling that his last Starship captain embodied both those characters but was an older man, whose passions, though tempered by time, were not diminished. That was Gene, too.

After two bagpipers in kilts played "Amazing Grace," Gene's recorded voice filled the hall, reminding us again that a glorious future awaited humankind if only we would make it so. The service ended, we adjourned outside to witness the final tribute, an Air Force flyby. There we mingled with hundreds of fans who stood in the bright autumn sunshine to pay their respects. At the distant roar of engines, we all turned and scanned the horizon. Against a gorgeous, clear-blue sky, four planes appeared and held formation before one broke away, traveling heavenward, symbolizing Gene, the missing man.

With all due respect to that beautiful tradition, I interpret it differently. To my way of thinking, Gene is not missing; he simply continued his journey to a place that he himself would not presume to name or imagine. Whether it is to a place where no man has gone before, we'll each have to wait and see for ourselves. But I do believe that wherever Gene may be, he will one day see his dream of the future unfold, not on a soundstage but in space, in a time when humankind's propensity for hatred and intolerance will be a memory.

CHAPTER ONE

My father had been waiting ever since he'd read the morning paper's headline: CAPONE GIN MILL SMASHED: SMALL TOWN BUSTS MOBSTER'S BOOZE FACTORY. From the porch of our large white Victorian house, the very one his parents had raised him in, he gazed across the lawn, over the large circular driveway, to the church across the street, and beyond. All day long he'd been waiting, and when the long black limousine crept into sight, he knew his time was near. He caught sight of the tall old alder trees, standing gracefully still and ominously silent, then the sultry magenta and lilac tones of the flowers, burnished golden in the last rays of the sinking sun. All so beautiful and familiar and safe. Until now.

"Get up quietly and go into the house," Samuel Nichols gently ordered his wife, Lishia. "Sit the kids down in the parlor. And don't make a sound."

Without a word she rose, and for once her children, Sam, Jr., and Frank, and her young stepdaughters, Olga, Billie, and Ruth, obeyed without question. As she lowered herself gingerly onto the overstuffed sofa, she placed a pillow protectively over her swollen belly and hugged her youngest child, Frank, close to her. The other four sat about the room, wide-eyed and still, and very much afraid.

From the veranda my father watched as the long black limousine turned into the driveway and glided to a stop. Four white men, all sporting nearly identical black camelhair coats and black fedoras, emerged wordlessly. As three stood staring up at my father, the fourth opened the back door. A fifth man, resplendent in a pearl-gray silk suit, white silk shirt, and tie, stepped out. He might have been a Chicago businessman, but his glistening diamond tie tack and pinkie ring and the threatening yet obsequious manner of his four flanking "assistants" gave him away.

"You Sam Nichols?" he asked.

"Yes. You've come to the right place. I'm Sam Nichols. I'm the mayor of this town."

"Well, you've got a problem, Sam," the stranger said calmly. "Do you know who I am?"

"I know why you're here. I read the newspaper. I just don't know why you've come to me."

"Allow me to introduce myself: My name's Mr. Capone, and I'm here because my brother Al is very displeased with you, Sam."

Not fooled by Capone's calm manner, my father asked, "Can we talk privately in my study? My wife is pregnant, and you've frightened my children. No need for them to witness this, is there?"

"Lead the way," Capone replied, snapping his fingers. Three men followed my father into the house, with two stopping to post themselves in the parlor with my mother and the children, and a third following his boss as my father led him up the stairs. The children watched nervously as Father disappeared up the steps, then turned their gaze to the pair of goons. Mother, hugging the pillow tightly, stared straight ahead.

"Brandy?" Sam Nichols asked.

Capone, fingering his pearl-gray homburg, studied my father for a long time before he accepted.

"As I said," the mayor began, "I know your mill was raided by one of my officers. He was a rookie and thought he'd make a good impression."

"He made a *helluva* impression, Sam," Capone snorted.

"Yes. Well. What I don't understand is why you're here to settle your displeasure with me. I didn't even know your mill was in my township." Capone's skeptical frown told my father he wasn't buying it. "Look," my father added, his rush of words betraying his fear, "I know you're here to kill me. But I ask two things: One, why hold me responsible, and two, whatever you do to me, don't harm my family—please."

My father could see Capone's patience ebb. "For five big ones a week is why you're responsible, Sam." He set down his empty glass with a deliberate, ominous thud. "Nice brandy," he remarked as he rose from his chair and turned. Then, almost as an afterthought, he softly commanded his bodyguard: "Be quick and clean."

Capone had his hand on the doorknob when my father quietly but firmly stated, "I never received a dime of your goddamned money!"

The gangster turned; his bodyguard relaxed his grip inside his jacket.

"Explain, Sam," Capone ordered.

"*You* explain. I should at least know why I'm about to die! Who did you give money to?"

"What are you, *pazzo?*" Capone exploded. "Your police chief, Sam! Two for him and three for you, in cash, on time, every week for the last eighteen months. Now, I've had it with this game. *Arrivederci!*"

My father jumped up from his chair. "I've had it too, dammit!" he shouted. "I never received a dime from that weasel, nor did he ever approach me about it! He knew if he had, I'd have handed him his head on a platter. Besides, this whole meeting would not be taking place, because I'd never have let you put your filthy gin mill anywhere *in* my township! This is a clean, honest town. My father helped found this town, and I'd rather die before I'd help it be corrupted, dammit!"

Capone and his button man exchanged a quick glance, before Capone replied, "You almost did, Sam." Then he continued, "I'll tell you what: We'll check out your story. It checks, we won't be back."

Numbly, my father followed the pair out of the study and down the stairs. The two bodyguards who'd stood guard over the family looked up in bewildered surprise.

Capone crossed the room and patted my mother's shoulder, his hand lingering as he said, "You can relax, sweetheart. Sam's okay. For now."

For the first time, Lishia's eyes met the visitor's, and as she stared through him, she slowly removed the pillow from her stomach to reveal a pearl-handled six-shooter, as cold, black, and shiny as a snake's eye, and fully loaded. The children gasped, and her husband held his breath.

"It's a damn good thing he is," she hissed.

Startled, Capone's goons all drew their guns, but their boss gestured for them to relax. "You had this all this time?" he asked incredulously, careful to remove his hand from her shoulder. "Why didn't you use it?"

"You hadn't done anything," she answered icily. "You were *guests* in my home."

Capone's nervous guffaw crashed the silence. "You're all *pazzo!"* he cried. Trying to muster a look of scorn for his inept bodyguards, he couldn't stop laughing. "Out of here, you goombas!"

Turning at the door, Capone said, "We won't be coming back, Mrs. Nichols." Then to my father: "You've got yourself one helluva little lady there, Mr. Mayor." Capone drove off into the Indian-summer night, never to darken our lives again. As the door swung shut, my parents rushed to embrace their children.

And where was I all of this time? Under the pillow, next to the gun, inside my mother, waiting to be born.

In 1932 there were hundreds of places across this country where a Black man might be murdered and never missed, but Robbins, Illinois, was not one of them. A small town about thirty miles southwest of Chicago, Robbins looks like any of a thousand small towns. Yet Robbins is unique, one of only four all-Black-governed towns in America, a rare social experiment that began in 1892. That year, land speculators, convinced a few years earlier that Chicago would spread beyond its city lines, unloaded cheap plots of land when the predicted boom failed to materialize. A white man named Henry E. Robbins, outraged by racial discrimination, bought up huge tracts, which he then sold for a fair price to Black and racially mixed couples, who otherwise had no hope of ever owning land.

My paternal grandparents, Samuel Gillespie Nichols and Lydia Annie Myers Nichols, came from the same world—the mid-nineteenth-century American South—but their paths were never meant to cross. At least not in a manner that suggested they were equal. Samuel Gillespie was born in 1849 in Natchez, Mississippi, a thriving bastion of the Old South until it was overtaken by the Union midway through the Civil War. His father, my great-grandfather, owned four hundred "head of" slaves, as they called them back then.

My grandmother Lydia Myers was born some years later, in 1862, to a family of ex-slaves. Time has washed from memory stories of how my grandparents met and fell in love. But Lydia and Samuel were married in the South the day after Christmas 1878. Slavery had been abolished—at least legally—for over a decade, yet the power of that unsavory institution endured on both sides of the Mason-Dixon Line. The notion of a white man legally proclaiming his love for a Black woman was unthinkable.

One reason why is that any child born to parents of the different races was automatically regarded as Black. To acknowledge the offspring of such a union in those days—which was usually by rape—would be to grant equality to a child considered Black. The white mother of a Black child lost her social "value," and a Black woman had none to begin with. To elevate either woman by marrying her and therefore recognizing her children as anything other than Black, and thereby inferior, threatened the very foundation of American society, North or South.

Whether my grandparents ran away from their families before or after their wedding, we do not know. Nor is it clear when Samuel S. Gillespie adopted the surname Nichols, although we might assume why. His father, a stalwart Welshman who'd made his fortune on his plantation, was heartbroken over Samuel's choice of a wife and the "disgrace" it cast upon the whole family. Infuriated by his heir's independence and rebellion, he not only disinherited him but dispatched a posse to return his son—against his will—to his "rightful" place.

A man of unshakable resolve and clear moral vision, my grandfather declared, "Nobody is going to tell *me* who to love and how I should live my life! Nobody is going to dictate that to me—no society, no family." As far as anyone knows, Samuel never spoke to his father again.

Samuel and Lydia Nichols loved each other passionately. You could not have found two people who looked less alike than my grandparents: Samuel with his ruddy white complexion, bright red hair, and green eyes; and Lydia, whose Spanish, Moorish, and African heritage glowed through her chocolate-brown skin and waist-length ebony hair. By adopting a new name and severing ties with his family, my grandfather started a new family—

his own family—one shaped by the forces of love rather than social convention.

Their first two children, my Aunt Blanche and Uncle Frank, were both born in Natchez, the first of a new breed. They moved north before the birth of their third child, my father, Samuel Earl Nichols, Sr., which came twelve years after Frank's birth.

My father was the baby of the family in every way. He was a breathtakingly beautiful little boy, and he basked in the love and attention of his doting and loving parents. Perhaps because he was an unexpected arrival, he gave them a renewed lease on life. With their older children almost grown and the fear of my great-grandfather's wrath long behind them, Samuel and Lydia could relax a little, and they delighted in their baby son.

While prejudice against Blacks might have been less prevalent up North (and that is debatable), the cultural taboo against interracial marriages and children was no less vehement. Finding a decent place to raise his family proved next to impossible, even for Sam G. Nichols. To Samuel and Lydia Nichols, and hundreds of other people, this new community offered a safe haven, a chance to live a normal life and raise their children free of the fear, the finger-pointing, and the disapproving glares interracial families knew too well.

There in Robbins, Samuel Nichols lived out the rest of his days with his beloved Lydia, whom he affectionately called "Lit," raising their three children, and never looking back.

Sometime around the turn of the century an attorney representing Samuel's father, my great-grandfather, arrived in Robbins to tell him that his father, James Gillespie, was dying and wished to reinstate him in his will. Although my grandparents were not poor, they weighed whether or not they were correct to deprive their children of their rightful inheritance. When Samuel asked Lydia to accompany him back South, she replied, "No, you must go see your father."

The attorney then blurted out, "Yes, that would not be wise. After all, your father wants to see *you* so he can forgive you."

Samuel's eyes flashed with rage. "Are those your words or his words?"

"My exact instructions," the attorney replied, "were: 'Tell my son I love him and I'm willing to forgive him for his mistake and reinstate him in my will.' " Naturally, the attorney did not come right out and say, "Don't bring along your Black wife or your mixed children"; he didn't have to. It was understood: They were definitely not welcome.

"Is that what my father said?" Samuel asked.

"Well, yes!" the attorney answered brightly. "What a wonderful man your father is! He is dying and wants to forgive you!"

"You go back and tell that old white man to die and go to hell," my grandfather growled. "He has nothing to forgive me *for.*" With that, Samuel G. forsook his fortune—again—to stand by his Lydia and their children.

To this day, none of us knows whether or not James Gillespie did reinstate my grandfather and his heirs in his will, although we certainly have the genealogical information we need to find out and to lay claim to his fortune as direct descendants. My grandfather remained steadfast in his rejection of the money, but he made it clear that his children, grandchildren, or great-grandchildren were welcome to pursue the issue if they so desired. The symbolism of collecting even a portion of a fortune earned from slavery—and donating it to the civil-rights movement—was not lost on any of us. Out of respect and in tribute to my grandfather, however, we never did. If living without his father's money was good enough for Grampa, it was good enough for us.

Their youthful passion tempered by years of struggle and joy, Lydia and Sam remained deeply in love. Before they died, Lydia and Samuel Nichols had been married almost half a century, seen two of their children marry, and had held six grandchildren. In their later years, they even had come to look like each other. Except, of course, for their skin colors. They even had a black-and-white dog, Patches. Although they were gone by the time I was born, their love for each other, their commitment to what they believed was right, and their refusal to compromise those beliefs informed and shaped us all.

My father attended Howard University, in Washington, D.C., and became a chemist. He was just over twenty when he married his first wife, Catherine Romena Minnie Cordoza, or Minnie, in 1914. Over the next six years, they had three daughters, my half sisters Ruth, Olga, and Thelma (whom we called Billie), but by 1924 they had divorced, and my father found himself raising three girls alone in Robbins. Every morning my father made the long drive to the North Side of Chicago, where he worked for Hydrox Chemical Company. He invented numerous cold creams and colognes; of course, the company he worked for held the patents. Back in Robbins, he became active in town government, first as a town magistrate and then as mayor. He had a good job, a respected position in his community, and his three lovely daughters. And the last thing he was looking for was a wife.

My mother, Lishia Mae Parks, was born in Oklahoma City in 1906. From the day of my mother's birth she was the object of curiosity and suspicion, since she had come into the world with a caul, or "veil," over her face. Neighbors whispered this was a sign that Lishia Mae Parks possessed unusual psychic powers, the ability to see the future, to know the unknown, which she did. This, coupled with her great beauty (she was half Cherokee Indian and half African) and extraordinary intelligence, marked my mother as being different from her neighbors, and for this, she was sometimes ostracized.

My mother was still a baby when her father died at age thirty-five, leaving her and her grieving mother to make their way. Like most women of her time, my maternal grandmother was ill prepared to earn a living for herself and her daughter, and on Thanksgiving Day, 1907, she married a William Humphries. Whether this marriage was born of love or economic necessity, I cannot say. But my mother spoke gravely of her stepfather being cold and cruel, jealously dismissing her accomplishments and taunting her: "Oh, you think you're so smart, don't you now, Missy?" Even with his presence, the family's economic struggles continued.

Knowing my mother as I did, it's sometimes difficult to imagine her ignored and psychologically tormented by parents who believed that children should be seen and not heard, who lacked the education to guide or encourage her. Unlike most children, whose self-esteem would have been decimated, Lishia always held her own and made her way in life.

When my mother was nineteen, she gave birth to her first child, Eric. It's a testament to her indomitable will that even with a young son, she refused to be held back. Because of her outstanding academic performance, she'd received a series of scholarships and attended the finest schools in the South. Even after Eric was born, she was determined to complete her college education and, she hoped, go on to law school.

Unfortunately, her first marriage was short-lived, and in her early twenties she found herself living in Chicago with her Aunt "Hun" and her two daughters. Mother went to work as an upstairs maid for a wealthy white family on Chicago's North Side. One day the lady of the house happened to find my mother and her husband in the kitchen discussing literature and philosophy. In Latin!

It seems that until the moment they met, both of my parents were resigned to raising their respective children alone. My father, still devastated by his first wife's desertion, had deftly eluded all of his well-meaning friends' and family members' attempts to find him a new wife. For over five years he'd been raising his daughters, holding down his job, and helping manage the town of Robbins. As far as my father was concerned, he was doing quite well, thank you. Meanwhile, my mother, like many women fresh from a divorce with a child to support, simply could not be bothered.

In the course of conversation, a friend of my father's mentioned to my mother's Aunt Hun that he knew a wonderful divorced father of three girls, who needed to get out and see people. To which my aunt replied that she had a niece who did nothing but work and take care of her son.

Once Aunt Hun laid eyes on my father—well-spoken, dignified, handsome, impeccably dressed—she roused my mother (who had gone to sleep saying she didn't want to meet anyone). "Now, Lishia Mae, you listen to me: I've set this up, and he just wants to take you out to a nightclub. Now you won't come out, and I'm so embarrassed, and the very least you can do, Lishia—"

"Okay, okay!" Mother replied. Telling the story years later, she admitted to me, "Something told me, 'No matter how much you don't want to do this, just get up and do it.' "

When my mother emerged, her hair was combed to the side so that it fell in finger waves seductively over one eye. A beautiful bracelet encircled her upper arm, and in her dress—a black gown of the finest georgette, with a hemline cut on the bias and large red roses gracing her hips—she appeared to her reluctant escort an incredible vision.

"When she stepped through the door," my father remembered, "my heart fell on the ground, and I never picked it up again." A few months later they were married.

Mom was a newcomer to the small, closed community

of Robbins, many members of which had drawn sides in the wake of my father's divorce or perhaps favored another woman he had been seeing. My father was very light-skinned, and my mother's skin was the color of bittersweet chocolate. The same prejudices that the white establishment used to keep Black people down found voice within the Black community as well. In marrying my father, my mother encountered another, more subtle form of prejudice because she was so dark. Even in an interracial town like Robbins, fewer white Negro men married dark women than light women married dark men. People marveled over the fact that Mayor Samuel Nichols, who had the pick of the crop—and "pick of the crop" was defined as light, like his ex-wife—would marry a woman so dark. At the time, many Blacks bought into the racist saying, "White, you're all right; yellow, you mellow; brown, stick around; black, get back." In those days, it was not uncommon for an accomplished Black man to marry a light-skinned woman, for she was a status symbol.

As I've lived and traveled the world, I've learned that every racial or ethnic group has its own peculiar list of desirable physical qualities, and Blacks are no exception. Interestingly, my father—who stood to benefit from this twisted "colorism"—most adamantly rejected it. Earlier in this century, among some higher-class and educated "Negroes" there existed what were called "blue-vein clubs," closed, secret societies of Blacks with skin light enough to reveal the blueness of their veins. While attending Howard University, my father was offered membership in one, which he angrily rejected.

One of the most insidiously cruel aspects of racism is how it poisons not only those who practice it, but its victims as well. It seems to make no sense, until you realize that many Blacks were simply reflecting what they knew firsthand: The lighter you were, the straighter your hair, the easier your way through the world.

Surely, given my father's lofty position in his community, however disapproval over their marriage was expressed, it was done subtly. Still it's impossible to diminish the pain and humiliation Mother surely felt, yet, paradoxically, I learned many years later that she herself was not immune to these very same beliefs. For all her intelligence, my mother passed it on to her children, who, blessedly, rejected it.

A family photo taken just a few years before my birth would reveal my father, gorgeously dressed, looking every bit like a well-off white man; his three teenage daughters—Ruth and Billie white as ivory with flaming-red hair, and Olga, olive-skinned with coal-black hair; his beautiful, young Cherokee-African wife, and their two almost-white baby boys. That single image would reveal all that we Nichols children were, where we had come from, and what we were made of.

Then there were the qualities you could not see: Mother's fierce determination and stubborn independence, forged from poverty and ostracism, and Father's patience, confidence, and love. In some ways, Mother and Father were almost diametrically opposed. Once they threw in their lots together, though, nothing of my parents' wisdom, knowledge, or experience would be wasted or forgotten, and all of it—for better or worse—formed the rich tapestry on which our lives were woven.

CHAPTER TWO

I suppose I had a wonderful childhood, except for the fact that I never wanted to *be* a child and I never truly felt *like* a child. From as far back as I can remember (and I can recall precise details of events that occurred when I was only a few months old), I was not your typical kid. For example, even before I could walk, I could sing. Until the day he died, my father delighted in telling how, when I was a baby, he would walk his baby Grace (I was named after his Great Aunt Graciella from Seville, Spain) to sleep by singing as he strolled up and down our long, dark hallway. Daddy swore that when he opened the icebox to get my baby bottle, and the light inside went on, as if on cue, I'd break into "Let Me Entertain You" or "There's No Business Like Show Business." (Now, it would be years before I noticed that each time he told the story, the song title changed, and that in most cases he had me singing the latest showbiz hit, a tune that hadn't even been written then.)

By the time I was five, my destiny appeared set, at least as far as I was concerned: I would be on stage. My mother told me that after only a couple of reads, I could memorize reams of poetry, which I would not merely recite but *dramatize* with great flair. Of course, my first love was singing, and my "concerts" were anything but impromptu. If you wanted to see my show, you had to sit down and be quiet. As I grew older, I developed a diverse repertoire (which was subject to change, depending on my latest fixation), and designed an act that opened with a slow torch song, followed by something up-tempo, with maybe a skit or two I'd written and rehearsed to perfection. Naturally, I always saved the best for last, and when it was over, I'd take my bow, blow kisses, and walk off to wait for the requisite applause to peak before I returned for my encore. But no second encore: Even then I knew to always leave them begging for more.

We had moved to Chicago when I was a toddler. When I was about seven, I spent a month or so in the hospital with a condition they eventually diagnosed as a dietary deficiency. I was a skinny little thing who skipped meals so I'd have more time to play, sing, and dance. I'd always hated milk and orange juice, and I guess with the brutal Chicago winters, I became anemic. The doctor prescribed a special iron tonic, lots of fruits and vegetables, and exercise to rebuild my muscles. My parents enrolled me in ballet lessons, and so began my love of dance.

My true love was ballet, and my first ballet teacher was Miss Virginia Reilly, a large, green-eyed blonde African-American woman. She taught at the Sammy Dyer School of Dancing, a school founded in 1931 by Sammy Dyer, a then well-known professional dancer. The entire class was composed of Black children, which was somewhat unusual at the time. Black mothers and fathers who wanted their children to be well-rounded would ensure they studied tap, acrobatics, ballet, and modern dance, but to encourage a Black child toward a career in ballet was considered a foolhardy indulgence. After all, as we were so often reminded, there simply were *no* Black ballet dancers. What was the point?

In her long, flowing skirt, sweater, and ballet shoes, statuesque Miss Virginia was the personification of grace, in full command of the class. She was a brilliant teacher, and you either loved her or hated her—sometimes both at once. Ballet came so naturally to me that by the time I was nine, I had advanced en pointe. Miss Virginia saw something special in me, and so she drove and pushed me to excel. From the first moment, I fell fully, completely under ballet's spell.

After only a few months of dance lessons, I'd regained my strength and before too long, actually became quite athletic. Sitting under Mother's window, making mud pies, skipping rope, and playing dolls with the neighborhood girls was not my idea of fun. I never accepted the prevailing notion that girls were supposed to stay close to home and learn to cook and clean. It was so unfair, it made me furious. I knew I belonged out there kicking ass with my older brothers, Sammy and Frank. This was one source of contention between my mother and me in my early years.

Nearly nine years elapsed between me and my next youngest sister, Marian, who was born in 1941. Although I also had a younger brother, Tommy (born in 1938), in my mind I remained my father's baby and the apple of his eye. I told him how lonely it was for me when Sammy and Frank went out with their friends, and so he told them, "You have to take your sister with you."

This was probably the worst torture a parent could inflict on two boys just entering their teens, and they and their friends made sure I didn't have an easy time. After we all met up together someplace, I submitted to my daily "initiation rites" as the boys would take turns punching me in the shoulder. I had to pay my dues, so the deal was that if I screamed or cried, I couldn't go with them. Each day I stood, and, true to my honor, never let out a sound; not a whimper, not a tear. Nobody was going to make me go home. Or cry.

Desperate not to give the boys a reason to exclude me, I did everything required—climbing trees, swinging from branches—as well as any of them. Thanks to ballet, I was more agile than most of them. You could say I was a tomboy; I thought I was a normal girl. Come four-thirty every afternoon, though, I'd have to get cleaned up for dinner, put on a clean frilly dress, and sit on the stoop with the other little girls and wait for the ice-cream truck.

One day the leader of our pack decided that we would all jump off a second-story landing. I agreed to go along, knowing that I shouldn't do it, but not really afraid of anything except the triumphant smirks I knew they would be wearing if I backed out. First one agile boy jumped and landed safely, then my brother Frank. An inviting soft emerald patch of grass lay right under the landing, and as I looked down, I figured I had to pitch myself ever so slightly forward in order to reach it. Gathered under the landing, the boys stood quietly and looked up at me. Unbeknownst to me, however, Mother happened to look out our first-floor window, and sensing something wrong, ran out into the yard. In the exact instant I let go and felt myself hurtling toward the ground, my mother's horrified scream—"Gra-a-a-ce!!!"—shattered my concentration. I hit the ground, driving my knee into my lip and splitting it wide open. A searing pain cut through me, and blood ran all over my bare legs, but did I let on I was hurt? Hell, no. I was too damn mad.

Furious and frightened, Mother promptly grounded my brothers and me for a whole week. As she hustled us back into our apartment, I choked back my tears and said, "Mother, you just don't understand!"

And, truth be told, Mother didn't really understand me at all. As I grew older, I came to realize that she knew me better than I knew myself. But throughout my younger years, I carried the burden of believing she did not really love me; or at least if she did, she didn't particularly like me. It would be years before I learned why. Learning to know and truly understand my mother would become, for me, the work of a lifetime.

Since I was sure my mother hated *me,* I constantly baited her. One day when I was eleven or twelve, Mother was bawling me out about something, when suddenly I blurted out, "Mom, was that Dr. Winston who stuck me in my arm?"

She wasn't sure what I was referring to, so I proceeded to tell her the story of when I was vaccinated for smallpox: "And we had that lightbulb—the same lightbulb we have in the hallway here—and you were holding me, and Frank was pulling on my blanket, fussing at you to pick him up. And I saw this brown man. Was that Dr. Winston who hurt me?"

"What are you talking about?" Mother asked impatiently.

"He did. He hurt me. He was standing there, and it wasn't my daddy, because he was brown. And he was standing there talking and smiling at you, and all of a sudden he hurt me, and I screamed bloody murder."

By then Mother had stopped stirring soup and was staring at me as if she'd never seen me before. "You can't remember that. You were only six or seven months old!" she exclaimed.

"Frank kept pulling on my blanket," I continued, "for you to pick him up."

" 'Put that little *woming* down and pick me up.' That was his word for you," Mother said slowly in amazement.

"And then I was screaming."

"Yes, and I knew you weren't hurt."

"No! I was furious. You were my protector, my mother. I decided then: I'll never trust you again."

"Yes," Mother said, smiling, "and you *didn't*. That was the beginning of it."

At the time, I was too young to see the bittersweet humor in what Mother told me that day. But she was right.

That was the beginning.

In March 1944 Mother gave birth to her sixth and last child, Diane. Given my mother's intelligence and strength, it would be too simple to say that she "settled" for motherhood, because it was much more complicated than that. It was not as if she could suddenly ignore her brilliance or her psychic powers and experiences, which continued throughout her life. Later Mother told me that she had wearied of her psychic dreams and visions, because more often than not the news they portended was disturbing. If she dreamed of fish jumping, someone in the family was pregnant. If the fish she saw was dead, a miscarriage soon followed. Mother endured the pain of seeing one of her stepdaughters, newly married, deeply in love, and basking in the early glow of her pregnancy, all the while knowing the young woman would lose the baby. Painfully, that's exactly what happened.

One day she was scrubbing the kitchen floor, which is one chore she *never* did. My father always said there were enough males in the house that Mother should never have to scrub or vacuum a floor. Yet for some reason she could not articulate, she was down on that floor on her hands and knees, scrubbing like mad, when she suddenly froze. In her mind she saw a long funeral procession and gasped, "My God! A funeral like that could only be for Reverend Clarence H. Cobb," a prominent, well-loved Chicago minister. A second later, jolted back to reality, she was asking herself what she was doing down there on the floor.

When my father came home that evening, she told him what she'd seen, and two days later Reverend Cobb, indeed died. He was important enough in the community that his funeral was televised, and as we watched, Mother predicted precisely what we would see as the long funeral procession rolled slowly down the street and exactly where the hearse would turn.

"It is a gift that you have, and you can develop it for great good," my father told her. Mother tried seeing it that way, but it took a lot out of her. Every major event that would occur in my life, my mother predicted. Later she would confide that all of her life she'd begged God to please take this "gift" away. Other times, perhaps thinking back on those instances when her ability had been a force of good, she wondered if denying this strange gift had been the right thing to do.

These characteristics of hers were intricately bound and in the end they would not be denied. But during the years we were growing up, Mother expended tremendous energy suppressing her psychic abilities, her ambition, her will. Although it was not so, my father often stated that, intellectually speaking, he could not hold a candle to my mother. He admired her, loved her, and respected her. Yet, oddly, he was extremely possessive of her, jealous, and terrified of losing her. And so, he held her back. What might she have become had she enjoyed the encouragement of her loving husband?

My mother's reserve—what I thought of then as her coldness—derived partly from her own less than loving upbringing. My father, on the other hand, had the confidence that comes from being warmly hugged and unreservedly loved, and so he loved us the only way he knew how. He instilled in each of us that we were special. Once, to explain to me the importance and inherent value of things that are different, he brought home a book illustrated with pictures of snowflakes. "See," he said, pointing to the starry white configurations, "each is different, yet each is uniquely perfect."

Despite the hardships and inequities my parents endured as Blacks, they were never bitter. It never occurred to either of my parents to feel inferior to anyone for any reason. My father taught us, "You are not better than anyone else. But there is no one better than you." Both my parents—and in my father's case, his parents as well—had defied the odds and bucked the system. They saw no reason why we could not become whatever we wanted.

Both he and Mother revered education and the arts, so our home was filled with books of every type, from Shakespeare and the classics to contemporary poetry and novels, and art. And there was music. Our living room always contained a piano, and the spacious South Side apartment reflected each child's passions: my brother Samuel's paints and canvases, Frank's violin and sheet music, my ballet slippers and scripts. No matter what our interests, my parents always made sure we had whatever we needed to excel. We were far from rich, but everything my mother and father had went into their children's futures. There was no question that we would each go to college. Yet my parents were very progressive, believing that you could learn just as much if you spent that time perfecting your particular talent, be it music, dance, painting, fashion, architectural design, or business. In our house it was understood that whatever occupation you chose was not important: You were.

My parents' progressive attitudes extended to religion as well. Every Sunday morning all of the children were obligated to attend church; sometimes it was a Baptist church, sometimes a Methodist church. We might attend Catholic services with one of our friends. To my spiritual but independent parents, the denomination didn't matter as much as the fact that you were in God's house. As my father often said, "God and church should be about loving and living with all people. You are going to pay your respects and tithe your time to God, not to the minister or the priest. It's there for you to set aside an hour to celebrate God and life, to give thanks for who you are and where you are. It doesn't matter what the philosophy of that particular church is."

We were taught that our faith came from within, that our talents were gifts to be cherished and respected. In this, as in almost everything else, my parents' purpose was to teach us that God blessed us with the power to think for ourselves, to ask questions, and to have the courage of our beliefs. The closest I came to finding a formal religion that coincided with my spiritual beliefs is the Church of Religious Science, or Science of Mind, to which I've belonged for some years.

Growing into adolescence I pursued and developed my love of singing and performing. In addition to appearing in school plays and recitals, I began creating and "directing" productions of neighborhood children. But, as I've said, my true passion then was the ballet. From the time I was twelve, I was sure I could be a professional ballerina. By the time I was fourteen, Miss Virginia told my parents that she had taken me as far as she could. In her opinion, my talent demanded more than the twice-weekly classes Sammy Dyer's school offered.

Sadie Bruce's Ballet School, another fine Chicago school renowned for its excellent ballet training, was one place I might have studied. At that time, the local Chicago papers would write up both schools' dance recitals, and for a while there an unofficial rivalry developed between me, Sammy Dyer's star pupil, and Sadie Bruce's top dancer, Frances Taylor. Frances went on to dance professionally all over Europe, and she later married Miles Davis. Miss Bruce's course included moving her best dancers to the country for three rigorous months of training each summer. It was obviously more intensive, but both schools were held in the highest regard, so much so that leading choreographers regularly visited each, searching for new, young dancers to join their troupes. That is how I first met the great Katherine Dunham.

Miss Dunham, as any aficionado of the dance knows, was then the leading Black choreographer and a great star. A native of Chicago, she had studied the ballet, but also researched the African roots of dance both in America and throughout the West Indies and Africa. Her company's 1940 performances in New York City, where she introduced her revolutionary mix of primitive dance forms, were a milestone in the history of modern dance.

Needless to say, for a twelve-year-old aspiring dancer, Katherine Dunham was a living legend, so we were all thrilled when we learned that we would be dancing for her. The day Miss Dunham came to our school was, I thought then, the greatest day of my life. Many of us took solo turns. For mine, I performed a ballet in addition to some exotic free-form dancing. Waiting to hear my name called, I felt as if I were going to die. You stand there wondering, *How will I begin? How will I end?* But once the music begins, the dance takes you over. It becomes your story, your song. It becomes you, and you are transported.

After I finished, Miss Dunham told Mr. Dyer that my talent was exceptional, and she promised to keep in touch with him and my parents, which, over the coming years, she did. For a young dancer, there was no greater compliment.

Still, my sights were set on the ballet, and so my father visited the Chicago Ballet Academy, where he met the ballet master and explained my situation. The ballet master made an appointment for my father to bring me down for an audition, promising that if I passed, I would be admitted. When Daddy told me about the meeting, I was ecstatic, and with great hope we traveled downtown on the big day.

The academy itself was quite impressive, but nothing compared to the ballet master, an older, imperious Russian man whose name I can't remember except to say that it sounded like "Karishkov." To me, however, he was simply "the Mad Russian." He took one look at my white-skinned father, then one look at me, and bellowed, "I thought you said the appointment was for *your* daughter! We don't take Black students. Black people cannot dance the ballet. No one is better at jazz and tap," he allowed, perhaps thinking he was being kind, "but the ballet? Never!"

"This is my daughter," my father replied tightly. I sensed in his voice a mix of humiliation and fury bordering on violence. "We have an appointment for you to see her dance," he stated in a firm, measured tone. "We are here."

It broke my heart to see my father try to control and hide his anger, his hurt, and his embarrassment. "Professor Karishkov" must have sensed my father's heat, for he wisely relented. "Of course, I will see your daughter dance, Mr. Nichols," he replied, then showed me where to change. As I put on my toe shoes and leotard in the dressing room, hot tears burned my cheeks. I would dance, all right, but for my father, not the ballet master. When I was finished, it would be the ballet master, I vowed, who would be humiliated, not Daddy.

With each command the ballet master barked, I danced—"*Assemblé! Grand jeté! Plié! Port de bras! Pirouette!*"—executing each movement with perfection and grace. The audition continued a little longer than necessary, as the ballet master looked for something wrong in my form. By the time we were done, I felt my muscles quivering from exhaustion, but I never let on. By then I didn't even care if I got into the academy. The only reason I danced that day was for my father, and for the look of pride in his eyes.

When we finished, my father was just about to triumphantly tell "Karishkov" where he could go with his academy, when the ballet master began speaking.

"Mr. Nichols, I should be honored to accept your

daughter in our ballet school," he said softly. I noticed a tear welling up in his eye. "If she works very hard, in two, three years, she will be ready for any corps de ballet in the world."

Before we went home, Daddy and I stopped at a restaurant, where we celebrated with ice-cream sundaes, gleefully laughing with pride and relief. For the next two years I worked tirelessly to master the Mad Russian's grueling course. But never once did I regret being there or getting the chance to prove to him that I could dance—could even excel in—the ballet.

Looking for a studio where I could practice between courses, my father discovered a dance studio not far from our house owned by a woman named Carmencita Romero. I usually practiced there in the afternoon, but one day I was rehearsing in the evening. I became entranced by the sound of drums coming from the large rehearsal room across the hall. I found Carmencita there teaching an Afro-Cuban dance to a group of twenty or more young men and women. I was spellbound by their bodies, their movement, their sensuality. It was very erotic and primitive. Noticing me, Carmencita invited me to come and join in as a guest, introducing me as "a young ballerina."

I hesitantly took a place, feeling almost hypnotically drawn to this new dance. I was mesmerized and I vowed I'd master this new and ancient art, too.

Each day after school for the next two years, I pirouetted en pointe by day for the Mad Russian at his academy, then jumped and whirled barefoot at night for Carmencita Romero. My dear Mad Russian would have been scandalized to learn that his Black ballerina had become Carmencita Romero's top Afro-Cuban dancer. My introduction to Afro-Cuban and primitive dance "saved" me from the life of the ballet, which, while glorious, is torturous. My sights were set on show business. I knew opportunity would knock, but I never imagined so soon.

One day I came home from school, and Mother met me at the door, saying, "Hurry, dear, come in! Your dance teacher, Carmencita Romero, just called, and you have to get down to the Sherman House Hotel. You have an audition."

Oh, my God! I thought, *the Sherman House Hotel.* In a city of luxurious hotel supper clubs and nightspots, the Sherman House was one of the finest, regularly featuring big-name entertainment and an audience filled with what back then we called "swells": the rich, the famous, the notorious.

My dance teacher hadn't offered Mother too many specifics but warned, "For God's sake, Mrs. Nichols, tell her to look as old as she can. I didn't tell them she was just fourteen."

In less than an hour, the transformation was nearly complete. Hastily I shed my much beloved high school couture—tight cashmere sweater, long, straight, plaid skirt, bobby sox, and loafers—for something more sophisticated. Mother pulled my long black hair up, tied it in a ribbon, and arranged big curls on top and helped me put on makeup, including the heretofore forbidden eye shadow. "I just don't know what you're going to wear," she said worriedly as she rummaged through my closet.

"I do, Mom: my salmon suit," I replied. It was a gorgeous, form-fitting outfit my older sister Ruth had given me which Mother had deemed too "sophisticated" for my age. I put it on, and it was perfect. Then we had to pick out shoes. When I produced a pair of what we used to call "whore shoes" that Joan Crawford made famous in her films—open-toed black platforms that laced up the ankle—she cried, "No! You will break your neck in those!"

"Mother," I replied, "I put them on every night and practice walking in them after you guys go to bed."

"My goodness," she said, shaking her head and smiling.

As I left the house, Mom took one last look. How I wish I had a picture of myself that day. I'd come in the house a little girl and walked out a woman.

It was the first time I ever traveled downtown by myself. I wasn't nervous or afraid, just excited. When I got to the hotel, Carmencita Romero introduced me to "the Great Boniface," as he was affectionately known, Mr. Ernest Byfield, a legendary restaurateur who owned and ran the Sherman House Hotel for many years and became famous for, among other things, inventing the club sandwich. To give you an idea of how great a job Mother and I had done transforming me, at first Carmencita did not even recognize me. When Mr. Byfield asked me my age, I answered, "Eighteen" with a perfectly straight face.

The show being cast was a lavish revue in which a group of about twenty talented young performers portrayed the great acts that had graced the stage of the Sherman House's famous supper club College Inn stage in the twenties: Fred and Adele Astaire, Duke Ellington, Al Jolson, Vernon and Irene Castle, Irving Berlin, Helen Morgan, Ben Bernie, and others. Miss Romero with the four of us—two girls and two dynamic Black male dancers—re-created the historic appearance by none other than Katherine Dunham and her troupe.

I danced and sang, and by the end of my audition I had the job. I rode the elevated train back home that evening, now not only a woman, but a professional performer. From that moment on, I knew I would not have to wait for "someday." Destiny had found me, and I embraced it. I was ready to receive.

CHAPTER THREE

As far as introductions to the world of show business go, mine could not have been better: I felt as though I'd started at the top. Of course, my being underage did not remain a secret for long, and so my mother or father had to accompany me to each performance. We were given a small suite in the hotel, where we could sleep over, which we did whenever a snowstorm struck or my father was too tired to make the drive home.

Waking up in the morning to room service and breakfast in bed was a special treat. Working at the Sherman House Hotel had its other perks, too. Walking through the kitchen, you'd see huge bowls brimming with the finest caviar money could buy, and champagne flowed like water there. After each week's last performance, I was allowed my one little glass of champagne and all the caviar I wanted. Sitting in our suite after the show, Mother and I enjoying our sumptuous "snacks," I knew this was the life for me. We also enjoyed stopping afterward at a little restaurant a block away from our house called the Welcome

Inn. We'd walk in and declare: "From the College Inn to the Welcome Inn!" There was no champagne or caviar here, but the best hamburgers, chili, and barbecue in the world.

So there I was—young performer by night, Englewood High School sophomore by day. I was one of four of Carmencita's "Katherine Dunham Dancers" in the show, and the baby. After I had been in the show a little over a year, Katherine Dunham returned to Chicago and asked my parents if I could join her troupe and move to New York City to study with her. In my heart, I feared my parents would say no, and they did. Of course, I added this to the long list of grievances against my mother that I had compiled. Not long afterward, when I read in the newspaper that my rival Frances Taylor got the spot, I was devastated. Yet, I wondered, what other possibilities were waiting out there for me?

Among the many stars who came to see our show were the cast members of *Lend an Ear,* a recent Broadway hit then playing in Chicago on tour. My first real beau was a young, blond Adonis and one of the show's stars, Ray Kyle. Every night after work he met me at the Sherman House and walked me to the train station, with my parents following behind. Ours was a sweet, brief romance that went nowhere, but years later I named my son Kyle after Ray.

Ray and other members of his cast took me under their wing. And it was through them that I got the opportunity to meet the great Ruth St. Denis, another pioneer of modern dance, in her elegant hotel suite. Miss St. Denis was first known for her elaborate Orient-inspired works, which she began staging in 1906. With her husband, dancer Ted Shawn, she founded the Denishawn schools in 1920, and continued to create rich, exotic works. Among those who studied and danced with the Denishawn group were several important choreographers, including Martha Graham.

By the time we met, she was around seventy years of age, yet she retained a dancer's exquisite carriage. This was a special day for me, and she was so gracious as she greeted me warmly and poured tea.

"Yes," she said, "I can see, you are a dancer." Then she stood up and took my hands in hers. "Follow me," she commanded as we began to move gracefully, and I followed her lead. We "danced," and I felt her incredible grace and power. "Oh, yes," she remarked as our arms moved in slow, rhythmic arcs through the air, "you have beautiful hands. You have the hands of a dancer."

Working at the College Inn, I was fortunate and honored to meet so many great performers, including Lena Horne, Sarah Vaughan, Peggy Lee, Stan Kenton, Mel Tormé, Ella Fitzgerald, and so many other notables. But for a young lady with dreams of the stage, there was no greater, more magnificent idol than the *grande dame des grandes dames,* Josephine Baker. Mr. Byfield knew her, and when she appeared at the Chicago Theatre (one of her countless "farewell tours") he kindly arranged for me to meet her. Anytime Josephine Baker came to town, my parents always took me to see her. With the passage of time, her legend has grown unabated, but everything about her—her Amazonian height, her pet leopard, her penchant for outspokenness and scandal, and her almost perfect command of the French language—was larger than life to begin with.

She swept onstage that night with her long, long black hair pulled up two feet high then cascading down in an incredible "ponytail," looking as if she'd been poured into a tight white jeweled gown that flared dramatically from the knees to the floor. Almost nonchalantly she dragged behind her an enormous white, diamond-studded ermine cape. The audience gasped, then began applauding wildly. When she began singing in that distinctive, odd, high-pitched, quavering voice, everyone was riveted. Her appeal was as enigmatic as she, and as she took her last bows, I began to quiver at the thought of meeting her.

Mother and I were shown to her dressing room, where she sat, wrapped in a silk robe, amid zillions of flowers. Though still sweating from her performance, she was so charming, so beautiful, so French, so Josephine! From the minute she exclaimed, "My darling! Ooh la la, you're such a beauty," I was speechless. In fact, I don't think I uttered a single word; she did all the talking in her high, throaty sweet French accent. As we were leaving, she said again, "How beautiful you are! You are *très magnifique*. She is so beautiful! And look at Mama! Such *je ne sais quoi, non?*" Mother and I floated out of there like a couple of intoxicated butterflies.

Without question, however, the highlight of my nights at the College Inn was meeting the great Duke Ellington. We had just come off the stage after our last number, and someone told me that Mr. Ellington had requested that I come to his table. Mother discreetly made sure that Carmencita Romero and the three other dancers in our troupe were invited to the table as well.

He was, in a word, magnificent: tall and arrestingly handsome, with penetrating eyes. As he took your hand or turned to face you as he spoke, his demeanor was regal yet totally natural, as if he had been born to the title Duke. Indeed, after a few moments in his presence, you felt as if you'd been graced by a king.

"You are an excellent dancer, Miss Nichols," Duke Ellington pronounced while I stood breathlessly entrapped in his gaze. "It's beautiful to see you perform, to watch you work. But you have a special voice: I could hear you above all the others. You're going to be a singer, I think."

I thanked him, *I think*. This chance encounter left me soaring for months to come. By the time the spell began to wear off, we would meet again. But that's another story.

Because of the places I worked and the high caliber of people I met, my parents supported my being in show business, because they knew how much it meant to me; it was my passion. However, for someone who never wanted to be a child, and more importantly, never wanted to be treated like a child, working among adults, meeting adult responsibilities, and making adult money made me mature beyond my years. After the College Inn, I put together a solo act, taking charge of every detail, from choosing my repertoire to designing and sewing my gowns. I signed on with a manager, who renamed me Lynn Mayfair, a name I used for only six months, because I hated it. Playing the Chicago "club date" circuit, "Lynn" was making quite a name for herself. But it was a point of pride for me, if only for my parents' sake, that my name be Nichols. I'd always hated the name Grace, so I asked my mother to please rename me. Perhaps subconsciously I knew my mother and I had more in common than I could admit, but then I thought it was simply because I loved her name that I asked her to rename me after herself, Lishia. She refused, instead choosing Nichelle because it was close to Michelle, which she had wanted to name me in the first place, and because my initials would then be "NN." Still I felt rejected.

My path stretched before me, shining and clear. Only Mother, I was convinced, was holding me back. By now she and I fought constantly about everything and nothing, and I was convinced without a doubt that she hated me. In my anger and frustration, I wanted to hate her, too, but how could I? Here was a woman who criticized me constantly—or so it seemed. Yet, at the same time, she was the same woman who made sure I had the finest clothes, that I mastered every detail of etiquette, who taught me to discern quality in everything from a pair of shoes to a work of literature. She encouraged me to think, to write, to be independent of everyone, including herself. It was she from whom I inherited my freedom of spirit, so why was she now denying it? Why was she trying to take from me all that she taught me to cherish? All that she cherished?

The answer was so simple and obvious, but, as worldly

as I felt at the ripe old age of sixteen, some things about being a child followed me like my own shadow. The mystery of my mother and our fiery love-hate relationship was one. Not seeing any solution to our problems, I decided to leave home—one way or the other. In that time and place, getting away from my parents was not as easy as all that. Even if I'd been eighteen, nineteen, even twenty, an unmarried young lady did not live alone, at least not a *respectable* one. And as much as I wanted to "hate" my mother, I respected, revered, and, yes, loved our family.

My deliverance arrived one hot August day, quite by chance. My niece Barbara, who was just two or three years younger than I, was visiting from New York. We both had big dreams: I would be a famous singer and dancer; Barbara was going to be a doctor.

A torrential rain washed in the first cool day that August. When Barbara and I finally ventured out late that afternoon, I was wearing a green cashmere sweater (they called me the Cashmere Kid), a long ballerina skirt, cut on the bias, and hoop earrings. My hair was cut then in a gamine style, with bangs.

The city streets gleamed in the cool breeze as we headed for the Chicago Art Center, where a theater arts festival, featuring guest artists from all over the world, was being held. We found ballet classes and a troupe of real African dancers on one floor, a comedy improvisational group and a dramatic repertory company at work on another. We heard that singers from Broadway shows and the opera would appear later, so we decided to wait around.

To kill time, we wandered up to the third floor, drawn by the distinctive *brraack-a-brack-brack* of tap shoes. There, inside a large rehearsal hall illuminated by a wall of fifteen-foot windows, stood thirty to forty dancers—all professionals, all of whom had traveled hundreds of miles for this particular workshop—staring in awe at the guest dancer-teacher. He wore a suit of copperish tan silk, and with his reddish-golden hair and amber honey-colored skin, he was a vision to behold. The waning sunlight behind him created a golden aura about him, and he glided so effortlessly across the oak floor, he seemed to float just above it. If you didn't hear the steady, mesmerizing flurry of taps you wouldn't even know his feet were moving.

"Barbara," I whispered calmly. "You see that golden man there?"

"Uh-huh," she answered absentmindedly.

"That's the man I'm going to marry!" That very second, the dancer turned to face me, his emerald-green eyes glowing, and locked me in his gaze. I beheld him, falling deeper under his spell.

"For cripe's sake!" Barbara hissed. "That old man? He must be thirty years old! At least!"

Yes, I nodded. *Yes.* At least.

His name, I soon learned, was Foster Johnson. A brilliant performer, who with his partner Bobby Johnson (no relation) had replaced the famous Nicholas Brothers in the National Company production of *Kiss Me Kate* and had toured in the play's national company, Foster was a legend among other dancers. He could make Fred Astaire look like he was standing still. He was beautiful, sophisticated, and elegant, and so charming he could talk the flowers off the wallpaper. He also suffered fits of self-absorption and petulance that, being young and naive, I viewed as artistic temperament and quite romantic. And I fell in love with him, madly, deeply, and completely.

I knew that my parents would never approve of our love, but from our first kiss, I also knew that my parents would never part us. Foster was fifteen years older than I, a man of the world in every sense of the term. I was too young, they would argue. I should go to college, they would say. And they were right. But I was seventeen, and Foster loved me. Together we would be the greatest song-and-dance team in the world. And—shades of my Welsh Grampa—no one was going to tell *me* what to do or who to love.

Well aware of my parents' resistance, I took the only

route I knew to circumvent their disapproval. You might assume that Foster was a cunning older man who preyed on innocent little me. Wrong. I entered our relationship with my eyes wide open. I had been waiting for and "saving myself" for someone intelligent, suave, and sophisticated, someone who understood my dreams, who would stoke my ambition and savor my success. And I found him. I also found the way to ensure that my parents would not drive us apart, that my father would not run Foster out of town or shoot him with those big black six-shooters he kept. Knowing my father would temper his rage toward the father of his grandchild, I made sure that by the time I presented Foster to my parents, it was a *fait accompli.* My mother and father were devastated, and their disappointment in me almost broke my heart. Yet I would not be denied.

We married shortly after my eighteenth birthday, in early 1951, and soon left to visit Foster's father in Chillicothe, Ohio. A sweet, hardy old Irishman, Will Johnson embraced us and fell in love with me. We spent the closest thing to a honeymoon in his rambling old Victorian house, sleeping and making love in a big brass bed so high I had to use a step stool just to climb into it. Pappa, as I called Foster's father, had sweetly tucked under the sheet a hot water bottle wrapped in a towel. Each night, lying next to my new beautiful husband, the father of my unborn child, I drifted off into the sleep of angels, never guessing it would be years before I ever knew such happiness again.

From there Foster and I embarked on a tour, performing our song-and-dance act in Cleveland, Columbus, Toledo, and Pittsburgh. We were a smash every place we played; it was all coming together just like I dreamed it would. But within a few weeks the bloom of our love began fading, and although I felt uneasy about some of Foster's habits, I was still content. If I chose not to smoke marijuana with him and his friends, why should it bother him? I asked myself. If he drank without me, well, that was because I didn't drink and, besides, alcohol wasn't good for our baby. I didn't really begin to wake up to Foster's true nature until the day he said, "I'm cutting your ballad from the act."

"But, it's always so well received," I argued, baffled.

"It's out!" he replied angrily. "It slows up the show."

I finally put my foot down when he "suggested" that I stay back in Ohio with his father while he played solo in Cincinnati. I refused. If they wanted the great Foster Johnson alone, fine. If he wanted me to stay away from the club, okay. At least, I told myself over and over, we're together. That's all that matters. For the entire two weeks in Cincinnati it rained torrents. I felt like a prisoner.

My salvation came from, of all people, my mother. We had not stayed in touch since I'd left, but my ever-resourceful, indomitable mother tracked me down to tell me that Duke Ellington's public relations person had called the house. Duke would be arriving in Chicago, and he wanted to meet with me. I was so excited, but when I told Foster the good news, his expression darkened. "We have other engagements, you know," he said.

"Yes, but not for another ten days. Why not go back and see what he wants?" I pleaded. Reluctantly Foster agreed, and we returned to Chicago and stayed at my parents'.

I went alone to the Palmer House Hotel, where I was escorted up to the Duke's private suite. "I've never forgotten seeing you two years ago in the College Inn show," he said warmly. "I have composed a new musical suite entitled 'Monologue Duet and Threesome.' The dancers who have been interpreting my Monologue segment are leaving the tour. Would you be interested in choreographing and performing that dance for me?"

My heart pounded so loudly I was surprised no one else heard it. I remembered reading when the great dancer Ann Henry got the part. And now Duke Ellington was asking me to replace her. In less than a minute so many thoughts flashed through my mind. I was two months' pregnant and not yet showing. The engagement would run six weeks. How would I look then? If I wasn't married, if I wasn't pregnant, I wouldn't have to worry about these things. But I was, and still dedicated to making marriage, career, and motherhood all work.

"What about the male dancers?" I asked, wondering if I would be working with Ann's, and if so, could I leave Foster the same way he was going to leave me in Ohio? Would he let me?

The Duke answered, "It's your responsibility to find two male dancers of your own, choreograph and rehearse them, and be ready to travel in two weeks."

I sighed. "I'll be ready!"

The Duke smiled his devastating smile and purred, "I know you will. You'll be great."

Ellington was, obviously, a fascinating man, but also one of great complexity. Regardless of how warmly you were received, you would be foolish to presume to know all that he thought and felt. And so even in my happiest dealings with him, there would remain an indelible trace of uncertainty.

I flew home to tell Foster, who seemed as thrilled as I was. He immediately phoned Bobby Johnson, and his former partner arrived in Chicago a few days later. The Duke sent me a tape of his monologue titled "Pretty and the Wolf" along with notes on what he wanted. To music that was classic Ellington, the Duke recited a poem that told the story of an innocent country girl who falls under the nefarious influence of a gold chain–swinging "wolf." He reveals to her "the various conditions and ways for her to get somewhere," which Pretty learns quite well. Indeed, by the end of the piece, it is Pretty swinging a diamond-studded gold chain; the tables have turned.

Once upon a time, there came to the city
A pretty little girl, a little country, but pretty

A little ragged, but a pretty little girl.
Then she met a man, a city man—
Smooth, handsome, successful, cool,
A well-mannered-type man.
And since she was pretty, he thought fit to give her
an audience.
So he talked to her for quite a while.
Naturally, she wanted to get somewhere.
He was standing on the corner, twirling his
diamond-studded gold chain
Around his finger.
And as he enumerated the various conditions and
ways
For her to get somewhere
You could hear her saying, "Yes Daddy, Yes Daddy,
Yes Daddy."
And so agreed, they danced.
They danced, they really danced.
They gave it a mad whirl—the maddest.
Their hearts danced,
They virtually spun each other around.
And as they came out of their spin—
Or, rather, as she came out of her spin,
Because I think he got caught in his.
As a matter of fact, he's still in his spin.
Obviously, he likes it.
Because there she is, standing on the corner,
Twirling her diamond-studded gold chain
Around her finger.
And as she enumerates the various conditions and
ways
For him to get somewhere,
You can hear him saying, "Yes, baby, yes, baby,
yes, baby."

It was a wonderful piece, and I knew exactly how I wanted to stage it. For two weeks I worked endlessly creating the choreography and rehearsing with Foster and Bobby. We needed costumes. The guys would wear zoot suits, I decided, but I had to whip up one complicated outfit: a simple country girl's dress that broke away to reveal the provocative costume of the sexy, worldly mama who, of course, prevails in the end. We would not have a full dress rehearsal with the band until the night before we opened in Omaha, but I was confident it would be great.

The night before we left Chicago, the Duke threw a big party. I entered the room so happy and proud, with Bobby and Foster on either arm. As I introduced Foster, the Duke's amiable eyes momentarily flashed surprise and disdain. The epitome of class and restraint, Ellington smiled politely and nodded. "Foster," he said graciously, "how good of you to join us." Turning to me, he gently but firmly took my arm and guided me to the piano, where he introduced me to the other guests.

"Ladies and gentlemen: Next week, you will see poetry in motion," he announced. "Please meet the lovely Miss Nichols—our latest, and I'm sure, finest, Pretty."

Everyone applauded and smiled, and I felt my face flush. "Oh yes," Ellington added, almost as an afterthought, "over there of course are the Pretty's wolves: the Johnson brothers." There was no mistaking Ellington's unmitigated contempt for my husband. As I later learned, Foster had bested him in the pursuit of a beautiful woman, and the Duke never forgave him.

Foster, who was livid, soon whisked me out the door. I was furious with him for not at least warning me, and I feared my big break would be torn up with our contracts. But the great Ellington was too big a man to do something like that. Seemingly, all was forgotten after opening night. Well, almost. Now visibly more reserved, Ellington observed me nightly from under hooded eyes. He never mentioned Foster to me again; he didn't have to. So it came as a great surprise when he summoned me to his dressing room one day after the matinee show.

He greeted me with an unusually warm smile and asked, "How does it feel to be a hit?" Before I could answer, he said, "Your dancing is quite beautiful. Sing for me. I know you can sing."

Caught totally off-guard, I blurted, "Well, sure!" For some crazy reason I recalled a self-denigrating joke the Black musicians would crack whenever anyone mastered a particularly difficult Ellington passage, and without thinking, repeated it in a lame attempt to crack the ice: "Hey, we all got rhythm, ain't we?"

The Duke smiled obliquely. "Fine, sing something for me."

"Now? There's no piano here."

Ellington smiled even more wickedly, then purred, "You don't need a piano. We all got rhythm. Ain't we?"

Waves of hot crimson washed over me, forcing tears into my eyes, but I would not cry. I felt like Pretty—naive and ambitious, asking for nothing but the ways and means of how to get somewhere. Ellington and his protégé, cowriter, and right-hand man, the genius Billy Strayhorn, sat silently, waiting. For the past several weeks, as I waited in the wings with Bobby and Foster for our cue, I had watched the tall, svelte singer who preceded our number and admired the way she caressed the Duke's "Sophisticated Lady" and "Satin Doll" or belted out "Take the A Train." I replayed in my mind the rhythms and timing of his arrangements, mimicking the singer's expressions and phrasing. Ellington and Strayhorn remained expressionless, almost Buddhalike, until I finished. When I finished, Strayhorn smiled slightly.

"Do you have that pretty little velvet dress you wore to the party in Chicago?" Ellington inquired.

"Sure, I do. And I even have the shoes," I foolishly gushed, thinking, *He wants me to sing at the wrap party after our last show.*

"Good," Ellington replied. "You go on tonight."

And so I finished out the tour as dancer *and* singer with

the great Duke Ellington. Given the situation with Foster, I entertained no illusions about Ellington extending our contract. Besides, by then I was having morning sickness, and though I still didn't show, it was just a matter of time before I would be unable to dance.

This was, however, meager consolation. I'd scaled the heights and for a few brief moments breathed the rarefied air at the top. It was everything I'd imagined and more, and as I stepped back down, I swore never to forget it. Just a year before, my future lay shining before me, a bright, open vista of limitless possibilities. Now I would go home with Foster, not as Duke Ellington's newly discovered star, but a young bride of a man whom I now suspected wasn't all I had envisioned, and with a baby on the way. I'd grabbed the reins of responsibility and made my choices.

After the show closed, we were supposed to return to Ohio for our next engagement, but Foster decided he had some unspecified business to attend to, so we returned instead to my parents' house in Chicago for a few days. The next morning Foster left for parts unknown, not to return until late the next evening. I was on the verge of calling the police when he sauntered in, bright as a penny, and kissed me. Ignoring my rage and speaking to me as if I were a child, he wondered aloud innocently, How could I doubt him? Why didn't I realize he was taking care of us?

I was furious, seething silently, when he announced proudly, "I've got twelve weeks of engagements in Montreal, Canada."

I should have been elated, but somehow I knew that this was it; I'd felt it coming for weeks now. Then he dropped the other shoe: He was leaving me behind with my parents and would send for me later.

I nodded, knowing it wasn't true, knowing it was over.

For the next five months I stayed with my parents, crying myself to sleep at night in what felt like an empty bed, exhausted from fighting with Mother by day, defiantly facing the questioning stares of relatives and neighbors, and worrying. As promised, Foster did send money, but that was hardly good enough for me. With every day that I spent alone, a little more of my love for Foster died. The next time, I promised myself, I would be wiser.

My only child, Kyle, was born on the morning of August 14, 1951. I vividly recall every detail of that day up until the point of his delivery. I thought I would die. I cursed Foster for every painful contraction, then something went wrong, everything went black and silent. Three days later, when I finally emerged from a coma, I found myself in the intensive care unit with Mom sitting at my bedside. I opened my eyes to see her there, like an angel, and in the seconds before she realized that I was awake, I caught her in an unguarded moment. I remember it so clearly. She was wearing her cocoa-and-blue-checked sundress and jacket, her long black hair shining in the afternoon light. Her face—filled with helplessness, vulnerability, and fear—was one I'd never seen before. The instant she realized I was awake, all that vanished, and she smiled at me sweetly. In that moment I knew in my heart that my mother loved me, and although we would continue to do battle for years, I would never doubt her love again.

Soon nurses brought in my son. Peering over the fluffy baby blanket, I saw his face for the first time. Fair and ruddy, with his golden-red hair, Kyle lay in my arms, his bright eyes staring up at me knowingly. Wrapping his tiny fingers around one of mine, he was so strong. So beautiful. So perfect. I went into my private self, as my father had taught me to do, and asked God to forgive me for cursing this beautiful baby's father. I had almost lost the most precious gift in life, and I gave thanks for Kyle's existence and his good health.

Slowly, as my strength returned, my parents insisted I let

them call Foster, but I refused to divulge his number. He should at least know that his son had been born, they argued.

Why? I asked. I had survived those five lonely months without him; I had given birth and nearly died in the process without him. I would raise my son without him, too. I made up my mind. And nothing could change it. That summer I planned my first professional comeback; I was eighteen years old.

CHAPTER FOUR

Cradling my newborn son, I began life as an independent woman right where I started: in my parents' loving home. Mother and I had fought a great deal during my pregnancy, and we were not the friends I wished we could be, yet we managed. It was so important to me to be there for Kyle, and living with my parents meant that I didn't have to get a job right away. Although Foster and I did not divorce for several years, our marriage was over.

Very early on, it became apparent to all of us that Kyle was special: bright, inquisitive, delightful. He first spoke when he was about eight months old, and instead of stumbling through something typical, like "Kyle want that," he said clearly, "Rama, I think I want that." (Rama was his name for Grandma.) If you put something down in front of him that he didn't want, he'd calmly say, "I'd rather not. Thank you." We'd look at each other as if to say, "Where did he come from?"

Kyle loved both of his grandparents dearly, and while he shared a special bond with his Rama, my father was his hero. To him Grampa was the source of knowledge and wonder, and I could not have found a better "father figure" for my son than my father.

It's often said that you don't fully appreciate your parents until you have a child of your own, and I can attest to that. I always loved and respected my parents, but I don't know that I ever appreciated them, especially my mom, as much as in those moments when I overheard Rama telling Kyle a story I'd learned as a child, or caught Grampa patiently explaining the intricate mysteries of snowflakes. To have been able to give Kyle the gift of my own childhood was truly a blessing.

I treasured every moment I spent with my son. Kyle was a sweet, lovely child with an insatiable quest for knowledge. I loved sitting for hours teaching him everything I knew, pointing out each word on the page as I read aloud. One of his first, favorite stories was about Babar the Elephant, and when he was still toddling, he spelled his first word for me: Babar. When he was a little older, he treasured the multivolume Book of Knowledge Rama had given him when he was five. He still owns it, in fact.

When Kyle was just about three, he became fascinated with colors, constantly asking, "What color is my shirt?" "What color is this?" "What color is that?" Before long, noticing different shades, he'd remark, "Mom, this is red, but it's not red like this," and I'd explain that colors came in "families," and some members of the family look a little different from the others, just like in our family. Usually with Kyle, all you had to do was explain it once. His grasp and love of logic was positively Vulcan.

I thought myself a competent, responsible mother, but, looking back, I was still a kid myself in many ways. One day, I admit, Kyle got the best of me. He was about three and getting ready to go out with his Grampa, when he asked me what shoes he should wear. I told him his brown shoes would be perfect, and after a few minutes he emerged with the shoes on and asked, "Are these shoes brown?"

"Kyle, of course, they're brown. You know your colors."

"Oh," he replied with a baffled look.

"Kyle, come here," I said. For several minutes, we played our color game, and Kyle correctly identified the color of about a dozen objects I pointed to. Until I pointed to his shoes.

"Don't tell me, I know," he answered. "Orange!"

Kyle was having himself a ball, teasing me. Every time I asked him the color of his shoes, he told me every color but brown. Of course, I didn't understand how clever my baby was, and, thinking he was just being difficult, I impatiently snapped, "What color are your shoes?"

"Um, um. Purple?"

That was it: Before I knew what happened, I'd whacked him across his bottom. "What color are your shoes?"

"Yellow?" Kyle was crying torrents of tears, but in sheer frustration, I hit his little butt again.

"What color are your shoes, dammit?"

"Pink!"

I could not believe how out of control I was. My parents came running into the room. "What the hell is the matter with you?" Mother asked, scooping up my crying and confused child in her arms.

"What the hell is going on here?" Daddy asked.

"Oh my God, oh my God," I cried. "I whipped my son! I'm so sorry!" I ran out of the room and lay down on the sofa, buried my face in my hands, and vowed I would never lay a hand on my son again. A couple of minutes later Kyle was standing by the couch. "Mommy? Mommy?" he asked hopefully. "Mommy, I'm sorry. I know what color my shoes are."

"Yes, baby."

"They're blue!"

I lunged for him, but he scurried behind his Grampa, smirking. Then it finally dawned on me: Kyle had been playing his joke on me all along. The brown shoes became part of our family legend. When Kyle was about thirteen, he once defused my anger by running into the shower in his clothes, turning on the water, and shrieking, "Don't beat me, Mommy. I know what color my shoes are!" (As you'll see, the brown-shoe saga didn't end there, either.)

In a way, you could say that Kyle and I grew up together, but while there was always an element of siblinghood to our relationship, there was never any question that I was his mother. Once, when Kyle was about five, I came home from a job out of town and heard him calling my mother "Mother." Then he called me "Nichelle."

I grabbed him and asked sharply, "What did you call me?"

Startled, my baby looked up at me with his big eyes and in a soft, uncertain voice answered, "Nichelle?"

"Don't you ever call me Nichelle. You may tell someone what my name is, but do you see this?" I pointed to my stomach. "You know where babies come from?"

"Yes," he said.

"I carried you in there. The entire time, you belonged to me. You are what God gave me as a gift, and I was able to bring you into this world. I am your mother. *I* am your mother! No one else is. Do you understand?"

Kyle stood there for a minute, then said, "But, Mom—your career."

"My career? You are first and foremost in my life. The most wonderful thing that ever happened to me, Kyle, is you, not my career. But my career is what I do, and it takes me away so I can provide the best for you. Not because it's where I want to be."

Kyle hugged me with all his might. And he never called me Nichelle again. When I was much younger, I'd always thought I'd like to have five kids. But once I had Kyle, I figured I'd better quit while I was ahead. He was, and is, the greatest accomplishment of my life.

By the time Kyle was about eighteen months old, I'd

reached the difficult decision to quit show business. I had responsibilities and no husband, so how could I be an entertainer, running all over the country? I got my first "real" job working as a file clerk at the Goldenrod Ice Cream Company. Despite the fact that I foolishly listed having appeared at the College Inn and toured with Duke Ellington under "job experience," the manager, Mr. McGregor, hired me anyway.

"You aren't going to be staying," he observed.

"Yes, I am. I'm married, and I have a child. I'm going back to school—" I argued.

"No, you're not," he replied calmly. "But I'll give you the job anyway."

"So why are you hiring me?" I asked, baffled.

" 'Cause I'm from Blue Island"—a small town adjacent to Robbins—"and I know your father is the one who put in the sewage system and the water when I was a kid. I have a lot to thank your father for."

"Is that the only reason you're giving me this job?"

"Yeah," he answered. "And take my word: You aren't going to stay." He paused thoughtfully, then added, "And you shouldn't."

For six months I reorganized the filing system, learned bookkeeping, and mastered the switchboard. (Are you surprised?) One day I was called into the front office and presented with what most young women in my position would consider the opportunity of a lifetime: the company was offering to send me to business school so I could take a higher position in the firm. I went home that night in tears, knowing that if I accepted, I'd be obligated to remain with the company for at least several years. Mr. McGregor was right: I just couldn't stay there. So I resigned and began taking some law courses at Cosmopolitan Law School as I made plans to return to the only profession I ever wanted to be in: show business.

I'd begun studying dance with Jimmy Payne, a leading

exponent and teacher of Afro-Cuban and tap dance. Many talented people studied with Jimmy, including Carol Lawrence. I'll never forget one young man who came from New York specifically to study with Jimmy and who often danced beside me in class. He was really good, but he moved in a quirky, jerky manner that always made me think of a dancing broken stick. Our paths didn't cross again until the mid-sixties when I auditioned for the movie version of *Sweet Charity*. I immediately recognized the director and choreographer as that guy from Jimmy Payne's class: Bob Fosse. Bob and I reminisced about Jimmy, and producer Robert Arthur and Fosse both told me I was their first choice for the role. I was devastated to learn a few days later that Paula Kelly, who'd created the role on Broadway and was promised it in the film version, had unexpectedly been freed from another production. Bob Fosse kindly phoned me to say how sorry he was and how great I danced.

Back in Chicago I returned to show business, headlining in Jimmy Payne's acclaimed and long-running revue called "Calypso Carnival" at the Blue Angel. Working nights, I was still home for Kyle in the daytime. Each night before I left, I'd tuck him into bed, and he'd look up, smile, and chirp, "Break a leg, Mommy!"

For over a year we played to sold-out crowds, which often included new up-and-coming performers in town playing Mr. Kelly's nearby: Bill Cosby, Phyllis Diller, and Joan Rivers, among them. Before the Blue Angel I did a few plays and a few nightclubs, including Mike DeLisa's showroom, another top Chicago club, where performers of the caliber of Nat "King" Cole, Joe Williams, and Sarah Vaughan sang. I opened for Joe Williams once, as a matter of fact.

As I soon learned, however, even the classiest clubs have their seamy sides. Given my limited and, I soon realized, sheltered show-business experience until then, it came as a shock to notice the dressing rooms reeking of pot. Then there was some of the gangsterish clientele. When a male singer tried to seduce me, I gave him the brush-off and sought the safety of a friendly female singer in the show, only to find out that she was a lesbian. Not only that, one of the chorus girls was sweet on her and, mistaking my intentions, threatened to kill me. It was just awful.

While I was making my name in the Chicago clubs, I became very close with Jimmy Payne. Kyle adored him, and I might have accepted his proposal of marriage were it not for his insane jealousy. By the time the show closed at the Blue Angel, I began to feel trapped, so the minute I got a two-week offer to open a posh new supper club in Milwaukee, I jumped at it. Jimmy was less than thrilled, to say the least.

In every way, this was a dream job: headliner status, a two-week contract with options for up to six weeks, and great pay. It was close enough that Kyle and my parents could come to visit. Most important, though, this was my first big break as a singer (though I still danced in my act), and I could not afford to pass it up.

The newly renovated supper club was magnificent: each gleaming white table set with candles and a bottle of fine Italian wine. At one end of the room, a long, elegant bar stocked with the finest liquor and glistening crystal glasses sparkled. The spacious stage was a performer's dream, as was the top-notch eight-piece band. During my first rehearsal I met the musicians, the chorus-line dancers, and Laura, a singer whose specialty number was a scintillating bolero. Everyone seemed like one big happy troupe.

The first week went very well—great reviews and packed houses—but I sensed something peculiar in the way the dancers giggled nervously between acts, then dashed from the stage, dressed in a flash, and went back upstairs to mingle with the customers after each show. Each night after my big closing dance number, I came off the stage, then collapsed in my dressing room, before getting ready for the next show. From my basement dressing room I would hear Louie the bartender snapping at the girls, "All right, let's move it. Ya know, Mr. B. don't like nobody bein' late. Let's go!" Within minutes, they'd be gone.

What I didn't know was that these pretty young girls were going upstairs to "B-drink." B-drinking was an old practice where the strippers mixed with the audience to coax male customers into running up a large bar tab. If you were B-drinking with a customer, known in the vernacular as the john, you might order a glass of champagne, then the bartender would pour you a ginger ale while the customer, who probably ordered champagne, too, got billed for two champagnes.

Not only did this allow the club to make a fantastic added profit on the bar, it also created an atmosphere conducive to the other "business" many of these working girls knew best: prostitution. Of course, prostitution was not openly practiced *in* the better B-joints, as they were called, or on the premises. But everyone knew which clubs were B-joints and which were not, and many a working girl made her "dates" on the side. I made it my policy never to play B-joints. Not only would my parents have died if they found out, but those places were not legitimate, and could be demeaning and dangerous. As I learned, though, appearances often proved deceiving, and some very posh clubs were fronts for this lucrative twist on the oldest profession.

I was sitting in my dressing room when suddenly the door seemed to jump out of its frame with rapid-fire pounding: *Bang! bang! bang! "Miss* Nichols! You're wanted upstairs!"

There stood Louie the bartender. Assuming he meant that a customer wanted to meet me, I said politely, "Thank you very much, but no thanks. I'm getting ready for my next show."

"Look," he replied firmly, "I'm not askin' ya; I'm *tellin'* ya: You're supposed to be upstairs. *Now.*"

"Excuse me? Who do you think you're talking to?"

Louie's mouth dropped, and the veins in his temples strained against his skin. Louie was small and wiry but tough. One look into his cold, black glaring eyes and I knew why the girls jumped when he barked.

"No, thank you," I said firmly and closed the door. During the next show I avoided his steely gaze, but I couldn't shake the feeling that something about this place just didn't add up. When I had a chance to speak with Laura, the bolero dancer, I found out why.

"Well, you know this used to be a strip club," she said matter-of-factly.

"Yes, but it was my understanding that the place was under new ownership."

"Leopards don't change their spots," she said, laughing ruefully. "They just change the decor."

"You mean this is the same owner who owned it when it was a strip joint?"

"Yeah, Nichelle. Who do you think *we* are?"

"Who?" I asked naively.

"All the girls. We were the strippers. Or did you think we were all legit?"

So there it was: Louie the bartender/enforcer, a bunch of ex-stripper B-girls, and johns everywhere. No doubt about it: I was working for the mob. I had to get out.

The next night the club's owner, Frankie Balistrieri, came to my dressing room. Frankie was not your typical-looking mobster. Small, stocky, yet always impeccably dressed, he had chiseled Nordic features, blond hair, and steely light-blue eyes.

"I understand from Louie that we're having a problem."

"I don't have any problems," I answered innocently. "I go upstairs every night, do my two shows, then I go home."

"Yeah, I know," he said patiently, then proceeded to explain to me what my job really was. "So you see, that's how we do it here."

"I'm sorry," I replied. "I don't B-drink and I don't play B-bars. My agent told me this was a legitimate supper club."

"But I want you should do this," he said gently as he calmly cracked each knuckle.

I knew now what I'd gotten myself into, but I wasn't smart enough to keep quiet. "Number one, Mr. Balistrieri—"

"Call me Frankie. Please," he said, smiling.

"Number one, *Frankie,* my father would die if he knew I was anywhere near a B-joint. I wasn't raised that way. You have a beautiful club here, but I don't drink and I don't smoke, and I'm not going to B-drink for anyone."

"Well, you don't have to drink," he said.

"I will not be part of anything like that. I have a beautiful young child, and I don't want him growing up to discover that his mother was a B-girl. I'm going to *be* somebody in this life, and it's not going to be as a B-girl. I'm very sorry, Frankie, but if that's the deal, I will just have to leave."

Frankie stood there silently, looking at me. "Okay," he said at last. "You're bringing in lots of customers. They like you, so it's okay. You always mind your mother and father, you will not go wrong. Anybody tells you anything, you tell 'em to talk to Frankie Balistrieri. I like ya. You got class, kid."

"Thank you."

He nodded and walked out the door. I breathed a sigh of relief, looked at the calendar, and counted down just a few more days before my two weeks were up and I would be back on the train to Chicago. But a few days before what was to have been my last night, Louie knocked again, this time softly. "Oh, uh, *Miss* Nichols," he said in his cretinous voice, "by the way: You're stayin' on. Frankie wants ya here anuddah two weeks."

Frankie exercised that first two-week option with a raise, then another bigger one, by which time I was dying to leave. I felt sorry for the girls, who could not have cared less, and a little depressed myself. But at least I knew I'd be getting out. I began to get the idea that Frankie was fond of me when he invited me up to visit his family. As I soon learned, his wife and children had never been seen at the club before. In Frankie's words, "The two"—meaning his beloved family and his sordid business—"should never touch." So for him to have brought them down to see me and then invited me upstairs to meet them was quite an honor, and I knew better than to refuse. As I greeted his gentle, lovely wife and their three chubby cherub kids, I saw how I could get to Frankie and maybe, just maybe, escape.

Once when I delicately broached the subject of leaving, he said, "Why? I'm not good to you?"

"No, you are, but eventually I want to go to New York and Broadway, maybe even Hollywood and make movies or do television."

"You got big notions for a little girl," he said, smiling.

"Well, big things come in little packages," I answered, relieved to see him laugh.

While staying at a very nice hotel just around the corner and up the block from the club, I began hearing stories about Frankie and the local rackets. Frankie was not yet the Midwest don he would become, but he was working at it quite assiduously. His gang and his rival's were entrenched in a turf dispute, I heard, and right before I got ready to leave, a stripper at another club was shot onstage and killed by a rival mob. They had no compunction about making sure that their girls never got away. The implied threat of a savage beating or a shattered nose kept all the girls in line. I was scared to death, but more determined than ever to get away. Ironically, my show grew increasingly popular, and for the first time in Frankie's career, one of his shows was reviewed in the local newspapers. The better I got, the deeper the hole I was digging myself into.

When I finally marshaled the nerve to tell him I was leaving, I saw the dangerous glimmer in Frankie's eyes. "You know," he said menacingly, "nobody quits on Frankie Balistrieri."

"But, it's my dad," I said, appealing to his sense of family. This was the performance of my life. "He's had a heart attack, and my family needs me back home. I have to go."

"Your dad, huh?" Frankie considered as he eyed me carefully. I think he knew I wasn't telling the truth, but he seemed to go along with it. "You don't smoke, you don't drink. Okay, here's what we're gonna do: You leave and go take care of your father. I respect you. After all, you love your parents. That's beautiful. Then you come back here. And bring your little boy. We'll find you a nice apartment. You'll love it here. *Then* we'll see about you going to New York."

"I'm not bringing my son here," I said, smelling the trap. "And I'm not moving to Milwaukee. I've been here ten weeks and I'm dying inside. I've got to go."

"Okay, go home, and come back, and you'll give me six weeks. Then you're free."

I went home for a couple of weeks, and told my parents about the B-drinking, but nothing else. Even hearing that, Daddy said, "Go back, pack up, and get the hell out of there." My father had had enough experience with the mob to know there was a smart way to go about that and a dumb way. Even without my mentioning the shootings and threats, he knew I couldn't just walk away. In the meantime, I'd torn into my agent, who never stopped claiming that he had no idea about the club. That may well have been, I told him, but how could he be booking the Midwest and not know who Frankie Balistrieri was?

I'd spent my time in Milwaukee observing Frankie carefully. He had his soft spots, and one of them was his ego. I had a plan.

So did Frankie. Thinking if I stayed the whole six weeks, he'd be able to convince me never to leave, he started turning up the heat. Enter Dominic, or Mr. F. as everyone at the club called him, Frankie's lawyer. In his thousand-dollar silk suits, Dominic was as slick, suave, and cunning as a snake. I often found him at the end of the night waiting for me. He'd offer me champagne, which I politely declined. This infuriated Louie, since Dominic was Frankie's personal friend, and a bottle of champagne was a bottle of champagne and a nice profit for the bar.

Dominic, however, seemed to be falling for me in a big way, and Frankie encouraged it, saying to me, "Ya know, he's real classy. Like you." One day Dominic gave me a little box. Thinking it was jewelry, I declined, saying, "I can't accept this."

"Go on," he urged. "Open it."

Inside was a little gold key to an apartment that Dominic described as decorated in white and pastels, with a beautiful view.

"No, thank you," I said, handing him back the box. "I'm not interested."

Dominic just smiled and kept on spinning his web.

A few nights later I was getting ready to leave the club when Dominic's driver, Tony, announced, "I'm here to take you home because of the storm."

The driver walked me to the black limousine in the pouring rain, and I got inside, where I found a large box on the backseat.

"Mr. F. says you should open the box," Tony said.

Inside was the most sumptuous sable coat I'd ever seen. When we got to the hotel, I opened the door and got out.

"Hey! You forgot your box!"

"No, I didn't forget it. Tell Mr. F. I thank him very much, but I cannot accept it."

"Whadaya, crazy?" the driver shouted through the thunder before driving away. I was beginning to wonder myself.

It was time for my plan. Three or four weeks into this run, I contacted a reporter who had given me a great review. I told him that I had a real scoop for him, and then proceeded to enthusiastically reveal how because of the terrific exposure I'd gotten working for the wonderful Frankie Balistrieri, I was on my way to New York. I owed everything to Mr. B., I gushed, because he was so kind as to feature me in his club—where a big agent had spotted me—I was getting the opportunity of my dreams, and so on and so forth. The writer ate it up, and when Frankie read the item in the paper, he did too.

"Why dincha tell me you were going to New York?" he asked proudly.

"Oh, I just found out about it, and thank you so much. I really owe it all to you." More lies, although peppered with some truth: I did find an agent, Dave Sobol, and I *was* opening out of town—in Minneapolis. Whether Frankie Balistrieri really believed that I really believed that he had discovered me—as he went around boasting for years—or was simply saving face and decided to give me a break, I'll never know. All I know is that my engagement was mercifully shortened, and in a few weeks I got away. However, not before a girl from another club was found dead one morning, her body disposed of in a trash can.

How big was Frankie? Well, let's move ahead about twenty years. We were on the set of one of the early *Star Trek* movies, and one day between scenes Bill Shatner was regaling us with a true story that he swears scared him to death. Apparently, Bill had committed to star in a summer-stock play in Milwaukee. When an attractive film offer came along, Bill instructed his agent to get him out of the play. His agent called back, very agitated, to say the owner of the theater intended to hold Bill to the contract and to ask if he would consider doing the play on the condition that the film be delayed to accommodate him.

"So I told my agent," Bill recounted tensely, " 'Tell him I said no.' " He then told us about a phone call he received on his private line from a husky-voiced man who said: "Bill, I want you should do this play. I'm a big fan of *Star Trek* and Captain Kirk. You won't regret it."

Bill had us all hanging as he told about calling his agent, screaming and cursing, only to calm down after he learned the theater owner's identity.

"So who the hell was he?" Leonard asked.

"Well," Bill replied slowly, "all I can tell you is when I found out who he was, I did that show, *and* they held the film for me." There were a couple of little gasps, then Bill continued, "He's a notorious Mafia don of the entire Midwest, but I can't tell you his name, since it was told to me in the strictest secrecy and confidence."

Wow! everyone seemed to be whispering. "Come on, tell us his name," someone said.

"Yeah, we won't tell," another person added.

Bill clearly relished keeping such a fascinating secret.

"Oh, Bill," I piped up calmly. "You mean Frankie Balistrieri."

Bill spun around and demanded, "How the hell would *you* know?"

I arched one brow conspiratorially, kissed my fist, and replied, "Simple. Frankie Balistrieri is my godfather."

Over the next several years Dave Sobol booked me throughout the Pacific Northwest and Canada. Although I was often on the road and away from home, Dave helped me get very lucrative jobs, and before long, club owners were inviting me back for return engagements. I'd vowed very early on to live by three rules: Never date the club owner, never date anyone in the band, and never date a customer. Instead I met a lot of great people, and before long I had friends in every town I played. It made life on the road much less lonely and gave it a semblance of normalcy.

Except for the necessity of being away from my son and my family, I enjoyed my work. But it wasn't always easy.

One winter day I arrived in Salt Lake City, Utah, and approached the reception desk at the hotel where I'd been told a reservation would be waiting for me.

"Good morning, I'm Nichelle Nichols."

The man behind the desk just stared at me expressionless. "Yes?"

"Yes, my reservation?" I replied, smiling.

"We'll have to ask you to leave," he replied. The words hit me like a thunderbolt, and for an instant, I glanced around the lobby to see who he was talking to.

"Do you have a reservation for Nichelle Nichols?" I repeated, thinking he must have misunderstood me. "I'm Nichelle Nichols."

"You don't have a reservation," he replied curtly. "We will have to ask you to leave."

"Are you saying what I think you're saying?" I asked, looking him straight in the eye.

"You are free to think whatever you want to think," he answered, then coolly looked down at his work as if I didn't exist.

"Are you giving me a problem about my reservations because of my color?"

Startled, he looked up and said nothing, yet in his face I read the whole message: "I'm being quite patient with you. You have obviously stumbled into the wrong place. Please do not continue to defile these premises."

"They called to make reservations for me," I said persistently. "I want to see the manager."

The man stepped back and looked me up and down carefully, appraising me in my expensive suit, fur jacket, and fine leather boots as if I shouldn't be wearing them.

"Very well, madam."

He walked away, leaving me standing in the lobby, speechless and utterly alone. Slowly, almost imperceptibly, the whole atmosphere in the room changed, as people who normally walked through, minding their own business, saw me, slowed down, then stopped and gaped. I felt myself shaking with anger at them and at myself. Why didn't I see this coming? Why couldn't I just turn around and leave? Time seemed to stop, and the looks on their faces spoke volumes of hatred: "Can you believe it?" the sidelong glances and disapproving nods seemed to say. "How could she possibly?" "They know better, don't they?"

Inside I heard my own voice saying, *Wait a minute. This is the United States of America. This is 1956, not the Deep South; this is Salt Lake City, Utah. Maybe I got off at the wrong town. Maybe this is the wrong hotel.*

At last the manager emerged from his office, and in a loud, clear voice said, "We have no place for you. There is no reservation for you here. You do not stay in this hotel."

"That's pretty damn clear," I answered through clenched teeth as I picked up my bag and strode out. I took a cab to the club where I was set to open that night, and when I told the owner, Red, and his wife what had happened, they were shocked and embarrassed. Red, a wonderful, tough little man who had made his fortune in the Alaska mines, assured me, "No way. Not here. This is a *Mormon* town. Don't worry. I'll take care of this."

His wife and I watched as he phoned hotel after hotel. With each refusal, Red grew paler and more agitated. Finally, he said, "If you want to bow out of your contract, you can. I will pay your salary and put you on a plane." Believe me, I was about ready to take him up on it, too. The poor man was almost in tears, he was so angry. He finally reached an Italian couple who, when Red angrily yet warily told them I was "colored" and asked if that made any difference, replied, "Well, what color is she?"

"She's brown and she's an American."

"If she doesn't mind Italians, she can stay here," they said. I did, and I had a wonderful time there. I stayed with them when I returned, too. It wouldn't be until well into the sixties before desegregation came to Salt Lake City.

Despite the occasional problem, the best thing about my working in those years was that it enabled me to send a lot of money back home to my parents in Chicago. I was deeply grateful to them for all they were doing for Kyle and me, but I knew it might not continue like this forever. They were getting older, of course, and Daddy had suffered a couple of serious heart attacks. While he had recovered beautifully, his doctor had warned him repeatedly that another Chicago winter would be the death of him. I had to make some changes, too. Sitting in countless clubs, I'd seen great singers ten, twenty, thirty years older than I still up on the same stage, still doing the same numbers for the same crowd, going nowhere. Working night after night I'd honed my art and paid my dues; it was time to move on. But where?

From the time I was in grade school, we'd all dreamed of one day moving to Southern California. As luck would have it, my agent got me a job in Hawaii and I had a couple of free months, so I decided to visit an aunt who lived in L.A. For a Midwesterner then, Los Angeles was as fabled a city as Paris, and within hours, I knew this was where I belonged. By my second day in town, we were out apartment hunting. It would be impossible to pay back my parents for everything they had done for me and for Kyle, but I wanted to try. Within a week I'd found, leased, and furnished a large apartment where they all could live. I was so happy I thought the phone would jump out of my hands as I placed the long-distance call back to Chicago to tell my parents, "You've got a big three-bedroom apartment with a swimming pool starting November first!"

Within a month, my parents, my son, my sisters Marian and Diane, and my brother Tommy were stepping off the *Super Chief* in Union Station.

Oh, to hold my little boy again, and to see the looks on

my parents' faces when they saw our beautiful new home with its palm tree–lined walks and aqua swimming pool glimmering in the sun. We embraced our fabulous new hometown, where my father would live six more happy, precious years. Everyone spent that Christmas Day splashing in the pool, so we took a picture, then taunted all our friends back in Chicago by making it into next year's Christmas card.

I couldn't spend more than a few days with my family in our new home before I reluctantly left town for my next engagement in Hawaii. I often toyed with the idea of staying in Los Angeles and concentrating on film and television, but by then I was simply earning too much money on the road to stop without lining up something closer to home. I was so sure the decision rested in my hands. In one long, brutal night shortly after the move, I learned that I was wrong.

To be a woman traveling alone was never easy. As I learned very early on, people—especially men—often made assumptions about my character based solely on the fact that I was in show business. For my own safety and peace of mind, it was my policy never to play what we called "smokers": men-only private functions. I wasn't the only woman performer who shied away from these, and one result was that the functions' sponsors often offered extremely attractive fees, far above what a singer might earn for a regular club date or private party.

Before I left for Hawaii, my agent had called with what sounded like a terrific booking to entertain at the annual dinner of a private Canadian club.* Having always loved Canada and having felt comfortable there, I agreed to go. When I landed, the Canadian agent met me at the airport

*To preserve the privacy of the innocent people involved in the incidents described in the balance of this chapter, the names and other identifying characteristics of all the people involved have been changed.

with a bouquet of flowers, and we drove to the home of a "Mr. Buckley." He was the event's sponsor, and he had kindly invited me to stay with him, his wife, and their five children. The kids were so excited to be near someone in show business, they insisted I show them all my costumes, autograph pictures, and answer a million questions. After a lovely dinner, we retired early since we had a long drive the next day.

Mr. Buckley and I left for the long trip. We shared a pleasant conversation, and I lost track of time. When we finally arrived at our destination, a large, beautiful rustic lodge, I looked up and said, "I didn't know I was performing at a lodge."

"Oh, your agent didn't tell you?" Mr. Buckley asked. "It's for our big annual charity dinner."

I must have looked a little perturbed, because he quickly added, "But you don't have to stay. You'll be taken back to my home after the performance."

"Thank you," I replied, relieved.

Inside, Mr. Buckley introduced me to several of the organizers and then showed me to my dressing room, one of the largest and best appointed I've ever seen. The realization that I had been tricked into playing an all-male function didn't hit me until I got onstage. I could see only as far as the first few rows, but it was clear from the whistles when I removed part of my costume to go into a dance number that I was the only woman there.

I left the stage to thunderous applause and returned to my dressing room to get ready to leave. I wasn't nervous exactly, but annoyed that my agent had accepted this job without telling me it was, in fact, a smoker. I just wanted to get back to the comfort and safety of Mr. Buckley's home. "I'm staying over here," he told me after I'd changed, "so I'm having you driven back to my house by a friend who has to be back into town early, 'Mr. Fedderson' " (not his real name).

A wave of relief washed over me, and I began to relax. As I made my way toward the front entrance of the lodge, the men called out, "Thank you for coming, Miss Nichols!" "You were great!"

Mr. Buckley introduced me to "Jordie Fedderson," and I got into his car, a Rolls or a Mercedes. It was too dark to tell, but it was warm inside. By his manner and the way the other men spoke to him, I quickly gathered that Mr. Fedderson was an important, respected man in his community; he seemed very much a gentleman. After a few minutes of polite chitchat, he mentioned it would be a two-hour drive back to town. I pulled my big wool coat up around me and started to doze.

I had just begun to drop off when I felt something. *His hand on my leg!* I opened my eyes to see nothing but darkness and instinctively screamed, "Don't!"

Fedderson looked at me as if I were crazy. From his surprised but determined expression, I knew I was in trouble. He was stocky, strong, and angry. When I screamed, he snarled, "Shut up! What are you screaming for? You be nice to me, I'll be nice to you, hey?"

He thrust his hand toward me again, and I slapped it away. "I don't want to be nice!" I shouted. "I just want to get back to the Buckleys', so stop this. Please? Okay?"

"Okay! Okay!" he snapped, pulling away, but suddenly he jerked the car to a stop at the side of the road, killed the headlights, and turned toward me. He reached to kiss me. I pulled back. Then I heard the sound of lace being ripped from my dress.

"Listen," he hissed between clenched teeth, "no one can hear you, and no one will know."

I thought, *Either he's rehearsed this speech or said it many times before, because he is fully in control. And he knows it.*

"We've got all night. You want money? Okay, I understand. How much?"

Before I could answer, he lurched across the front seat and pinned me against the door. Kicking and screaming, shaking my head, I evaded his kiss, but by then he was furious.

"Okay! Get out and walk!" he screamed, red-faced. "You're miles from nowhere. Good luck!"

I looked out the window at the deep, seamless blackness. *How far out were we? How long had I slept? I had to get out—* I grabbed my bag and reached for the door handle when suddenly he revved the engine, I felt myself thrown back into the seat, and the car turned sharply back onto the road. Now he was driving so fast and so recklessly, I was sure we were going to crash. I cringed against the passenger door, my heart pounding, my mind racing: *I can't get out now!*

"You're lucky I'm such a nice guy!" He laughed. "You wouldn't get far: This is bear country, and there are wolves out there. Want to see some bears and mountain lions?"

It was like being in a nightmare. He veered off the main road and soon we were in a thickly wooded, mountainous area. After a mile, or two, or three—how could I know?—he slammed on the brakes, cut off the lights, and got out of the car. *I can't think. I can't think.* Where did he go? I can't see anything. Suddenly a flashlight beamed in my face, blinding me.

"Get out!"

"No!"

"Get out, or I'll drag you out!"

Shaking, I made myself slide off the leather seat, made my legs move through the grass and brush. I saw a cabin among the trees in the near distance, and the soft glow of a fire burning inside. I realized then that this wasn't a sudden whim. Fedderson planned this. *This isn't happening to me,* I kept repeating to myself. Then he brusquely grabbed my arm hard and pushed me inside.

"Don't touch me!" I screamed.

His eyes flashed anger, then uncertainty. Maybe he was thinking this wasn't such a good idea after all. *Maybe,* I hoped, *he will take me back. Maybe I can bargain with him.*

"Please, please, I won't tell. I swear I won't tell. Just please take me back."

He regarded me coolly.

Reason with him, I told myself. "They'll know you didn't take me back. If anything happens to me, they'll know it was you," the words ran out of me. "What will you tell them?"

"Shut up! I'm thinking!" he said and released my arm, but he was not thinking at all. This was part of the game, and as I, tricked by this momentary show of hesitancy, backed away, he charged me. "Don't fight me and you won't get hurt!" he warned, then he hit me hard. Grabbing a small, heavy statuette, I raised it.

This is not going to happen to me, I heard myself saying inside. "I've made up my mind!" I screamed, just inches from his surprised face. "You'll have to kill me!"

Fedderson stopped again.

"I'd rather die than let you touch me!"

"You're crazy!" he bellowed, but he backed off.

"Yeah, I am. Try me." And I watched him as he paced back and forth and back and forth like a caged animal, waiting for him to come near me again. Suddenly, inexplicably, he stormed out the door. The car drove away, and I was left there alone.

I have to survive, I told myself over and over as I huddled in a corner of the cabin, on the cold wooden floor, holding myself and rocking back and forth. The sound of steps—perhaps a bear, perhaps a wolf—outside the cabin, the howls and calls tore through the silence. The musty smell of the blanket I wrapped myself in. That was all there was to my world for that night. And there I was, in the middle of nowhere, without food, without water, without any way out except to die. *Who will find me? And when? And what if he comes back?* . . .

Just before dawn the cabin door creaked open slowly, and there stood a man I'd never seen before. By that point I was running on pure instinct, and the only way I could react was to scream hysterically as I pushed myself against the wall. The stranger seemed alarmed by my response, but he kept walking toward me, talking softly, trying to disguise the panic and fear on his own face. Whoever sent him, I realized then, didn't know it would be like this: I'd been bruised, my eye blackened, my clothes torn, hysterical.

"My name is 'Lloyd' (not his real name), Mr. Fedderson's law partner," he said. "I'm here to take you back."

He told me to calm down and asked me what I wanted. Then his tone and demeanor changed. He said "they" had the power to send me back to the United States. When I didn't respond he finally threatened me. And when that didn't work, he said, haughtily, certainly, "No one will believe a little colored showgirl from the States."

With great trepidation, I got into Lloyd's car; I had no choice. We drove in silence until we approached the town. It was around six A.M., and as the Sunday church bells pealed, Lloyd slowed down and proudly pointed out the school named after Fedderson's father and their family bank, the peaceful, perfect town square, and the mansion Fedderson lived in.

By the time we pulled into the driveway of a large, attractive but unfamiliar house, I'd gotten the message. "This is *my* house," Lloyd announced as he drove into the garage, so his neighbors couldn't see me. I pleaded with him to call Mr. Buckley to come for me, but he refused. I started to cry and slumped over in my seat. I was so tired, scared, and bruised, it took every ounce of concentration I could muster just to keep from falling apart. I had no fight left in me. His wife took me upstairs, practically carrying me. She bathed me in the tub, like a baby, then gave me something hot to drink. I felt myself floating down a long, dark tunnel. And I slept.

Not long after I awoke, Lloyd finally called Mr. Buckley, who came for me. Though I felt totally alone, I decided that Sunday night that I had to report what happened to the police before I returned home. There was no way that bastard was going to get away with this. Perhaps I was naive, but nothing could have prepared me for what happened next. The two detectives assigned to my case, "Dowdell" and "McDonald" (not their real names), listened to my story and questioned me carefully, but I could see that despite my bruises and my fear, they didn't really believe me. Next I was taken to a hospital, where I was examined and my injuries treated. The nurse and doctor there seemed sympathetic until I mentioned Fedderson's name. Then their attitude seemed to chill.

On the flight home, I replayed the incident in my mind and vowed not to tell anyone about it, not even my parents. During the weeks between the "incident," as I came to think of it, and the trial, the full weight of what had happened threatened to crush my very soul. For one interminable night I knew what it felt like to know I was going to die, and the fear of that knowledge—the fear of the power one person could wield over another—swirled around me. For weeks, no matter where I was or what I was doing, in my mind I was standing in a dark, howling vortex, gasping for breath as the winds forced my screams down, down, down, back into silence.

Over the next few weeks I received many ominous, threatening phone calls. Some clearly from Lloyd himself, telling me not to come back to Canada, offering me money, and threatening me with what could happen if I didn't cooperate. Finally, the day before I boarded a flight to Canada for the trial, I told my parents. They were angry, hurt, and devastated. They knew the trial would be painful and difficult. But they also understood that I had to do it.

The stewardess's voice jerked me out of my reverie. I had

been gazing numbly out the window, envying the sky its nothingness, remembering how I used to feel as the plane crossed the border: welcome, loved, accepted. But today, when this flight touched down, there would be no friends bearing flowers or ribboned bottles of champagne. Just two Canadian Mounted Police detectives, Dowdell and McDonald.

Standing at the top of the stairs, I looked down as the other passengers deplaned ahead of me. Dowdell's and McDonald's eyes met mine, and each heaved a small sigh of relief. They knew I didn't have to come back, that I couldn't have been forced to return against my will. They knew I could have been paid off, like Fedderson's other victims. Or scared away with threats against my life. What were the odds that a "little colored showgirl from the colonies" would voluntarily go up against a powerful man whose family counted among its allies the town's top law-enforcement officials, judges, and lawyers? Many of the detectives' colleagues back at the police station were placing bets on what the circumstances suggested was a sure thing: that I wouldn't show. Yet there I was.

Dowdell and McDonald escorted me through customs and into their car, then drove me to a small out-of-the-way hotel. The prosecutor stopped by, and we briefly discussed the case before the detectives took me to dinner. We talked a little about our plans for tomorrow, when they would take me to court, and after dinner, they saw me safely to my motel room.

Inside I took a long, hot bath, creamed my face, set my hair, and laid out my clothes for the next day: a soft gray wool suit, white silk blouse, black alligator shoes and matching bag, gray leather gloves. As I did, I recalled how impressed—actually, surprised—the investigators were to see an entertainer so conservatively dressed, and how the prosecutor remarked, "Just look as classy for court as you do right now." Without anyone saying it, I knew what they were thinking: *She is not the little colored showgirl we were expecting.* No, I was not.

I fell asleep that night and dreamed. Suddenly I jerked myself up off my pillow, and sat there in confusion, my heart pounding, *Where am I?* I hadn't had that dream for weeks, but why shouldn't I have it now? The clock read 3:30, and the room was so cold, spotting the radiator under the window, I reached for the lamp, then froze. A man was standing not more than ten feet from the window, the motel's blinking neon light casting an eerie bluish shadow. Without thinking, I pulled back the drapes to get a better look.

Stupid! He looked straight up at me and began walking quickly toward me. I ran for the phone. *Where did I put McDonald's number?* Barely breathing, I fumbled across the dark desk, the phone crashed to the floor, and then came a loud rap at the door.

"Are you all right, Miss? It's 'Officer Mooney.' " (Not his real name.)

No sooner had I gingerly replaced the receiver than the phone emitted a shrill, piercing ring. By then I was so scared I couldn't even speak.

"Hello! Are you there, Miss? This is Officer Mooney. If you're okay, please say so. Inspector McDonald will be worried."

My chest ached as I let out a breath, barely recognizing the tiny little girl's voice I heard as I said, "There's someone outside, watching my window."

"Oh, right. That was me," the officer said. "Was going to let you know. McDonald sent me over to watch over you, but your lights were out and I didn't want to bother you. Don't worry. Be right outside if you need me, Miss. Try to get some sleep now, hey?"

"Sure. Sure." *Sure.* Ten minutes later the phone rang again. It was McDonald, apologizing for not telling me, wishing me a good night, what was left of it. I was relieved they were taking the threats I'd received seriously; I just wished they'd told me about it. Knowing I'd never fall back to sleep, I wrapped myself in my robe, got a soda from the little refrigerator, and settled in a big chair. Shivering, I nervously started taking the curlers out of my hair, wondering if maybe I should learn to smoke for times like these. And, *How do we women sleep in these damn things?*

I drifted off again, and had the same nightmare—or should I call it a sleeping memory?—all over again. When the alarm rang I found myself still sitting in the chair. Looking out the window, I saw Mooney sitting drowsily in his car. It had been a long night. I stretched, showered, and dressed, and promptly at six-thirty, McDonald arrived. Over breakfast, the middle-aged detective and Dowdell, his inquisitive, boyish partner, reminded me, "You'll be the Crown's main witness, but don't let his attorney throw you. He'll try to discredit you. But remember: Just tell the story as you told us. Don't let him rattle you, hey?"

I looked at McD and D, as I'd come to think of them. "What made you guys believe me?" I asked. "Fedderson is such an important lawyer, from such a powerful family."

Dowdell met my gaze evenly, and with great candor, he replied, "We didn't—at first. We couldn't figure out why you waited so long after you finally got back from the cabin, until late Sunday night, to report it. It just didn't figure at first."

I nodded, and we finished our coffee and left.

"All rise."

Standing in the courtroom, it almost didn't seem real. And then I saw him sitting there with his wife and his children, his father, and around him many other well-dressed, privileged people. *Which is his mother?* I wondered. *What does she think?* Then I noticed Lloyd, Fedderson's lawyer, staring at me, trying to fathom me, to intimidate me, and I returned his gaze. *No, not the "little colored showgirl" from the States!* I wanted to shout in his face.

I thought back to the morning he found me in the cabin, the threats, the tour of his nice, clean little town, the bribes, the phone calls. *That was you, Mr. Attorney Lloyd!* I wanted to shout in the courtroom.

"State your name, place your hand on the Bible, please."

I swore to tell the whole truth, and I did, for hours, as the courtroom clock clicked like a metronome. I felt detached, almost calm as I told the story, but it was a protection I needed as I took everyone in the courtroom with me, step-by-step through that horrible weekend, until I heard myself saying, "Then Mr. and Mrs. Buckley picked me up and took me back to their home."

"And what time was that?" the prosecutor asked.

"About seven o'clock in the evening."

"You say you were brought to Mr. Lloyd's house around seven A.M. After he gave you a tour of the town?"

"Yes."

"And the Buckleys came and picked you up at seven that evening."

"Yes."

"Why so late? Why did you wait so long to get out of there?"

I'd been waiting for this, because, as the prosecutor had cautioned me before, this was the weak link in my story. I found Mrs. Lloyd in the crowd, and, focusing on her face, replied evenly, "I'd not slept since six-thirty Saturday morning. I was bruised, both physically and emotionally, and I didn't really know where I was, or the Buckleys' phone number. After Mrs. Lloyd bathed me, I passed out from exhaustion. When Mr. Buckley finally came for me, he said he had only just returned from the lodge and received the message that I was at the Lloyds'. He had no idea what had happened to me."

"And then what did you do?"

I felt my face flush and my eyes sting. I had been holding up so well, but the terror and confusion of those hours welled back up inside me. *Just tell the story,* I told myself.

"I didn't know if Mr. Buckley had been part of it until I got back to his home," I began evenly. "His wife was frantic. She had expected me that night before, or rather two or three o'clock in the morning. Mr. Buckley had called her, and she'd waited up for me. She had not heard anything until Sunday afternoon. Then her husband had not returned until six-thirty or so. That's when he picked me up."

"And then," the prosecutor said, knowing full well what was coming.

"Well, then they knew something was wrong. I just wanted to get on a plane and go home, but I couldn't. And then it just all came out, and I threw up, and finally I truly cried. Great heaving gulps of pain came spewing out, and they held me and they cried and begged my forgiveness, and then they called the police, and I had to go through it all over again."

I stopped, feeling myself swept away in the awful memories. But I had to go on. "And they took me to the hospital, and a female officer talked to me, and a male doctor examined my bruises and made sure I'd not had sex or been raped. And I knew from their faces and their questions and their tone of voice, they didn't believe me. From the moment they heard his name, they changed. They just didn't believe me."

"Would you like to stop for a while, Miss Nichols?" the prosecutor asked kindly.

I shook my head no.

"Well," he continued gently, "we're all here today. Someone must have believed you."

"Yes," I whispered.

"Why do you think you were finally believed?" the prosecutor asked. He meant it rhetorically, of course, and Attorney Lloyd was jumping to his feet to object as I blurted out, "Because I believe they discovered he'd molested other girls who were frightened off or paid off!"

Pandemonium erupted, and over it all Lloyd shouted, "Objection! Objection! Nothing of that sort is in evidence, Your Honor! Objection!"

"But he told me himself," I said, staring Lloyd right in the eye. "And so did you, Mr. Lloyd."

"Order in the court!" the judge shouted over the noise. "Fifteen-minute recess!" Then he ordered Lloyd and the prosecutor into his chambers. Within seconds the prosecutor's assistants were leading me into an anteroom, and McD and D came running in soon after. The prosecutor was furious, pouncing on the detectives the minute they entered. "Where the hell did she get that information?" he demanded, glaring at the pair. "You know it was ruled out of evidence!"

The detectives convincingly protested their innocence, but they could barely disguise their pleasure at this turn of events.

"I don't understand," I said. "I only repeated what they both told me."

"*Both* of them told you there were other girls before you?" the prosecutor asked, angrily eyeing the detectives again.

"Fedderson and Lloyd, dammit!" I replied. "Fedderson that night and Lloyd later in the cabin and in the car on the way back to town. When he tried to buy me off. 'Take the money,' Lloyd said. 'They all do, sooner or later.' I told you that before, didn't I?"

"Stay here," the prosecutor said wearily. "I've got to see the judge in his chambers."

Court reconvened, and the statement was ruled inadmissible, but the prosecutor didn't seem to mind. "Your witness, counselor," he said to Lloyd.

Lloyd approached the witness stand, and beneath his

professional veneer I could see he was seething. Now everyone knew he was more than a defense attorney, he was practically a defendant. He recounted my testimony, tinting my words with innuendo and doubt. The more he tried to trip me up, the calmer and more detached I became.

"Yes, your wife was very compassionate. . . . Yes, I talked with your children when I awakened. . . . No, I was not able to eat the nice dinner you offered me. . . . Yes, I did ask you to call the Buckleys. . . . No, I didn't know if you really had until Mr. Buckley arrived. . . . No, I did not ask you to call the police. No, not even once."

Lloyd paused for effect, then turned to me and said slowly, "Do you recall when you finally awakened after eight hours of sleep? Oh, you did sleep eight hours, did you not? Yes? Well, you certainly must have felt safe enough in our house to sleep peacefully and soundly for hours that day, did you not?"

"Objection!" the prosecutor cried.

"Withdraw the question, Your Honor," Lloyd replied before circling back to renew the attack. "Now, you do recall when you finally awakened, it was around what—four? Four-thirty? And we had dinner, and then a neighbor stopped by. Do you remember?"

"Yes."

"Fine. And I introduced him, do you recall?"

"Yes."

"Good. Do you recall my telling you what his profession was? Take your time please," Lloyd rattled in one breath.

"You told me he was a policeman," I shot back. "It was that man sitting in the second row," I said calmly, pointing. " 'John Carver' [not his real name]."

Everyone turned to look at Carver, gasping, but Lloyd knew exactly what he was trying to achieve.

"Well," he began smugly, "if you had been so violently molested against your will, and imprisoned against your will; if you didn't trust us—where you slept for six to eight hours and ate and played with our children, as you admit—why did you not scream, 'Officer! Officer! Help me! I've been violated. Help me!' Why, dear lady, when you had the perfect opportunity?"

I felt myself freeze, as I saw the self-satisfied smirks on Fedderson's and Lloyd's faces. They had me, they thought. And in a way, they did. But I decided that nobody who tried to make me feel like something less than a human being was going to succeed. Nobody.

I took a deep breath, then fixed Lloyd in my gaze and replied firmly, "Because I did not trust you. Even if he was a policeman, he was your golf buddy. Your children played with his children. He lived across the street. After what happened to me by two of this town's 'finest,' I didn't trust you or your cop friend."

Embarrassed and visibly stung, Lloyd appealed to the judge. "Your Honor, the witness is not being responsive to my question. Please instruct the—"

"Counselor, you opened the barn door with a fusillade of interrogations. Let's just let the witness have her turn. Please proceed, Miss Nichols."

How awkward Lloyd appeared when things didn't go his way. Now feeling the sympathy of the court resting on my side, I continued.

"When you tried to buy me off, Mr. Lloyd, you called me 'a hot potato.' You tried to scare me. I was born and raised in Chicago, Mr. Lloyd, where Al Capone's brother almost killed my father for raiding one of his gin mills. Cops were a dime a dozen back then, and you didn't strike me as being much better.

"I wanted out of there. *Alive.* So I kept quiet until Mr. Buckley came and got me."

Lloyd stared at me for a long time, as if he didn't know what to do, before he muttered, "No more questions, Your Honor."

Seizing the moment, the prosecutor requested and was granted permission to ask one more question on redirect.

"Will you tell the court why you've filed these charges against Jordie Fedderson?"

"Yes. I want him to know that money and position do not give him the right to violate another human being for any reason. And when a woman says no, she has a right to say no. And that means no!"

I stepped down from the stand and sat alongside the prosecutor as Mr. Lloyd trotted out a parade of character witnesses, who spoke in defense of Mr. Fedderson's fine character. In the end, however, it was up to the jury, and four hours later, they returned with the verdict: "Guilty on the charge of attempted rape. Guilty on the charge of violent assault. Guilty on the charge of illegal detention."

Jordie Fedderson lost his license to practice law, was fined an enormous sum, and received five to ten years in prison. The latter was reduced to probation. The judge was his father's lifelong friend.

That night changed my life in ways innumerable and yet unknowable. Despite the passage of years, despite changes in attitude toward violence against women, I still find speaking about this painful. The texture of these memories stands out from everything else, assuming a bizarre, almost cinematic quality. When I recall everything else in my life, I am *there.* When I force myself to think back to this, however, I cannot simply "remember." Instead I become a horrified spectator who sees it all as if for the first time yet is powerless to turn away or to make it stop. After that night, my days on the road were over.

CHAPTER FIVE

I had no choice but to begin building my career in Los Angeles. Certainly the prospect of starting over again, as it were, in a town crawling with talent was daunting. And then I had to think about money, for I was supporting not only Kyle but my parents as well. My decision to focus my sights on film or television wasn't an easy one. I knew that months, perhaps even years, of sacrifice and discipline lay ahead, but something inside me told me I could make it work.

Of course, I could always sing, and despite being a virtual unknown in my adopted hometown, I managed to get a few bookings. On one of my very first engagements, I opened for comedian Redd Foxx at a little jazz joint on Western Avenue. At the time Redd was known for his hilarious "party" records and blue jokes, and, believe me, he had a filthy mouth. But he was so incredibly funny and charming that even when he hit on me, I couldn't get mad at him. Sensing my opening-night jitters, he introduced me as "fine, brown, and terrific."

"Don't mess with her," he playfully warned the men in the crowd. "This is my little sister and I don't play dat shit!" Everyone laughed and gave me a warm reception when I hit the stage, and I never forgot Redd for that. Slowly, jobs came my way, and soon Kyle and I were able to get our own place a few blocks from my parents'.

Not much time passed before I got what felt then like the break of my life: a small part in the Samuel Goldwyn production of *Porgy and Bess,* George and Ira Gershwin's Black "American Folk Opera." This was the break I'd been waiting for, though not because it brought me sudden fame. In fact, by the time the film was edited, I could be easily missed in the blink of an eye. No, *Porgy and Bess* brought me together with the greatest Black stars of the day—Sammy Davis, Jr., Pearl Bailey, Dorothy Dandridge, Sidney Poitier—and opened doors for me that I might have otherwise been knocking on for years.

I had auditioned for the music director and won a place in the first chorus, whose members would also play characters in Catfish Row. I was ecstatic, for all the other singers chosen had just come from appearing in a production of *Porgy and Bess* that toured Russia. Then, to my dismay, I was called back by another agent to come in and try out as a dancer. I was so new to Hollywood, I jumped at the opportunity, not realizing that once hired in this second capacity, I became a singer-dancer-actor and what is known as a "must join" in the Screen Actors Guild (SAG). Unwittingly, I did the right thing and became a full-fledged card-carrying screen actor rather than an extra.

About fifty of us auditioned for the legendary Hermes Pan, who had been Fred Astaire's personal choreographer and the architect of some of Hollywood's most memorable, lavish musical production numbers. While waiting for the audition to begin I noticed one dancer in particular, who was strikingly tall and very African looking, not a glamour type at all. We struck up a conversation, and during the hour or more we waited for Pan to arrive, I learned that this six-foot-tall woman had been the lead dancer in the show's road company. I found her quite friendly and engaging, but I couldn't help but compare her slightly gawky movements with my years of dance training and suspected that she was telling me a "story." As she recounted having toured Russia with the show as the lead dancer, I remember thinking to myself, *Sure, and I'm the prima ballerina of the Bolshoi.* Yet she had such stature and eloquence, and a peculiar grace, that by the time Hermes Pan and his entourage finally showed up, I didn't care what the truth was. Her name was Maya Angelou, and we began a close friendship that continues to this day.

Pan was gentle and friendly and moved with a lanky grace that gave the impression that he was much taller than he actually was. I got the sense that he regarded the Black dancers as exotic and challenging, and he saw in us the means of taking his choreography in new directions. Pan put us through our paces, and I watched as Maya did some funny footwork that transformed her into an African Dahomey queen. Pan, impressed by my unusual combination of classical ballet moves and Afro-Cuban pelvic contractions and Maya's unique style, made us his first two choices for the select ten or twelve dancers who comprised the main dance corps.

Our director was the great, infamous Otto Preminger, a very tall, frightful man with a massive bald head and piercing ice-blue eyes who was quite accustomed to having his way. He roared like a lion and seemed to delight in watching the cast and crew scatter. Preminger was notorious for having crushed some of the biggest egos in town, but he soon realized that this wasn't just any cast. With the exception of poor, beautiful Dorothy Dandridge (with whom he was having an affair and whom he seemed to enjoy reducing to tears daily), the stars of this show were not about to be intimidated. Invariably something would set off one of

Preminger's infamous tantrums, and Sidney, Pearl, Sammy, Diahann Carroll, and Brock Peters would simply stop and look on calmly as he ranted and raved at any and all, whether they were involved or not. When Preminger finally wound down and regained his self-control, one by one they would silently walk off the set and retire to their respective dressing rooms, refusing to emerge until he apologized or went on to a scene that didn't involve the offended star.

Fed up with Preminger's condescending attitude toward everyone in the all-Black cast, Sidney Poitier called a full cast meeting. He carefully planned it for a time when Dorothy Dandridge was not on the set. She was a delicate, beautiful woman who deserved far better treatment than Preminger gave her, and Sidney didn't want to cause her further problems with our director.

As Preminger stood there baffled, Sidney expressed his annoyance in no uncertain terms. "Otto! We are not Stepin Fetchits. We are artists!" he roared. "And we will not tolerate your bullying, white slavemaster tactics!"

"Hear! Hear!" Brock Peters growled.

"You do not *listen,* Otto," Sammy added, somewhat more gently. "Otto, baby, you gotta listen, man."

Surprisingly, Preminger did listen without arguing. But to make certain that he fully understood the problem, Pearlie Mae settled it once and for all.

"Look, Otto, honey," she began. "There ain't no use goin' through this over and over. You've got professional people here, from the stars to the singers and dancers, even the *extras.* We know our business and we all workin' hard, but you are not givin' us the respect that is due us. And the way you treatin' that poor child Dandridge is disgustin', with her breakin' down every day in tears and holdin' up production. You better figure this out, honey: We are human beings, not slaves! If you don't, you ain't gonna have no picture."

"Miss Bailey, vat do you vant from me?" Preminger finally asked.

Pearlie Mae's eyes narrowed. "Dahlin', I know you ain't stupid, and I know you know what *respect* is. But just in case, I'll tell you. You can start with this damned script. It's written by some silly-ass white boy who's trying to write colored. It's insulting. First, he's written all these 'dees' and 'dems' and 'dose' and 'Ises' and 'weeses' and 'beeses.' Well, we've tried to act this dumb crap, but it's all ridiculous. Besides," she added, chuckling, "they're all in the wrong places!"

"Vat do you suggest, Pearl?" Preminger asked, truly befuddled.

"Honey, just let 'em write the script in plain English without your white version," she replied. Lapsing into a stereotypical Southern dialect, she quipped, "Wese knows where dem 'deses' and 'doses' and 'I's' 'sposed to beses, Mr. Charlie. We don't need no white boy tellin' *us* how to be cullud . . . *suh!*"

She held Preminger in her gaze, and he stood speechless while the rest of us gaped awestruck. Until then Sidney had maintained a formidable stance of righteous indignation and fury, but Pearl's cutting, hilarious performance was simply too much, and suddenly his deep, unbridled laughter broke the silence. Soon we were all laughing until tears rolled down our cheeks, while Preminger, unsure whether to be amused or insulted, stood looking absolutely baffled. The next day we received revised scripts, sans the offensive dialogue, and from then on, the actors themselves added the appropriate antebellum figures of speech and pronunciations where they saw fit. And Otto Preminger, probably for the first time in his career, treated actors as human beings.

Shooting on location always changes a production, and I don't mean just geographically. Location is to actors and crews what summer camp is to teenagers—a chance to make fast, often short-lived friendships and romances. Maya was my roommate, and she and I, along with a tall, lanky, beautiful baritone named Joe James (also from the Russian company), talked, sipped wine, and laughed through almost every night. Maya was a drinking buddy one minute, a philosopher another, Pagliacci the next, but always a provocateur. Even then, I was in awe of her. Later, when I read her first volume of autobiography, *I Know Why the Caged Bird Sings,* I recalled her having told me those same stories years before, with the same depth and spirit the rest of the world soon discovered.

Then there was Sammy Davis, Jr. He struck me as one of the sexiest, most sensuous men I'd ever seen. He was so enormously talented and charming, and at the same time so vulnerable. Sammy let it be known that he was stuck on me and couldn't understand my attraction to Joe, whom Sammy referred to as "Ichabod Crane." He was just jealous. On the plane to Arizona Sammy had asked me to have dinner with him that night, but when he didn't call, Maya and Joe consoled and distracted me, and I decided to hell with Sammy. When he emerged in the hotel lobby the next morning with his arm around the very prominent fanny of an extra and asked, "And how was your night?" I surprised myself with how furious I was.

One of the important scenes we shot while on location in Arizona was the Kittiwah Island scene. In it Sammy, as Sportin' Life, does a big dance number after seducing Bess and convincing her to go with him to New York. Sammy was to pull me up on a barge, then we were to dance together before I took a solo turn. It was a wonderful number, and although it was later substantially edited, there was enough left in to give a newcomer a real boost.

We returned to Los Angeles to shoot the last scenes, and already everyone was laying plans for the next job. Of the leading cast, only Sidney and Dorothy were true box-office film stars; everyone else was a top star on stage, in concert, or on record. Both Pearl and Sammy would be going straight into Las Vegas, so every night they rehearsed their shows after we closed the set.

Sammy loved my dancing, and he often visited rehearsals and joined in. Hermes Pan welcomed his arrival, since he knew that whenever Sammy was around, all of us dancers did our best, showing off for him. Because Sammy always worked out with me and did nothing to keep his feelings for me a secret, Maya and Joe teased me mercilessly about him. We were not romantically involved then, but by the time Pearlie Mae asked me to join her show, I had already accepted Sammy's offer to do a big special number with him in his Vegas show and then tour with him.

Unfortunately, Sammy's doctors cautioned him against mounting a big production, and with great regret he informed me and several other cast members that he had to cancel his tour. Sammy and the rest of us were very disappointed, but Pearlie Mae couldn't have been happier: At last she had the pick of the talent pool Sammy had raided before. My big break now blown away, I gratefully accepted her second offer.

Pearlie Mae held her rehearsals in Hollywood, at seven P.M. sharp. I, along with other performers, would hurry over to her place, only to be left standing outside waiting twenty, forty, sometimes even ninety minutes until she arrived inevitably, unapologetically late. Soon I learned that not only would I not be a featured performer, but I would have the distinct "honor" of carrying Miss Bailey's train and bowing to Her Majesty. They say art imitates life, and Pearlie Mae's imperialistic manner did not stop at the footlights. I was shocked to see her address some of the other singers—most of whom were classically trained—as if they were stranded burlesque gypsies.

Marching across the rehearsal space, handing out contracts, she admonished, "Your call will be ninety minutes before showtime. Be bathed, dressed, and don't be wearin' none of that cheap Balalaika perfume."

She stopped suddenly, then added, "And no fraternizin'

in my show, or your checks will be docked for each infraction!"

I started to laugh but quickly realized she was not kidding. I thought for a moment of her eloquent speech to Preminger about respect, then I looked around the room. Each face registered stunned resignation. Maybe they would endure this disrespectful treatment, but it was not for me. I took a deep breath and, handing her my unsigned contract, said, "Pearl, I'm really proud that you want me in your show, but I've decided to stay in L.A. and work on my own singing career. I hope to be a star someday, like you."

My knees grew weak as I braced myself for her blistering reply. Instead she looked at me and softly said, "That's beautiful, dahlin'. That's the way to do it." Smiling, she put her arm around my shoulder and said, "You got class, honey. You gonna make it, and you got a friend in Pearlie Mae. Don't you forget it!"

I never did.

After we finished filming *Porgy and Bess,* Sammy called me at home several times, then began sending flowers. And more flowers, until my apartment looked like a nursery. I picked up the phone one day and heard him croon, "Dinner on Sunday. I'll send my driver for you. Want you to meet my folks. Sunday, around five?"

"Fine," I replied with a gulp.

"Fine," he purred and hung up.

That Sunday I dressed and redressed a few times before settling on the white silk dress I'd originally put on. Limousines were not an everyday sight in my neighborhood, and as Sammy's driver accompanied me down the sidewalk to the waiting car, I could hear blinds opening, curtains being pulled back, shades rolling up.

A short while later we arrived at Sammy's home in the Hollywood Hills, where I was greeted by his mother, Elvera Davis, a former Cotton Club chorus girl, whom everyone called Baby. Even though I soon found out she wasn't expecting me, she was extremely gracious and personable. I looked around for Sammy as she introduced me to their family and a couple of friends and made me feel at home.

"Well, Sammy ought to be back any minute," she stated hopefully but without much conviction.

"Back? Am I too early? He said—" It was clear that none of us knew what was going on, and so rather than prolong everyone's discomfort, I thanked Mrs. Davis and everyone else and suggested that the driver take me home.

"I will not hear of it!" Baby replied, dismissing the driver and instructing the cook to serve dinner. "You are a guest in my home. I insist you stay for dinner as *my* honored guest. We girls got a lot to talk about. We girls got a lot to teach these boys, hmmm?"

She was right, and I had a wonderful evening. At eight I thanked Mrs. Davis for her hospitality and said my good-nights. The driver was as professional and courteous as before, but he seemed to be in a rush to get me home, and that suited me. I sat in the soft, plush backseat, blinking back bitter tears and thinking, *To hell with Sammy—and all men!*

The driver pulled the limo smoothly to the curb, jumped out, and opened my door. "Good night!" I snapped curtly, then started up my driveway. I was fumbling for my keys when I sensed someone nearby. I looked up at the stoop, and there sat Sammy, wilted roses in hand.

"What took you so long?" he asked smoothly.

"I had dinner with friends."

Our eyes locked for a long time, both of us knowing precisely what had happened. Once again, Sammy was putting me to his own quirky test. He grinned that silly grin of his, and I broke up laughing. So began a short, stormy, exciting relationship, but one without enough room for my career ambitions as well as Sammy's demanding needs. His loyalty to Frank Sinatra's Rat Pack and its swinging life-style weren't for me. We did, however, remain friends.

Years later in the seventies, he and his wife Altovise lived up the hill from my house, so close we used to wave to each other.

I began performing at the Ebony Showcase Theatre, a small all-Black theater owned by Nicodemus Stewart, whom most people know from his portrayal of the shiftless handyman Lightnin' on the early-fifties television series *Amos 'n' Andy*. By the early sixties, that show and the negative Black stereotypes it had presented were anathema to most Blacks, so people are often surprised to learn that Nick Stewart was an extremely serious man who was almost militant in his support of Black culture and Black theater. Through vision and perseverance, he built the Ebony Showcase Theatre into a major theater.

I was just reemerging from the ashes of my brief fling with Sammy and diligently working on my solo singing act. Nick and his wife Edna cast me in the lead of their new play, *Carnival Island.* We were in the midst of rehearsing a big musical number when suddenly the music stopped and everyone glanced toward the door and began whispering. I turned to see a strikingly handsome man talking to Nick and Edna. He had amber skin, silky, straight black hair shocked with gray, and a face that appeared at once roughly hewn yet sensuously soft. Our eyes met, and I was captivated.

"This is Frank Silvera, Nichelle," I heard Nick saying to me.

"You have a beautiful voice," Frank said graciously.

Nick called a wrap for the day, then explained that Frank had agreed to direct *Carnival Island* and asked if I would stay and work with him. Over the next few hours I listened as Frank shared his insight into the characters and the script. He was an actor's actor, and he spoke with great conviction and authority, though always in a self-effacing, almost shy manner. I was transfixed by his every word and enthralled by the mystery of his voice—velvety and warm, yet tinged with a roughness—his seemingly contradictory demeanor, and his magnificent face.

That night he asked me to dinner, and we never parted for the next six years. This was the love of my life.

Frank was born in Jamaica in 1914. His father was a Sephardic Jew, and his mother, African. Although throughout his long, distinguished career he played characters ranging from Italian mafiosi and Mexican bandits to Jewish rabbi, Southern white gentlemen, and even King Lear, he always considered himself Black. He had first made his mark in New York, where he appeared on and off Broadway, then in films and television. Within the acting community, however, Frank was revered as a great teacher and director, and his counsel was sought by some of the greatest actors of the time. "Papa," they called him affectionately.

In Frank I found not only a wonderful man but an inspiration. Each time I sang, danced, or acted for him, he proved an enthusiastic, supportive audience and an astute, honest critic. He never sought to undermine or diminish my talent. When I was stung by rejection, he praised me lavishly and celebrated my achievements. I remember sitting up in bed one night after opening at Ye Little Club in Beverly Hills. "She sometimes reminds you of Lena or Eartha, until you realize she is uniquely Nichelle," critic Rex Reed wrote, and we read it over and over again, savoring every word. I felt myself soaring under his wing.

Frank was incredibly bighearted and generous, and my son, Kyle, then around nine, loved him. Those two Leos took to each other from the start, and before long they truly were father and son. Whether discussing what we'd done that day at Disneyland, astronomy, politics, or Kyle's latest passion for prehistoric animals, they were totally in sync. Frank respected and encouraged Kyle's tireless pursuit of knowledge and understanding. My parents adored Frank, and in short order we became a family.

In 1960 Frank was cast as the Tahitian chief in the remake of *Mutiny on the Bounty.* He knew it would require at least several months away on location in Tahiti, and he was reluctant to leave me. But his friend Marlon Brando had asked for him, and Frank felt he could not say no.

Brando asked Frank to come by the studio where they were doing some preliminary filming, and when Frank invited me along, I was thrilled. Even as he sat in a makeup chair being transformed into Fletcher Christian, Brando was formidable, charismatic, intimidating. After the introductions were made, Brando slowly turned his gaze on me and asked, "What's a beautiful young thing like you doing with the Old Man?"

My jaw dropped open. It wasn't until later that I learned that "Old Man" was another title of respect bestowed upon Frank by Brando and some of the other "Strasberg kids" from the Actors Studio in New York.

"The Old Man, indeed." Haughtily, I'm afraid, I responded, "I love every inch of his magnificent being."

Frank, I learned later, flinched with embarrassment, but Brando roared with laughter. "Nichelle . . . Nichelle . . ." he said thoughtfully. "Hmmm. What's your real name?"

"Nichelle," I replied.

"I see. I will make you a bet that that is not so."

"How much are you prepared to lose?" I asked.

Brando smirked, sure he had me. "A half of a cookstove."

"What color?" I retorted.

Brando laughed. "Hey, Pops! You got yourself a smart kid here." Then he abruptly turned to me and stated, "Pink!"

Several days later Brando invited us to dinner at the Japanese Gardens on Sunset Strip. There Frank and I were shown to the private dining room where Brando and some other guests were seated on low pillows. Brando had saved the pillow across from him for me, and when we entered, he gestured to it, smiling, without a word. Halfway through the meal, he said, "How is your memory?"

I smiled, beckoned the waitress, and a few minutes later she placed a large, elaborately wrapped gift on the table between us, bowed, and left. Brando glanced at the box, then seemed to ignore it until we were served ginger ice cream. Then slowly, deliberately, he pulled at the satin ribbon and peeled away the wrapping until the "box" itself—designed to break away once free of the wrapping—opened to reveal half of a small pink cookstove cut perfectly down the middle. Brando's girlfriend read the enclosed card: "I always pay my debts. Nichelle, a.k.a. Grace Nichols."

Brando stared inscrutably into my eyes for a long moment, then mumbled, "Touché" and broke into gales of laughter.

During the weeks before Frank departed for Tahiti, we held each other as if for dear life. Looking back now, I see that for Frank our love wasn't quite so idyllic. He was twenty years older than I, and it bothered him much more than I realized. I'd always been attracted to older men—from my first dates in high school to Foster Johnson. My mother and my grandmother both married men significantly older, so it simply wasn't an issue for me. Had I been wiser, though, I would have seen Frank's fear of losing me whenever he inquired if I didn't want more children.

I couldn't imagine staying alone in L.A. without Frank, so I was relieved when my agent called with a four-week booking in Hawaii. I'd been back in town just a couple of days when two of my friends, actors Major Conak and James Edwards, parked their bright blue Cadillac convertible under my bedroom window and blew the horn. I stuck my head out the window, ready to tell whoever they were where to go, when I saw the two of them, singing at the top of their lungs, "Nichelle is going to New York! Nichelle is going to star in *Kicks and Company!* And we're not going to stop blowing on the horn 'til she comes out!"

For several weeks the two of them had been pressuring me to audition, but I didn't see the point of a Hollywood actress auditioning for a Broadway play that Cicely Tyson, Diana Sands, and other good New York actresses had already read for. But, bless them, my friends had faith in me, and before long my neighbors were screaming in exasperation, "Go to the damn audition already!"

"Get out of here!"

"Go to New York!!!"

How could I say no? I auditioned that afternoon for the show's director, Vinnette Carroll, and choreographer, Donald McKayle, and was given the script to study that night. Could I be ready to read by nine the next morning? Would I go to New York and audition for the show's creator, Oscar Brown, Jr.? And, if things went well, would I be willing to go to Broadway? Yes, yes, and yes.

A week later I was in New York City, auditioning for Oscar Brown, Jr., a brilliant singer, songwriter, and playwright who'd made quite a name for himself in and around Chicago and among the musical theater cognoscenti. With this new play, *Kicks and Company,* he was destined, many predicted, to break into the big time. There was no question but that this show was Broadway bound. It had run at a small theater with Oscar in the role of Mr. Kicks, and he was fabulous as a modern-day Satan. Oscar, however, felt that he needed a bigger name in the title role, and so he relinquished it to Burgess Meredith, a highly regarded serious actor. Given that the cast of the play was largely Black, this seemed an unusual decision.

Later, Burgess, a lovely, brilliant man to whom I became quite close, confided, "They're crazy; Oscar should be doing the show. This play is going to get some bad reviews, and I can handle it, but the play cannot. The only one who's going to come out of this with any good reviews is you, Nichelle." It was as if Burgess had a crystal ball.

Going into it, though, we had nothing but high hopes. As Hazel Sharpe, I played a lovely, naive college girl who quits school and goes to Chicago to make her fame and fortune as a singer. She gets involved with and turned out by the satanic Mr. Kicks. But before she becomes a prostitute, she gives it all up and returns to her small hometown. There she waits tables in a restaurant frequented by college kids, the scene of one of my big showcase numbers, "Hazel Hips." In the words of Silky Satin, a modern-day Sportin' Life, "It's her hips that get the tips," and his spurned advances and Hazel's noncapitulation formed the premise of a very hot, sexy dance that had me doing a hundred high kicks and being thrown up in the air by a troupe of sixteen male dancers fresh from *West Side Story*.

Kicks and Company was plagued by a thousand different problems, but its fatal flaw was its concept. Or, rather, its principals' inability to agree on what that was. Oscar Brown wrote a provocative, sexy, modern allegory about the wages of sin and the personification of evil (as embodied in Mr. Kicks and a Hugh Hefner–type character). Another Chicago native, playwright Lorraine Hansberry, invested a tremendous amount of her own money to produce the play. Coincidentally, I had known Lorraine since I was a child. We were next-door neighbors, her father, Carl, was one of my father's best friends, and, being several years old than I was, she'd often walked me to school.

It had been just two years since her *A Raisin in the Sun* premiered, making her indisputably the most important Black playwright of the time. I so looked forward to seeing her again. That is, until she arrived. She immediately fired Vinnette Carroll, who'd done a wonderful job, and brought in Burgess Meredith's friend William Saroyan as a script doctor. He made several excellent suggestions—among them recasting Oscar Brown, Jr. as Mr. Kicks—

which she ignored. Instead Lorraine decided that the play's problem was that it was "too undignified, too Black," an interesting comment coming from her, of all people. Rather than improve on the show's strong points—the underlying blues of the score, the hot, show-stopping numbers—she set to work making the play "better." That meant replacing the blues passages in the score with innocuous string arrangements and taking all the high kicks, lifts, and hip twirling out of my dances because they were "demeaning" to Black women. At the very last minute, she demanded new choreography, new arrangements, and new staging. Then, after making everyone absolutely crazy, she proceeded to lecture us on dignity.

In rehearsal we followed her directions, but during the previews we reverted back to the old, scintillating choreography, which the audience loved. Lorraine, furious over my insubordination, sewed up the slit in my costume. That night, just as I went into the dance, I simply pulled up the skirt a little bit higher and kept going. The next night when I put on my costume, you could still see the threads where I'd pulled the stitches out, but her threat of firing me still hung over my head. As it turned out, she didn't get the chance. We opened at Chicago's then new Arie Crown and closed in a matter of days, although, as Burgess predicted, my reviews were spectacular. "Her body is a work of art," Dorothy Kilgallen wrote, "and she uses it with tact and grace."

Although the show died a quick, painful death, neither it nor I had gone unnoticed. After a successful run at the Chicago Playboy Club, I returned to Los Angeles, then came back to New York. With its great musical stage and a plethora of top clubs, New York City was every singer's dream, and it wasn't long before I began seriously considering moving there and pursuing my first love. Every day I studied voice with a teacher, who lived in a grand old building with the old-fashioned "cage"-type elevators.

After my lesson, as I descended into the lobby, I'd look across and wave at the young woman ascending in the other elevator, his next student. Her name was Barbra Streisand. That was not the first or last time our paths crossed, though.

While in New York I had the pleasure of opening at the famous Blue Angel, one of the most respected, sophisticated rooms in the world. The stately, formal, almost dour demeanor of the club's owner, Herbert Jacoby, was reflected in the all-black cocktail lounge, the uncomfortably small tables, and the tiny stage. Yet this odd little room on Fifty-fifth Street and Third Avenue was *the* place to be seen, one of the few top New York clubs that had always welcomed Black patrons. Jacoby launched the careers of countless stars—among them Pearl Bailey, Eartha Kitt, Harry Belafonte, Barbara McNair, and later, Woody Allen, Lenny Bruce, and Barbra. In fact, during my run there, the pianist in the lounge was none other than Bobby Short. I opened at midnight, and among the audience were William Saroyan, the Duke and Duchess of Windsor, Frederick Loewe, Burgess Meredith, and Pearl Bailey. Reading the next morning's papers, I knew I could not have garnered better reviews if I'd written them myself. "If you were permitted to use but one word to describe Nichelle Nichols," wrote the reviewer from the *New York Journal-American,* "that word would have to be fascinating." I left the Blue Angel and moved to the Bon Soir; the singer I replaced at the Bon Soir then replaced me at the Blue Angel: none other than Barbra. Later, she would record one of my numbers from *Kicks and Company,* "Like a Newborn Child."

During that period I was back and forth between Los Angeles and New York City, while Frank continued to work on *Mutiny on the Bounty.* I had barely unpacked my bags when composer Richard Rodgers asked me to serve as standby to the lead in his *No Strings,* the first musical he wrote after the death of his longtime partner Oscar Hammerstein, and the first for which he wrote both the music and the lyrics. Diahann Carroll had been playing the role for several months to great acclaim, but he was not certain she would stay with the show and wanted the role covered if she left suddenly. In four days I learned the entire show. The star-crossed love affair between a successful Black model (played by Diahann) and a white photographer (played by Richard Kiley) was, for its time, quite provocative. And the score, especially the oft-covered "Loads of Love," was sumptuous. Although it was not an overwhelming hit with critics, the show, which opened in March 1962, ran for over a year.

When Richard Rodgers discovered that I danced, which Diahann did not, he had a special dance choreographed for "Loads of Love," just in case. I had known Diahann since *Porgy and Bess,* and was dying for my chance to go on in her place. Who wouldn't be? One day backstage she said, "Nichelle, I understand they're creating a dance for you."

"Yes, I'm very excited about it."

"Well, don't be *too,*" she cautioned. "I have no intentions of being sick while you're here, my dear."

"Why, Diahann, that's okay," I replied, a little wickedly. "I keep a bag of banana peels in my dressing room. Just in case."

"What?" she asked. Then it hit her.

"Break a leg, baby," I said.

While I never appeared in *No Strings,* I did open the New York Playboy Club to more raves. Each night I had to wait backstage for half an hour to be sure Diahann would go on in *No Strings,* then rush over to the Playboy Club. It sounds like a logistical nightmare, but it proved to be a publicist's dream. Through 1961 and 1962, Frank was shuttling back and forth between Los Angeles and Tahiti, as the cursed *Mutiny* production forged on in the face of every conceivable disaster, from monsoons to defecting directors. Between the success I'd found in New York and my close friendship with Burgess Meredith, Frank feared he was losing me. He arrived in New York, with Kyle in tow, determined to win me back, and he did.

We planned to settle in New York temporarily; Joseph Papp cast Frank in the title role of King Lear in his Shakespeare in the Park series. Frank sublet an apartment from an actor friend, and after a meeting with Papp, Frank, Kyle, and I shopped for food and then took a cab to our new home. We were surprised to discover that the key Frank had didn't seem to fit the lock. A heavy Polish woman emerged from the manager's office, and with her arms folded across her broad chest sternly said, "No sublease!"

Frank was baffled, since he'd spoken to her before and thought everything was settled.

"You okay, you can stay," she said. "But no niggas!"

"What are you talking about?" Frank shouted. "You think I'm white? You think I'm white! You're white! Do you understand what white is? How dare you speak that way to this precious princess, and this young prince!"

By then the woman was shaking, and soon a Puerto Rican man who worked for her arrived, and began shouting, "You got to leave! You got to leave! Man say no Negroes!"

Our things were already in the apartment, and Frank's friend was not returning from Europe for three months. The woman would not let us in even to collect them. When Frank threatened to break down the door, the Puerto Rican man gestured as if he were pulling a gun. With my young son there, it was enough to scare us to death. Controlling my anger and speaking the little Spanish I knew, I assured him we would leave. We returned later and entered through an open window to get our things. The Puerto Rican man came out and helped us load the car. When Frank tried to point out to him the irony of the fact that both he and his boss were discriminating against native-born Americans when the two of them could barely speak English, he hung his head, shrugged, and replied, "I know, man, but I just work here."

It was a horrible, denigrating experience for all of us, but nothing Frank or I hadn't seen before and learned to live with, as much as one ever does. For Kyle, however, this was a hard, quick lesson in the real world his grandparents and I had protected him from. Over dinner Frank and I discussed it openly with Kyle, who examined and analyzed the incident with the critical detachment of a sociologist. Still, I sometimes wondered if I hadn't protected him too much.

While in New York Frank introduced me to his friends—Jane Fonda, Geraldine Page and her husband, Rip Torn, Shelley Winters, and the great acting teacher Lee Strasberg. Strasberg invited me to join his Actors Studio, but, oddly, Frank did not encourage me, and for the first time ever, I felt like a fifth wheel in his life. Perhaps amid the celebrity and the nightlife of *my* new world, he felt the same. We had reached a crisis in our relationship and could have easily ended it there. Instead, Frank asked me to marry him and return with him to L.A. We lay in bed at night talking about something that we could do together back in Los Angeles, and so we conceived our "child," the Theatre of Being.

We found a little ninety-seat theater with an apartment above near Olympic and Robertson. First we opened an actors' workshop, then Frank and I began producing plays in which one or both of us performed and he directed. It was extremely hard work, but I was never happier in my life, creatively or romantically. Kyle who, with Frank's encouragement, had begun acting, was thrilled and anxious for us to marry. All the pieces were falling into place: I didn't have to choose between love and my career. I could have everything. And for a while, I did.

Late in the summer of 1963 my father was diagnosed with advanced prostate cancer. The attacks of angina pectoris he experienced since his first heart attack continued, and he suffered another heart attack. It was not an easy time for any of us, especially my mother. She had been taking care of a neighbor's large, heavy little boy and developed some muscle strain in her chest area, which she had convinced herself was breast cancer. So I had my father in a downtown Los Angeles hospital, and about thirty miles away, in Santa Monica, Frank was recovering from a near-fatal accident. Those weeks became a blur of driving from one town to another, of pacing hospital corridors, and waiting.

One day in October my father told his nurses he was dying. Then, they later told us, he raged, throwing bedpans and dishes around his room, and yelling, "Go away! I'm not ready! She has to get here!" For three full hours, he fought. But there was no one in the room.

When my mother arrived, the nurses told her he had been raising hell, and she entered his room a bit annoyed. She was certain he was throwing a tantrum just because this one day she wasn't there; I'd taken her to the doctor, who assured her she didn't have breast cancer. Given the nurses' warnings, Mother was surprised to find him sitting calmly in his bed, smiling.

"Oh, darling, I waited!" he cried, relieved. "I waited for you! Death tried to take me and has been trying all afternoon to take me. But I told him I couldn't go with him until you got here." As Mother held him in her arms and kissed him gently, he asked, "You did love me all those years, didn't you?"

"Well, if I didn't, Sam Nichols, the joke's on me."

Daddy looked into her eyes for the last time. "I never told you enough, and I never, ever could, how much I love you. I'm leaving you now. But I'll be back for you when it's time. I'll always be with you."

Then he closed his eyes.

As always happens in the aftermath of a family death, some survivors cope a little bit better than others, and that was certainly true for us. My mother, always the pillar of strength—we had nicknamed her Rock (as in "of Gibraltar")—bore her grief with dignity amid a storm of hysteria. On the day we buried my father, one of my brothers took it upon himself suddenly to move Mother, my sister and her small son, and the contents of my parents' three-bedroom apartment into my two-bedroom house before he got on a plane and returned to Chicago. My son was asleep, and Diane, Marian, Mom, and I sat silently, crammed into my living room, surrounded by piles of furniture and boxes, trying to reconcile the horrible tragedy of losing Daddy with the series of near-comic events that had transpired in the past few days. I found some brandy and poured us each a drink, as Diane rocked her fretful baby Brett to sleep.

Mother finally heaved a great sigh, then said, "Well, Nick . . ." We all tensed, expecting her to break down and scream, "Darling, I always loved you! I can't live without you!"

Instead she said, "This is another fine mess you got me into."

My sisters and I looked at one another in disbelief, then the dam burst, and we laughed until we cried. Then we'd stop laughing, and the baby would cry. Then we'd laugh at that, and as Mother wiped tears from her eyes, she caught her breath and said, "Daddy understands, you know?"

Yes, we nodded, almost becoming solemn again before Mother added, "He should understand! He got us into this!"

We were in near-hysterics when my youngest brother came in, saw us, and in a voice choked with disapproval, demanded, "What the hell are you all laughing at? I just buried my father!! And you women are sitting around here laughing?" We fell silent for a moment, then burst out laughing again as he stormed out of the house. It was this moment that got us all through the terrible months that followed.

Naturally, Daddy's passing left a void in all our lives that will never be filled. This was especially true for Kyle, for whom my father provided such a fine example of love, caring, and responsibility. Less than a month after my father died, Kyle was devastated when his other hero, President Kennedy, was assassinated. One day a few years earlier, when Kyle was around nine or so, he asked, "Don't you think it's about time I met my father, Mom?"

All Kyle's life I'd told him that his father was a great artist, but I deliberately made no effort to seek out Foster Johnson. As always, though, Kyle's logic was indisputable, so I tracked down Foster in Montreal and, against my better judgment, invited him to stay with Kyle in our home while I went to sing for the first time in Europe. When I returned, I got two surprises. The first was that Foster interpreted my invitation as an indication that I wanted to renew our relationship. I immediately corrected that impression, and he later married a lovely woman, who was also a singer, named Jean King. We had worked together in *Porgy and Bess,* in fact, and her group the Blossoms toured with such great singers as Tom Jones and Ray Charles. She and Foster had two beautiful daughters, Kyle's half sisters, and she and I remained friends until her death.

The second—and most wonderful—surprise came when Frank took me to see a production of *A Raisin in the Sun.* There onstage was my son, Kyle. He received magnificent reviews, and from that point on, was cast in every television, film, and stage role he went up for, including starring in his first major motion picture as Newt in Gordon Parks's classic autobiographical coming-of-age story, *The Learning Tree.* On several occasions Kyle and I auditioned for parts in the same production, although we never let on that we were related. Once, in fact, I was flattered yet furious to be informed that I could not possibly play Kyle's mother because I looked too young. Kyle was a fine actor, and could have continued had he not found other interests, such as music.

I was always proud of my son's accomplishments, but prouder yet of him as a person. He mastered not only knowledge, but understanding. As he said once when he was quite young, "I've got a photographic memory and an X-ray vision mind." Once when we were in Chicago, Kyle was impressing a roomful of adults with a lecture on what happened to the dinosaurs when the Ice Age came. Even I was amazed. I was standing there looking at my own son as if he'd grown two heads, when Tony Bennett, who'd just wrested himself from my son's conversational grasp, remarked, "See that kid over there? Don't go near him. He's weird. He's either a genius or a midget."

"That's my son."

"Oh my God, Nichelle! Where did you get him from?"

After Frank recovered from his accident, we decided to produce James Baldwin's *The Amen Corner.* Jimmy wrote his highly autobiographical first play in the early fifties, before *Go Tell It on the Mountain* was published in 1953. Set in a Harlem storefront church, *The Amen Corner* concerns an older religious woman minister named Sister Margaret who tried to save her beloved, sexually confused teenaged son from the temptations and degradations of the ghetto and the example of his shiftless father. It was Jimmy's first play but had not yet been professionally produced, which was odd, given his stature. Having read all of his works and just completed his controversial collection of essays *The Fire Next Time,* I considered myself among his most ardent admirers. Frank and I were talking about the news that his *Blues for Mr. Charlie* was being produced on Broadway by Strasberg's Actors Studio when Frank said, "You know, he did another play before that, and I think I have it."

He dug out an old copy of *The Amen Corner,* and Frank and I stayed up late, with me reading all the women's parts, and he reading the men's. "This would be a wonderful play for you," Frank said. I pointed out that Sister Margaret had a grown son, and while I could try to play a fifty-eight-year-old woman, in my opinion, it wouldn't be good for the play.

"I trust everything you say, Frank, but now I'm a producer, and I wouldn't cast me in it. This is our first big production, and it's going to be reviewed. I'm in my early thirties, and I don't want this to be miscast."

"You can't be a glamour girl all your life," Frank snapped. *A glamour girl!* I thought. Dealing with actors and agents, seeing that sets got built, tickets got sold, bills got paid? I even cooked meals for the cast (including one that two mischievous actors spiked with marijuana, resulting in one of our more interesting shows). This was hardly the glamorous life. To my mind, I was simply turning down a role I wasn't suited for. But to Frank, my refusal to play an older woman represented a rejection of age, of his authority, of us.

Frank knew Jimmy quite well, and one evening he phoned him in New York to tell him about the play. We caught Jimmy during the pre-opening-night party he was throwing for the cast of *Blues for Mr. Charlie.* When Jimmy heard who it was, he shouted to the noisy room, "It's Frank Silvera in L.A.!" Over the extension I heard a loud, friendly chorus of "Hi, Frank!" before Diana Sands picked up the receiver to flirt with Frank and playfully meet me. "Are you that little gal who stole that juicy role of Hazel Sharpe from every actress in New York City?" she asked. "Well, keep your little narrow behind in L.A., honey."

Jimmy expressed amazement that anyone would want to produce *The Amen Corner*. "*Blues for Mr. Charlie* is the important play," he said. "Why not wait, and I'll give you this for L.A. after New York?"

Before Frank could answer, I interrupted, "Oh, but this way you'll have a Baldwin play running on each coast at the same time. It will be great!"

Jimmy laughed as I caught Frank scowling at me from across the room. "Okay! What can I say, Frank? You've got it. Do whatever you want. In your hands, Papa, it can only improve."

Realizing they were about to hang up, I hastily added, "Jimmy, would you please send us a telegram giving us permission to produce the show so we can get started right away?"

Before Jimmy could answer Frank broke in, "Hey, forget it, Jimmy. Shelley doesn't know how far back we go." Glaring at me angrily he assured Jimmy, "Your word is good enough for me, Baby."

"I just think it's good business," I stated, holding my ground. "If something happened to you, Jimmy, your estate wouldn't know you gave verbal permission."

By then Frank was livid, but Jimmy began screaming with laughter. "You got yourself a corker, there, Frank, old boy! I simply can't wait to meet her. I'll get that wire to you post haste, dear lady. I think I'm in love, Frank! Oh, Nichelle, ma belle . . ." Chortling madly, Jimmy returned to his party.

"You shouldn't have done that, Shelley," Frank admonished. "That was an insult to the mutual respect and integrity that I share with Jimmy. That was very embarrassing to me." The next day when Frank received the telegram, he angrily spat, "It's just a damned piece of paper!" before wadding it up and throwing it away. I retrieved the small yellow sheet from the wastebasket, carefully smoothed it flat, then proudly filed it away: our first official document under "Amen Corner."

Lacking sufficient financial resources, our biggest challenge was casting. We were fortunate to cast as three church sisters Academy Award–nominee Juanita Moore, Maidie Norman, and Isabel Sanford, who would become known to millions later as television's Louise Jefferson on *All in the Family,* then *The Jeffersons.* We still had no Sister Margaret, though I recalled a wonderful actress I'd seen in New York in *Purlie Victorious,* Beah Richards. When I proposed asking her, Frank exploded. "Why would an actress working in New York, on Broadway, want to come to L.A. to do a little-theater, non-Equity play?"

The tension between us was unbearable, and through a torrent of tears, I cried, "For the chance to work with Frank Silvera, damm it!" He held me, kissing away my tears, wiping away all the pain and doubt. He picked up the phone and called Beah Richards, who was only too happy to take the part and work with Frank.

The Amen Corner opened to fantastic reviews. We were a hit, and before long we had moved twice to larger theaters to accommodate the crowds. Frank and I were sitting on top of the world. Then Jimmy Baldwin came to town.

By then his beloved *Blues for Mr. Charlie* had bombed in New York City. Even the gallant efforts of Jimmy's supporters—including a fund-raising drive to keep the show on the boards—failed to save it from the savage and, Jimmy believed, racially motivated reviews. Frank and I really expected that seeing his critically lauded *Amen Corner* in our new four-hundred-seat theater would cheer him up. We were wrong.

Jimmy was witty, charming, and everything I'd expected. We hit it off right away, and we sat with him through the first act, bracing ourselves for his praise. At the intermission he rose, his large eyes blazing, and announced, "I hate this show! I hate the father, I hate the son, I hate Sister Margaret! It's all wrong—entirely miscast. Frank, how could you do this to me? I'm closing the show!" We were stunned.

The second-act bell sounded, but Jimmy refused to take his seat and instead marched off to a very chic restaurant across the street. Frank was absolutely crushed, but I convinced him to stay in the theater. I would go talk to Jimmy.

I found him at the bar and had no sooner sat down than he began railing about the play. I threw myself at his mercy, pleading, cajoling, crying, all to no avail.

"Nichelle, the play closes, and that's that. My lawyers will see to that!"

"Well, Jimmy, you *can't* close the show," I retorted. "And that's that!"

"What?"

"You sent us that telegram, granting us the full rights to produce, cast, rewrite, direct, do everything as we saw fit. And we did, and we produced a hit. Could it be, Mr. James Baldwin, that you're jealous of the success of this play because your other play didn't make it on Broadway? You'd make a terrible parent, wouldn't you?"

Furious, Jimmy sat there looking as if he might explode. I held my breath as his eyes seemed to grow wider by the second and the veins in his neck pulsed. He was so angry it would not have surprised me if he'd slapped me. Frank had just stepped in the door when Jimmy suddenly began laughing.

"This is an incredible woman, Frank. I'm going to marry her. She'll make a fucking man out of me." Ironically, Baldwin did finally see *The Amen Corner* on Broadway, staged and directed by Frank, and starring Beah Richards (with Isabel Sanford) in 1965. And ironically without me.

And so *The Amen Corner* played on. Our love would not be so lucky. Even though Frank had bought a house in Pasadena as a wedding present and bought me a wedding ring, our future together got cloudier and cloudier. I had begun thinking of a life without Frank. *The Amen Corner* kept us back together for a time, but we fought constantly. In the middle of all this, I got my first television role, a part that would take me out of Frank Silvera's world and into Gene Roddenberry's. Ironically, it was Frank who set into motion the events that culminated in my being cast in *The Lieutenant.*

He was teaching a class in 1963 in which one student, Don Marshall, seemed to be having trouble opening up. Frank asked if I would work with him on a scene from *A View from the Bridge,* and I agreed. Another of Frank's students happened to be Joe D'Agosta, who worked for a production company at MGM. Joe was so impressed by the scene Don and I performed in class, he told his bosses, who were seeking a Black actor and actress. Joe, bless him, convinced them that they couldn't simply interview us for the part; they had to see us do this particular scene. They agreed, and after Don and I finished, six wizened MGM executives sat there in silence with tears in their eyes. I knew right then we had the parts.

CHAPTER SIX

I first met Gene Roddenberry in 1963, when I was cast in an episode of his television series *The Lieutenant,* entitled "To Set It Right." The program set out to depict the maturing of young Marine Lieutenant William Rice (played by Gary Lockwood) as he confronts the problems that arise with the men under his command. I was pleased to learn recently that of the twenty-nine episodes produced, "To Set It Right" is one of two now preserved at the Museum of Television and Radio in New York City. With its gritty realism, powerful dialogue, and provocative themes, this is a fine example from television's golden age.

I played Norma Bartlett, the fiancée of Ernest Cameron (played by Don Marshall who later starred in *Land of the Giants*), an exceptional young Black Marine recently transferred to Camp Pendleton. Within minutes, Ernie recognizes one of his fellow officers as Peter Devlin (played by Dennis Hopper), a white racist who'd once led a gang that had beaten him and left him for dead back in their hometown. Without warning, Cameron attacks Devlin.

When the lieutenant demands to know why, Ernie explains to Rice, "I was just another nigger that didn't know his place."

The script sensitively yet frankly dealt with the many facets of racism, from the lieutenant's decision to make the two work together to his commanding officer and an older Black sergeant (played by Woody Strode) cautioning him that some things may never change. Norma urges Ernie to control his temper, while he refuses to assume the role of an "Uncle Tom." When Ernie demands to know why he can't defend himself and be "a man," Norma replies, "Well, if jumping somebody is all it takes, why not trade that nice uniform in for a funny white sheet with a pointed cap and a burning cross?"

Cameron and Devlin are torn apart by their hatred yet bound to each other by the Marine code of honor. The episode concerns not only how they learn to come to terms with their attitudes, but how those around them—Norma, Lieutenant Rice, his commanding officer, and other officers—overcome their own preconceived notions about how to bring these two men around. There was no mistaking that Gene used the Marines to present a microcosmic view of society at large. In its themes, its message, its passion, *The Lieutenant* was pure Roddenberry yet great entertainment. That was his gift.

This being my first job in episodic television, I couldn't have asked for a better part, a nicer cast and crew, or a more considerate director, Vince McEveety. Work seemed to go smoothly the first three days, with the only problem being Vince's occasionally calling "Cut!" and then asking me to please stay in my key light. I didn't know what he was talking about, but since I seemed to have been doing the right thing most of the time—and, honestly, because I was a bit intimidated—I never let on. I assumed I would discover what it was on my own.

Toward the end of the fourth day we were shooting a

crucial two-shot scene when Vince's patience finally snapped. "*Cut!!*" Everyone stopped. I turned to face him. He was fuming.

"Nichelle, you're ruining another beautiful take," Vince began, obviously exasperated. "You're out of your key light and in his." I stood there speechless with embarrassment. As I would quickly learn, in film and television every actor in a scene has his or her own light keyed just for them; sometimes you may share it with another actor, depending on the scene. But there is always a light focused specifically on you to take out the shadows cast by other actors and objects in the scene. When there are two actors in one shot, each has to be especially careful not to get into the other's light. In the theater, where I'd done most of my previous acting, the entire set is lit, and the actress finds her best light. Except in specific instances, a soliloquy, for example, you never give the light a second thought; it's simply there.

"Dear," Vince continued, "you're a fine actress, but for God's sake, please be considerate of your fellow actor."

Choking back my embarrassment, I replied, "I will, if you just tell me where my key light *is.*"

A beat of dead silence followed as everyone turned toward me. "Oh, for heaven's sake! You act like you never did TV before!"

"I haven't," I simpered.

I'm sure Vince meant his statement to be taken rhetorically, so my answer caught him totally by surprise. The cast and crew snickered quietly, though it wasn't clear then which of us they found so funny.

"This is your first—" Vince gasped.

Feeling every bit the amateur, I admitted, "Well, I sang and danced in *Porgy and Bess,* and I've done a lot of theater, but this is my first speaking role—on film, I mean." Unable to fight back my tears any longer, I turned away, but when I looked up at Vince, I saw him crying, too. He let out a whoop, laughing heartily, then called, "Fifteen minutes, you guys!" Putting his arm around me, he said gently, "Come here, little lady."

We went outside, where we sat on a grassy hillside while the crew reset the scene. "We've been working almost a week now," Vince said, laughing. "Kid, you're so good, none of us had any idea you didn't know what a key light is! We thought you were intentionally upstaging the other actors." I started to relax. In those few days, Vince taught me so much about filming, from both before and behind the camera. You can bet I never forgot my key light again.

Since the final scenes were night shots, and I now believed myself to be very much the seasoned pro, I felt confident and assumed I'd encounter no more embarrassing problems. I was wrong. In the next scene, I was to give my fiancé an ultimatum: either get his anger under control or I was leaving. The scene ended with my dramatically getting into my car and driving away. Simple enough, except that the car, an old forties-era Ford, had a standard shift. I remembered my father once explaining the intricacies of driving a stick, but I'd never actually tried it. I was beginning to despair, just imagining the snickers I'd get over that. Then, to make matters worse, I was distracted by a creepy-looking guy with a big hook nose, whom I'd noticed hanging around the set.

By then it was early evening, and there was very little light except for what was on the set. Trying to concentrate on how I was going to drive that damn stick shift, I kept getting distracted by this weird stranger just before I was to do my final drive-away scene. He kept hovering near me, trying to make conversation, getting so close that his shapeless tweed coat and smelly cigarettes threatened to asphyxiate me. Politely I explained that I had lines to study and asked him to please leave me alone, but nothing could dissuade him. When I couldn't stand it another minute, I complained to the assistant director.

"Ah, he's harmless," he replied, "a relative of the producer; he always hangs around the set when a pretty girl is working. Just ignore him."

It wasn't easy, but I almost managed to forget about the stranger until I felt him push up against me. That was it: I didn't give a damn whose obnoxious relative he was. I spun around with an upraised fist and came within an inch of socking him right in the nose when I noticed something else very odd about him. Only on one other occasion had I seen anyone hold his cigarette between his two middle fingers, and that was during my one brief meeting with the series' creator earlier that week.

"Mr. Roddenberry!" I screeched.

"Cut!!" Vince shouted.

Oh, God! I've ruined another scene, I thought. *I'll never work in this town again.* As I waited for Vince to devour me, I heard the cast and crew break into laughter as the creep yanked off his big fake nose and red wig and became Gene Roddenberry. This was my first—but not the last—experience with Gene's elaborately planned and carefully executed practical jokes. Ever the good sport, ha ha, and so relieved I could cry, I joined in the laughter, though deep inside I wanted to throttle everyone there but Gene. Him, I wanted to kill.

Thus began my long and fascinating relationship with the man who would come to be known as the Great Bird of the Galaxy and who would change my life. He was a large man, over six feet tall, with jagged good looks and piercing blue eyes that seemed to gaze right through you. He was unpredictable, imaginative, determined, possessive, and thoroughly infuriating. He was also kind, charming, gentle, generous, and immensely sensuous. Like the typical Leo that he was (oh, God, another Leo!), he had passion and the courage of his convictions. His appetite for life was insatiable. He was one of the most interesting people I've ever known, and throughout the years I have always been proud to call him my friend.

The next day Gene said, "I really want to apologize. Let me take you to lunch." And that was the real beginning for us. I thought to myself, *This man really is incredible.* Little did I know . . .

Eugene Wesley Roddenberry was born in Texas in 1921. When he was still a baby, his parents moved to Los Angeles, where his father—whom he later described as a bigot—joined the Los Angeles Police Department. Gene and two younger siblings, a brother and sister, grew up in a strict Baptist home. But not long after Gene reached his teens, he began questioning his parents' beliefs, and soon everyone else's. He had been a sickly child, and so often spent his free time reading, especially science fiction.

Between then and when he finally became a professional writer, Gene was a B-17 pilot in World War II, a commercial pilot for Pan Am (he survived a crash in 1947 tha. killed fourteen), and an LAPD motorcycle policeman. All the time, though, he dreamed of writing for television. One day in the fifties Gene, fed up with agents either ignoring or rejecting his work, roared up on his motorcycle to the Cock and Bull, a Hollywood restaurant famous for its showbiz clientele. In his full motorcycle cop uniform, complete with mirrored sunglasses and black leather boots, he pulled up to the entrance, gunning his engine so loudly everyone inside stopped to see what was going on. Gene dismounted, marched up to the bar, and with the sun shining behind him, demanded, "Are you Irving Lazar?"

Hollywood's most powerful agent, better known as Swifty Lazar, said yes, and Gene dropped one of his scripts on the superagent's table and commanded that he read it. A stunned Lazar, who admired Gene for his guts, if nothing else, did read it. When Gene told me the story years later, he added that this was the scariest moment of his life, because he knew everything he ever wanted was riding on it. Within a short time, though, Gene had a top agent and soon began writing scripts for a number of television series, including *Naked City, Have Gun Will Travel, Highway Patrol,* and *Dr. Kildare.* Eventually Gene was earning enough to quit the force and concentrate on his passion.

Around 1962 Gene attempted to sell his first television series, *333 Montgomery,* which starred DeForest Kelley as a famous criminal lawyer. It failed to sell, as did two subsequent pilots, *Defiance County* and a World War II show, *APO-923.* By now Gene was determined not to be just a writer, but a producer so that he could control his work. Approximately a year later, Gene sold his first series, *The Lieutenant,* the only one he would produce before *Star Trek* got the final green light in 1966.

While working on *The Lieutenant,* I witnessed firsthand his uncompromising commitment to his work and how his tenacious dedication to what he believed was right took its toll on him. Through the years, so much has been said and written about Gene. Perhaps because he was so complex and intense, and so stubborn in his beliefs, he inspired very strong emotions in others. If you liked him, you loved him, warts and all. Those who didn't tried to destroy him, in life and in death.

To his great credit, Gene Roddenberry was one of the precious few people I've known, outside of my son, my parents, and a small handful of others, who held unstintingly to his principles. More than anything else, Gene was a philosopher, a man who felt compelled to share his unique moral vision for the future of humanity with the world. In another time or another place, he might have been a great teacher of history or philosophy. But in the mid-twentieth century he instinctively sought access to the most powerful communications medium in history: television.

At the time we met, Gene was still married, although unhappily, a situation he endured for the sake of his children. Our early relationship, a close friendship, began casually. His offices were at MGM, and after *The Lieutenant*

I was often on the lot auditioning or working. I'd drop by his office, just to say hello. We might have lunch together, and before long I found myself seeing him more often. I have many fond memories of our taking long walks on the beach; Gene piloting us on wonderful, crazy last-minute flights to Palm Springs or Santa Barbara just for lunch; and holding his waist tightly on hair-raisingly mad motorcycle rides through Benedict Canyon. Gene was alive, and he made you know you were, too. I loved every minute of it.

The Lieutenant lasted just one season, but even before it ended, Gene was already formulating new series he wanted to produce. The networks rejected two possible concepts for new shows because, they said, they were "too cerebral." As much as anyone, he clearly saw and understood the limitations of commercial television and network front-office "suits" who seemed dedicated to preserving the status quo. Even during what today we longingly refer to as television's "golden age," the networks and other powers that be catered to a lower common denominator (and today it is the lowest). At the same time, though, the industry's resistance to change, to challenge, drove Gene that much harder to buck the system, to create and produce shows that would express what he wanted to say.

Clearly, the seeds of *Star Trek* had begun to take root when I first met Gene. And although we didn't fully discuss his ideas for what he would refer to as "a *Wagon Train* to the stars" in great depth, on several occasions he remarked, "I've got something in mind that I think is going to come about. And if it does, I think there will be something important in it for you."

"It's a movie, right?" I asked.

"No," he'd reply teasingly. "But you'll find out."

Still being somewhat new to Hollywood and naive to its ways, I sat by the phone for weeks before I realized what Gene had referred to was still just a dream. But what a dream it was.

The enduring constant in our relationship was the sharing and exploring of ideas. We passed countless hours together discussing everything, from the Civil Rights Movement and feminism to the feasibility of space travel. Gene took nothing lightly, and if you dared express an opinion, you'd better be ready to defend it. He could be maddeningly provocative when it came to certain subjects, yet he could graciously concede a well-argued point. One subject we often went back and forth about was the existence of God.

"God is scientifically undefinable," Gene would say.

"But you see proof of God every day," I'd insist. "A baby is born; that's a miracle. Or a jet plane takes off; that's a miracle."

"No, that's biology and aerodynamics."

"No!" I countered. "Steel flies through the air? *That's* a miracle. And that's God."

Gene laughed. "I've got to tell you, you've got a compelling, crazy way of thinking, and I like you even when I don't agree with you."

Soft-spoken and intense, Gene could catch you up in his gaze and in his dreams. I couldn't help but be taken with him, and before long—and despite our respective circumstances—we fell in love. Contrary to what some people now claim, our romance remained a secret for decades. It came to be fairly well known in *Trek* circles only in the last years of Gene's life. Until then, both he and I, out of respect for each other and the important people in our lives, were highly discreet. Certainly our relationship was over long before *Star Trek* began, and no one there except Majel Barrett had a clue we had even met before (and that's quite another story).

Despite my love and admiration for Gene, I sensed that our destinies were not to be together. Exactly why I felt this way, I cannot say—call it intuition. His divorce wasn't yet final, and while he vociferously denounced any form of racism, we still lived in a time when interracial couples in the industry were not accepted warmly, to say the least. Gene and I had discussed that aspect of our relationship several times. Sounding very much like my grandfather Samuel G. Nichols, he'd declared that what he did and whom he loved was nobody's damn business. I know that had we married, Gene never would have looked back. Although it would not have been a major issue for me either, I was not so idealistic as to fool myself into thinking everything would turn up roses for us, either.

Fortunately, or unfortunately, circumstances conspired so that that particular decision was never ours to make. One day several months into our relationship, which had become uncomfortably intense for both of us, Gene picked me up for a lunch date and announced with uncharacteristic nervousness, "There's somebody very important I want you to meet."

"Okay," I answered, sensing something strange in his mood.

As he turned into one of the roads that wound through the Hollywood Hills, I asked, "Where are we going?" He deftly evaded the question, and as we approached Laurel Canyon, I began to get the distinct impression that it wasn't a director, producer, or friend of Gene's we were about to visit. It was a woman.

"There's something you haven't been telling me, isn't there?" I asked bluntly.

"Yes," he replied tersely as we pulled into a driveway.

Gene rang the doorbell, and we stood for what felt like an eternity, during which I didn't know what to feel. I had grown accustomed to Gene's little surprises, but this one threatened to top them all. The door swung open, and it was a woman all right. A lovely woman, with big gray eyes and mounds of thick sable-brown hair. We stared at each other like a couple of owls.

"Majel?" I asked, hardly believing my eyes.

"Nichelle?"

After a few more seconds of gaping at each other wide-eyed, we both broke up laughing and hugged. You can only imagine what was going through poor Gene's mind.

"You know each other?" he asked incredulously.

"What are you doing here, Nichelle?" she asked, ignoring Gene.

"What are *you* doing here?"

"I live here! Come on in."

We spent the afternoon together talking and laughing over drinks, and sizing up each other. Majel was clearly unnerved by what this might portend, but we each covered our discomfort. I filled Gene in on how we'd met when I auditioned for *The Singing Nun,* and we discussed everything except what we most feared. As we said our good-byes, I told Majel it had been great seeing her. I was truly disconcerted, for I realized the depth of this woman's feeling for this man, but I meant it.

I was furious with Gene, though, for setting the stage for what might easily have been a painful, embarrassing situation for all concerned. Back in his car, I lashed out at him. "Gene, why did you do that?"

"I didn't know any other way," he answered softly. "I couldn't go on behind either one of your backs. I love you both too much. I didn't know any other way to bring—to tell—the two women that I love that I'm in love with two women. And I don't know what to do about it."

Gene's bewilderment and pain actually touched my heart; he was, at times like this, so much like a little boy. At the same time, though, he was not off the hook. "You've got to do something about it," I said. "Number one, you've got *three* women—"

"No," he interjected, "two. The divorce is only a matter of time. I have no home life."

"You have to decide, Gene. I cannot go on like this."

"I can't make that choice," he protested.

I knew that the last thing Gene wanted was to hurt either

of us. But I also knew that he wanted what he wanted, and it was conceivable that we might continue in this triangle indefinitely. I loved Gene, but the situation was simply untenable. Maybe it was my ego, maybe it was my commitment to my career—I don't know. What I did know was that Gene had placed the decision in my hands, and there was no choice for me but to end our romance. Out of deference to Majel, who I soon realized was dedicated to Gene above all else, and for my own salvation, I could not be the other woman to the other woman. And so I fled. Typical of Gene, however, he could not accept my rejection of him.

"How can you *do* this? How can you just walk away?" he asked me several times. Granted, it was not easy. It broke my heart. But it sure as hell was not the end of the world for me, either. How I could and did go on without him is something Gene never quite understood.

No matter what our personal relationship, Gene always believed in me. Shortly after I appeared in *The Lieutenant,* he brought me to the attention of some MGM executives. Very few Black actresses were under contract to major studios, the few exceptions including Lena Horne and Ruby Dee, and perhaps later Dorothy Dandridge, so I was astounded when MGM made me an offer. For an aspiring actress, the deal the studio proposed after seeing my screen test was something out of my wildest dreams: seven years at $750 a week with an option for renewal; daily voice, dance, and acting lessons; a wardrobe designed by the great Edith Head; personal hairstyles by the legendary Sydney Guilaroff.

One studio executive in particular was instrumental in the deal. His name will go unmentioned, since he's still working in the business, and his wife and children are famous in their own right. I'll call him Mr. X. From the moment we met, throughout the "courtship," he and I hit it off quite well. He was so handsome and so charming, and I found myself attracted to him. But being enamored with Gene, I never considered anything there. Nor did I think he was being anything more than flirtatious in a meaningless Hollywood way anyway. I thought nothing of it then when he called the morning my agents and I were to meet in his office for the final signing to say the meeting had been rescheduled for a couple of hours earlier.

That morning, I combed out my lovely new Guilaroff hairdo, donned a chic new black suit and matching alligator bag and shoes—all provided for by MGM—and walked out my front door with my head in the clouds. This was the day my life was going to change forever.

I'd been to his office several times before for business meetings, so I was a bit taken aback when his secretaries, who usually greeted me cheerfully, were so formal and avoided looking me in the eye. Once inside his elaborate office, I soon found out why.

I was surprised not to see my agents there, but, figuring they would be along any minute, we got started, with Mr. X going through the contract provision by provision. When he finished, he stated exactly what the final, unwritten provision was: He demanded that I sleep with him.

"I thought this contract was for my talent as a performer," I said, disbelievingly.

"Oh, it is. It is," he assured me. "It's just that I want to be sure that we both understand all the terms."

"Then you're putting the casting couch between me and this contract?" I asked, on the verge of tears. "Is that what it is?" I demanded.

"You must understand, I adore you," he responded, then gave a little shrug, as if to say, Hey, it's just good business.

Time seemed to stand still, and I felt myself grow cold and numb. It was like being in Canada all over again. As I gazed around his lavishly appointed office I'd so admired, I thought of all the dreams I'd indulged. I'd be able to afford private school for my brilliantly gifted son. I could replace my rickety Renault, pay my rent on time, maybe even buy my mother a home of her own. Then I thought of what the contract meant to me: stardom, security, a chance to let the world see me at my best. I felt my professional future running through my hands like beads of quicksilver. All the glitter tarnished before my eyes. Regretfully I knew what I had to do.

"Okay," I said, hearing my own voice as if it were someone else's, "I'll make *you* a deal."

He leaned forward, leering expectantly.

"You can have my talent for that contract. Or you can have my body for that contract. But I'll be damned if you get both, you bastard!"

I stood up, barely knowing how I forced one foot in front of the other, and walked out, slamming the heavy door behind me. One glance through the outer office told me that the secretaries either had heard us or had been through this many times before; probably a little of both. As I strode angrily by, not daring to look at anyone, one of them said softly, "God bless you, Miss Nichols."

Walking through the lobby, I stared straight ahead, doing all I could not to stop and cry my eyes out. *Don't you dare,* I told myself. As I reached the exit, I saw my agents Hy Sieger and Harry Lipton coming up the steps.

"Hi, babe," Hy said gleefully.

Of course, they didn't know the meeting had been moved up, and when I told them what had happened, Hy angrily drew up and charged past us fully intending to punch out Mr. X's lights. It was all Harry and I could do to hold him back. After consoling me and offering some much appreciated encouragement, they decided to take me to lunch, where we could talk about our options. Sure, I said.

"Where would you like to go?" they asked.

"The MGM commissary," I replied.

Hy and Harry were both surprised and apprehensive about my choice, but they appreciated what Hy referred to as my chutzpah. Apparently word of Mr. X's rebuffed proposal had spread across the lot like wildfire, and as we walked through the commissary to our table, I could feel all eyes on me. I walked through with my head held high. No matter what I'd lost—and believe me, I did lose—it would be his shame, not mine.

Once we were seated, several producers, directors, and agents came over to commend Hy and Harry and me, their incredibly brave client. Soon the news was all over town, and before long independent producers, some of whom just hated Mr. X, hired me for their films. The industry has its own way of meting out justice. I appeared with Ann-Margret in *Made in Paris,* and James Garner in *Mister Buddwing,* and soon I was being considered for parts with actresses whose stature I had, until then, only dreamed of reaching.

Yes, I was too proud to demean myself, but I admit I cried for months over that contract. Whenever Kyle needed something I couldn't afford, my fussy little car wouldn't start, or my checkbook came up short at the end of the month, I'd hear a little demon inside my head ridiculing me: *You dummy! You liked him anyway. So what if you slept with him? What was the big deal?*

But I knew what the "big deal" was: It was me, who had to get up in the morning and face myself, look my son and my family in the eye. I had to feel proud of who I was and what I was. I had not sold myself for a damn job so far, and I didn't intend to start now.

⸻

That said, I still had to pay my rent. Well, I figured, I always had my singing to fall back on, so reluctantly I packed up and hit the road. Only now I was bound for England and Europe. I'd just finished a marvelous engagement in London and gone on to Paris, where a charming

Italian textile merchant offered to show me around during the few days I had to pass before I was to meet some friends there. I hadn't even unpacked my bags in the City of Lights when a couple of telegrams forwarded from London found me. "Come home immediately," my agent had wired. The next one read: "Come home immediately. Call me immediately. They're doing *Star Trek.*"

Star what? I wondered. When he finally got through on the telephone, he implored me to return at once.

"But why?" I asked. "Listen, Hy, I've been working very, very hard, and here I am in Paris, having a wonderful vacation. And I've been invited to go skiing in Kitzbühel by a man who owns his own castle there. We're all going, and besides, I don't see the point of flying back for one more interview for a part that I might not get anyway." Hy knew that I'd been a bit discouraged at having just missed several roles I'd auditioned for. He had patiently explained that while it was great for me to now be considered alongside other longer-established actresses, it might take a little while before I got my big break. I understood, but after weighing the fabulous nights of Paris yet to come against further disappointment, I was less than eager to come home.

"Nichelle," Hy said, "get on the plane! Or I'm going to come and drag you back!"

"But, Hy—" Hy Sieger was not a man who took no for an answer.

"Okay, I'm going to make you an offer you can't refuse."

"Try," I dared him.

"There will be a first-class round-trip ticket at Air France. You be on that plane tomorrow. You get your little brown butt back here, and if you don't get this part, you've got a round-trip ticket on me.

"This is important," he added. "I know you're going to get the part."

It was an offer I couldn't refuse. Unbeknownst to me at

the time, the Starship *Enterprise* had barely made it out of space dock before she encountered subspace turbulence. Or, to put it in more familiar Terran terms, the network brass. Not long after my great escape from Gene, he set to work selling his idea for a futuristic weekly television series with an ensemble cast that would travel on a mission through the galaxy to, well, boldly go where no one had gone before. Unlike the majority of science-fiction films and the future-oriented series that preceded *Star Trek* (perhaps with the exception of *The Twilight Zone*), this show was pure Roddenberry: less about science and special effects than about the human condition, and more about the present than the future.

Though a fan of good science-fiction writing, Gene never considered himself a science-fiction writer. But he had learned through experience that playing out universal human philosophical and moral dilemmas in a familiar contemporary setting, as on *The Lieutenant*, for example, hit too close to home and was considered too smart. As a setting for the thought-provoking and idealistic series Gene had in mind, the future had everything. By virtue of its being unknown and unknowable it offered infinite possibilities for character and plot development. Through Mr. Spock, for instance, *Star Trek* explored story lines concerning his mixed heritage (half human, half Vulcan), the challenges of his parents' mixed marriage (which the network abhorred), and his father's rejecting Spock for his "human" attributes. Speciesism, racism—call it what you will—the point is that Gene created in *Star Trek* a multidimensional, multiracial, multipurpose metaphor through which he could express his personal, progressive ideals. He might have made exactly the same points writing the same stories with Spock being the mulatto human child of a Black parent and a white parent living in the sixties. The problem is that it never would have gotten on the air.

Anyone could conceive a cast of characters, give them a

weekly challenge, and dispatch them through and beyond the United Federation of Planets. In fact, several programs did just that, including CBS's *Lost in Space,* a sort of shipwrecked *Father Knows Best* where despite technological advances, Mom still cooked dinner. Interestingly, before Gene sold *Star Trek* to NBC, he had been invited by several CBS executives to discuss his brainchild. Thinking this was a pitch meeting, Gene held forth for quite a while, divulging how such a show would be put together. Only after they had thoroughly picked Gene's brain did the executives reveal that they already had a space series in the works. Naturally Gene was furious. The only solace he might have taken was in the knowledge that the program CBS deemed superior—*Lost in Space*—incorporated very few of his ideas.

Within the year, however, Gene had sold *Star Trek* to Desilu Studios and had begun to cast the show and write the first scripts. The first pilot, "The Cage," was rejected for a number of reasons. Viewing it today, however, the show stands as the purest early representation of what Gene hoped *Star Trek* would achieve. In light of how far the *Star Trek* universe has expanded, the pilot is akin to looking through a painter's sketchbook or an author's diary. Actor Jeffrey Hunter, fresh from having starred as Jesus Christ in *King of Kings,* was cast as Captain Christopher Pike; Leonard Nimoy, who had guest-starred on an episode of *The Lieutenant,* played Spock; and Majel Barrett portrayed the oddly named Number One. There was also the older, paternal ship's physician, Dr. Boyce, played by John Hoyt.

"The Cage" established the *Yorktown,* its mission, and the key crew members, and the story line brimmed with provocative ideas and concepts. In this story, the Starship is lured to the planet Talos IV, where a telepathic race of beings faces extinction. Its only hope of survival is to find a suitable mate for a beautiful human woman named Vina, the sole survivor of an earlier shipwreck. Through controlling Captain Pike's mind, the Talosians create a series of illusions in the hope that he will surrender his will, allow himself to be seduced by Vina, and father the human offspring that will inherit and advance Talosian culture.

Now toss in the half-Vulcan Mr. Spock; place as second in command a woman, Number One (who in Gene's truly gender-liberated world is referred to as "sir"); and bring the story to an intelligent, peaceful resolution, and you had not only the basic pattern for countless future *Star Trek* episodes but a blueprint for the future of civilization. After viewing what was purported to have been the most original and expensive television pilot ever produced, NBC executives weighed in: "The Cage" was *too* original, too cerebral, and decidedly lacking in "action" (i.e., violence). What's more, two characters in particular left them cold. It must have been difficult for them to determine which offended them most: the purely fictional pointy-eared, mixed-blood alien (whose appearance, they said, audiences might find frightening) or the intellectually gifted woman in charge of the ship (whose existence they might find threatening). Either way, they were determined to eliminate both of them. And so was launched the first of what would become an interminable series of conflicts between Gene and the "suits" overseeing *Star Trek*.

Knowing he couldn't hope to win on all fronts, Gene forfeited Number One to save Mr. Spock. He often quipped, "I compromised and still won: I kept the alien and married the woman." Now a blonde, Majel was recast as Nurse Christine Chapel. Oddly, no one at the network ever realized she was the same actress they'd hated and rejected before. Captain Pike "died" after Jeffrey Hunter refused to return to work on the second pilot, and William Shatner, as Captain James Kirk, took over the captain's chair. Also brought on board were George Takei as Sulu, James Doohan as Scotty, Grace Lee Whitney as Yeoman

My paternal grandparents, Lydia and Samuel G. Nichols, with their black-and-white dog, Patches. *(Author's collection)*

My mother, Lishia Mae Nichols. *(Author's collection)*

My father, Samuel Nichols. *(Author's collection)*

By my teens I had fallen in love with Afro-Cuban dance. At fifteen, appearing in "The College Inn Story" show, portraying one of Katherine Dunham's dancers. *(Author's collection)*

With my husband Foster Johnson while we were on tour with Duke Ellington in 1951. I was ecstatically pregnant with my son, Kyle. *(Author's collection)*

My family, newly arrived from Chicago, poses before the palms in their new hometown: Los Angeles, 1957. *Left to right:* my baby sister Diane, Dad, Mom, me, brother Thomas, a friend, and my sister Marian. *(Author's collection)*

As a Balinesian queen in a photo taken by my friend Joe James during the filming of *Porgy and Bess*, 1957. *(Author's collection)*

Through the late fifties and early sixties, my singing career soared. This is how I appeared during my engagements at New York City's prestigious clubs, the Blue Angel and the Bon Soir, in the early sixties. *(Author's collection)*

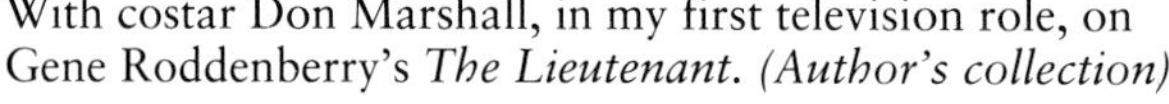

With costar Don Marshall, in my first television role, on Gene Roddenberry's *The Lieutenant*. *(Author's collection)*

Gene Roddenberry, the Great Bird of the Galaxy, the man who was and will always be the personification of *Star Trek*. *(photo © 1994 Paramount Pictures)*

The United Federation Starship *Enterprise*, the ultimate starship, where our adventurous souls abide. *(photo © 1994 Paramount Pictures)*

The big four in the early years *(clockwise from upper left)*: me as Lieutenant Uhura, DeForest Kelley was Dr. "Bones" McCoy, William Shatner as Captain James T. Kirk, and Leonard Nimoy as Mr. Spock. *(photo © 1994 Paramount Pictures)*

On the bridge of the first Starship *Enterprise (left to right)*: Captain Kirk, Mr. Spock, and Lieutenant Uhura. *(photo © 1994 Paramount Pictures)*

"Hailing frequencies open!" *(photo © 1994 Paramount Pictures)*

Mr. Spock, Charlie X (Robert Walker, Jr.), Captain Kirk, and Uhura, from the first season's "Charlie X." *(photo © 1994 Paramount Pictures)*

In the first season's "The Naked Time," Sulu (George Takei) fell victim to the Psi 2000 virus and fancied himself my swashbuckling savior: "I'll save you, fair maiden." Uhura: "Sorry, neither!" *(photo © 1994 Paramount Pictures)*

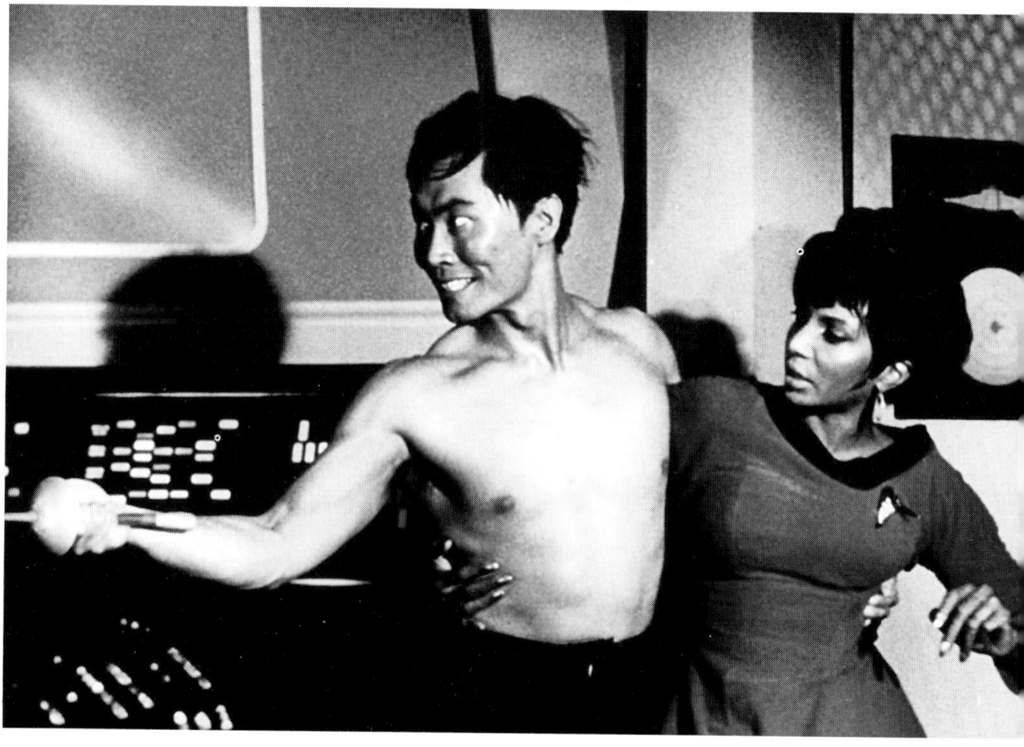

In a parallel universe from the second season's acclaimed "Mirror, Mirror," my cunning alter ego lets the lecherous "evil" Sulu know his romantic advances are not welcome. *(photo © 1994 Paramount Pictures)*

Uhura and Chekov (Walter Koenig) on shore leave with her new friend, a Tribble. How was Uhura to know that "The Trouble with Tribbles" was that they were born pregnant? *(photo © 1994 Paramount Pictures)*

On the set of "Plato's Stepchildren," the third-season episode that made history by presenting the first interracial kiss ever shown on national television. Cleopatra, eat your heart out! *(photo © 1994 Paramount Pictures)*

Just before the climactic moment when Captain Kirk and Uhura kiss—and we did kiss—in "Plato's Stepchildren." Bill deliberately destroyed the "nonkiss" take, so the network had no choice but to air the real kiss. *(photo © 1994 Paramount Pictures)*

In a quiet moment, soon after *Star Trek*'s cancellation, around 1970. *(Author's collection)*

Uhura in the animated, Emmy-winning *Star Trek* television series, which first aired in the 1973–74 season. Working with many of the series' writers, we had some very good scripts and even better parts. Uhura even got to take over the ship! *(photo © 1994 Paramount Pictures)*

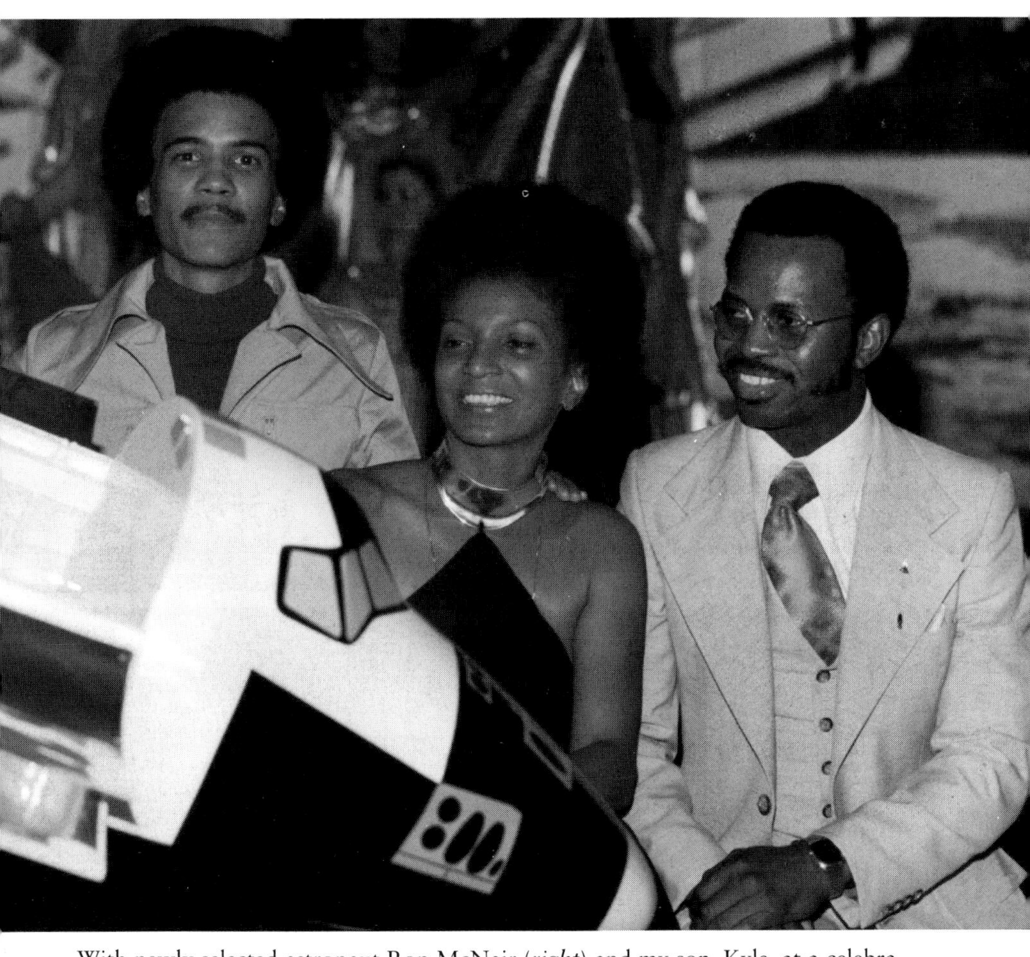

With newly selected astronaut Ron McNair (*right*) and my son, Kyle, at a celebration honoring Ron. *(Author's collection)*

Before I embarked on my whirlwind cross-country astronaut recruitment drive, I underwent briefing and astronaut training at the NASA Center in Huntsville, Alabama. *(photo courtesy of NASA)*

With astronaut Judy Resnik, who presented me with NASA's Public Service Award in October 1984. She was one of three Space Shuttle astronauts who applied in response to the recruitment drive I headed, and who were killed in the *Challenger* disaster in January 1986. *(photo courtesy of NASA)*

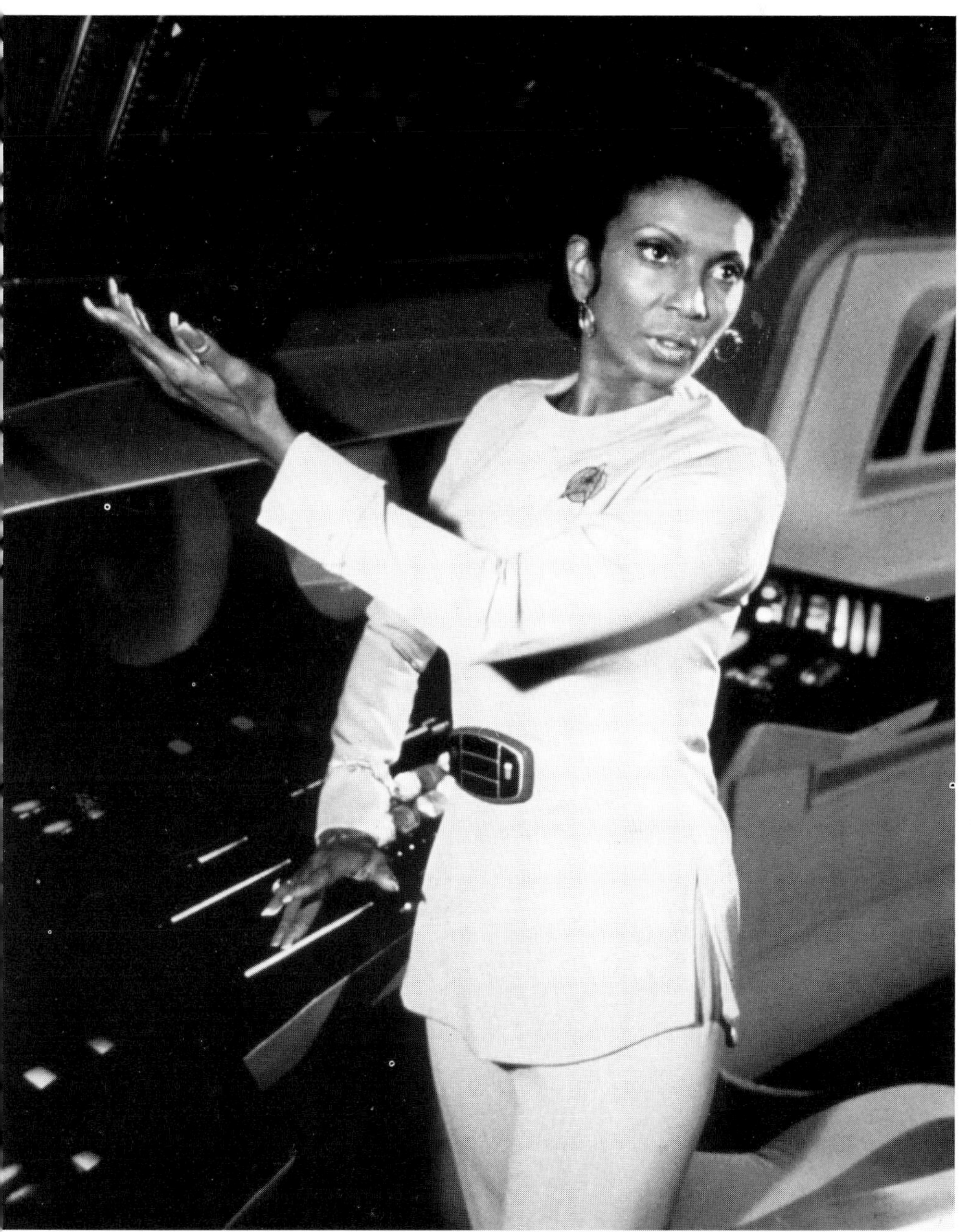

It took nearly a decade, but at last the U.S.S. *Enterprise* and her crew set course for the final frontier in 1979's *Star Trek: The Motion Picture*. It was great to be back on duty again. *(© 1994 Paramount Pictures)*

With my friend Jim Meechan at the premiere of *Star Trek: The Motion Picture*, December 1979. *(Author's collection)*

With Grace Lee Whitney and Leonard Nimoy at the first movie's premiere, December 1979. *(Author's collection)*

A new director and a new look for Uhura and the crew for one of the fans' favorite films: *Star Trek II: The Wrath of Khan*. *(photo © 1994 Paramount Pictures)*

Star Trek III: The Search for Spock found Spock's real-life alter ego Leonard Nimoy behind the camera as well, making his directorial debut in feature films. Here he helps me bring humor to the scene where Uhura "persuades" a young Starfleet cadet to retire to a closet while she aids Kirk and company in their plan to hijack the *Enterprise*. *(photo © 1994 Paramount Pictures)*

On the last day of shooting *Star Trek III*, Nichelle *and* Uhura gave Leonard a big kiss for his wonderful work. *Left to right:* Me, Leonard, Dee Kelley, George Takei, Jimmy Doohan, and Walter Koenig. What a team! What a family! *(Author's collection)*

It was with great pride that I helped Gene celebrate in 1985, when he became the first writer to receive a star on Hollywood's Walk of Fame. *(Author's collection)*

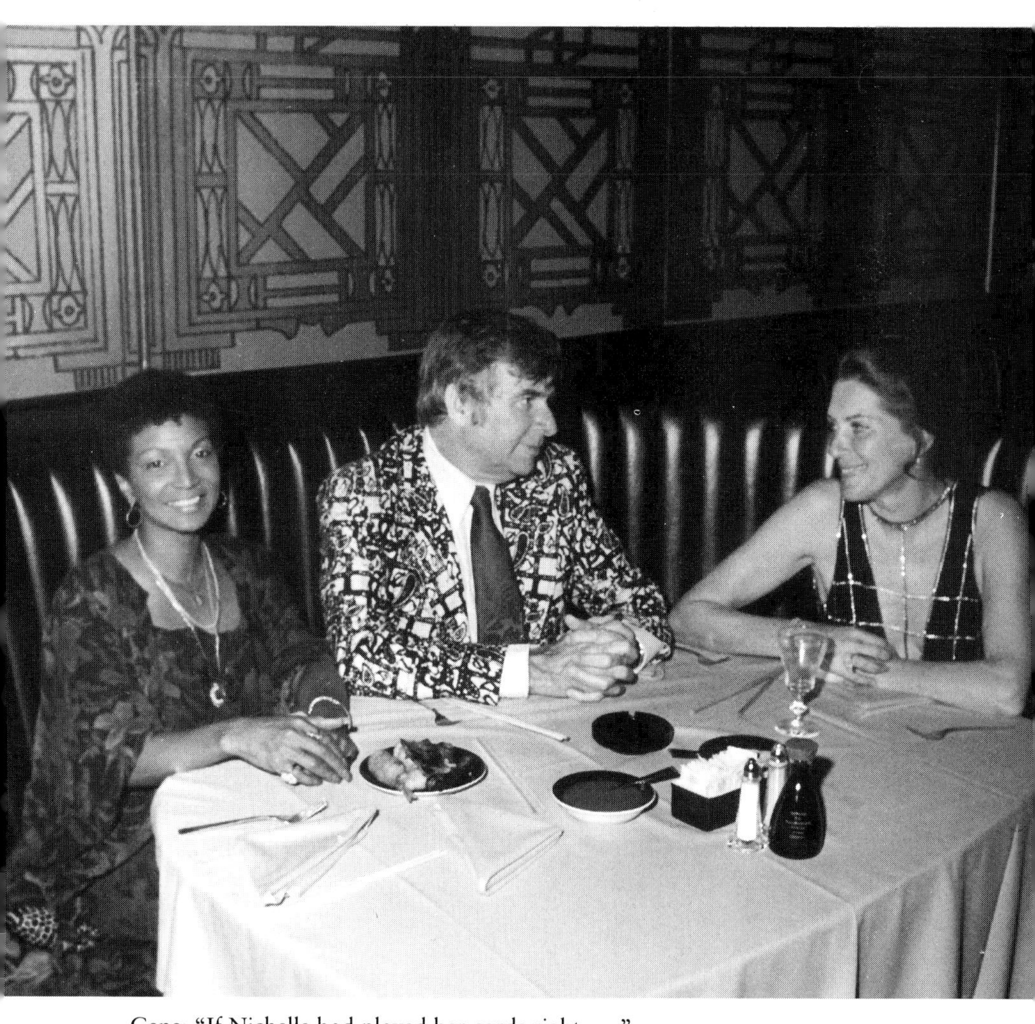

Gene: "If Nichelle had played her cards right . . ."
Nichelle and Majel: "Sure, Gene . . ."
Through the years, I remained close friends with Gene and his wife, Majel. We go back a long, long way. *(Author's collection)*

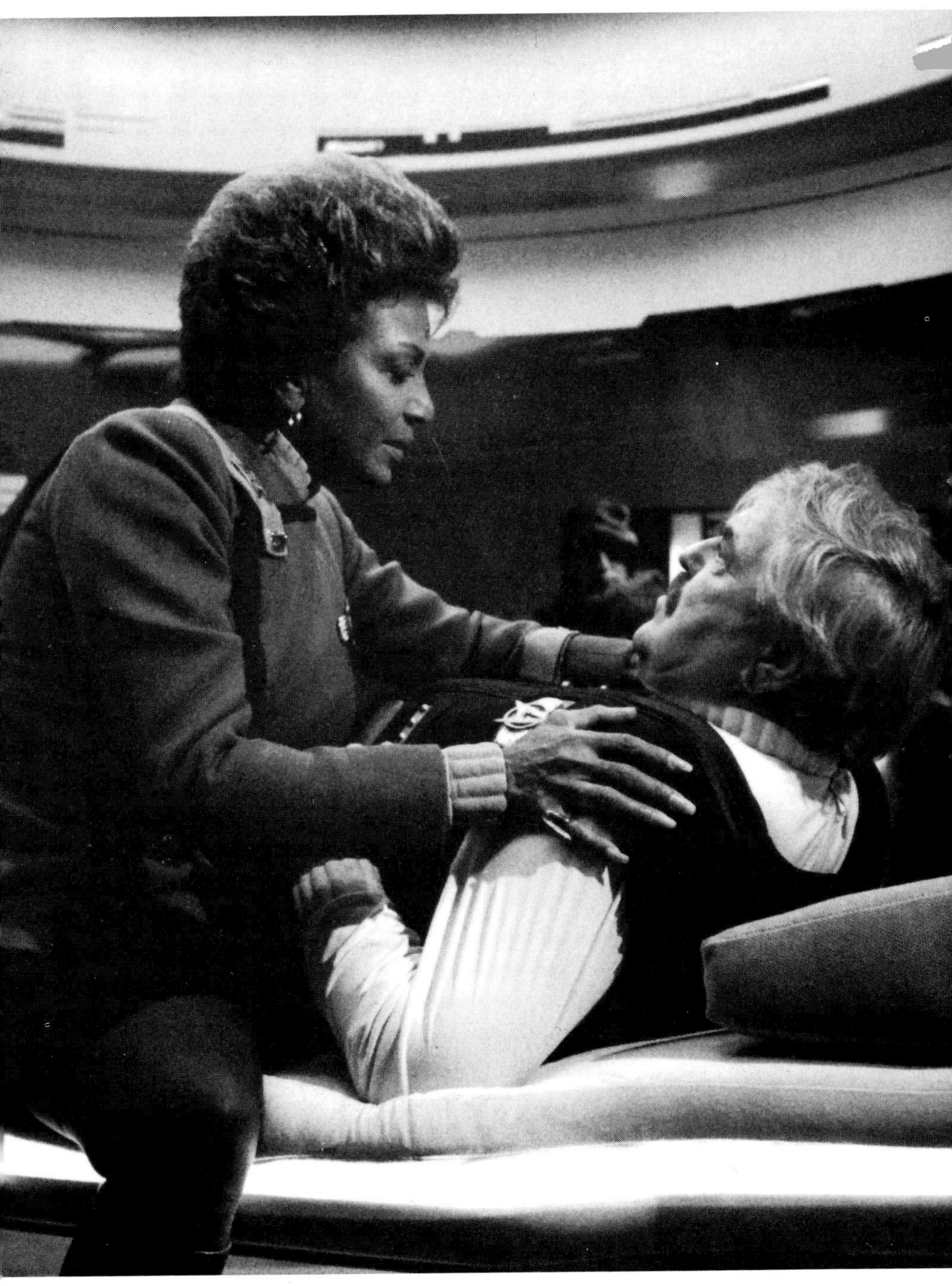

Some fans were surprised at the romantic turn Uhura and Scotty's relationship seemed to have taken in *Star Trek V: The Final Frontier*. In fact, Uhura's concern for her shipmate parallels my enduring love for Jimmy Doohan; we are best of friends forever. *(photo © 1994 Paramount Pictures)*

As the legendary Josephine Baker in my one-woman show "Reflections." *(photo courtesy of Jim Meechan)*

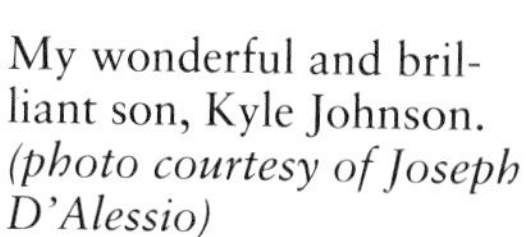

My wonderful and brilliant son, Kyle Johnson. *(photo courtesy of Joseph D'Alessio)*

With my friend Whoopi Goldberg, a gracious, funny lady and, as Guinan, a member of the Star Trek universe. Her acknowledgment of Uhura's inspiration has been an inspiration to me. *(photo © 1994 Paramount Pictures)*

Nineteen ninety-one, the year that marked *Star Trek's* twenty-fifth anniversary, began a period of beginnings and endings, joy and sadness. Here are two of my happier moments: receiving my star on the Hollywood Walk of Fame in early 1992 (that's my mother seated to my right, with my brother Frank). *(photo courtesy of Brian Meechan)* Shortly thereafter, I was Celebrity of the Week at Walt Disney World, where, after this parade down its version of Hollywood Boulevard, I became the first African-American to cast her hands in the cement of its make-believe Mann's Chinese Theatre. To my right is my friend and partner Jim Meechan. Along with my *Star Trek* costars, I had left my mark at the real Mann's in late 1991, when our last film, *Star Trek VI: The Undiscovered Country* premiered. *(photo courtesy of Disney Studios)*

Janice Rand (Captain Kirk's love interest), and the barely seen and rarely heard Lloyd Haynes—later better known for his starring role in the series *Room 222*—who appeared only in the pilot, as Communications Officer Alden.

Gene and his staff prepared three scripts, from which "Where No Man Has Gone Before" was chosen. Again, the script explored an intriguing question: What if a man was suddenly imbued with the powers of a god? Guest-starring Gary Lockwood (the title lead from *The Lieutenant*) and Sally Kellerman, the episode held true to *Star Trek*'s loftier goals while offering a few concessions in the form of fistfights and phaser blasts. Even with Spock still on the bridge, NBC felt confident that *Star Trek* would fly and reserved a spot in its upcoming fall 1966 lineup: eight-thirty P.M. Thursday, opposite *My Three Sons* and *The Tammy Grimes Show*.

My interview was scheduled for early the following week, and it was the weekend already. If Hy Sieger—who was my confidant, Svengali, and dear friend—had this much faith in me, I figured I had nothing to lose. The worst that might happen? A free trip back to France. I agreed to meet him in Los Angeles, and packed for what I expected to be a short detour home.

During my brief stay in Europe, I'd taken on a lot of the chic Continental styles: classic Chanel suits, dramatic eye makeup, and a short Afro hairstyle, which had not yet caught on in the States. This "Euro Afro" was Afro all over, except it had long, straight "sideburns" and came to a point in the center front. It being the sixties, and Californians tending to be somewhat laid back to begin with, God forbid anyone should think that you might get "dressed up" to go read for a part. I'd forgotten this, and so the minute I stepped into the outer office in my Paris chic and saw about a dozen other casually dressed actresses, I thought, *Uh-oh*. I received a number of cool stares and several smirks.

Knowing how auditions go, I'd brought along a book I'd discovered in Europe, a bestselling treatise on Africa entitled *Uhuru,* which I found absolutely fascinating. I settled down to read and wait my turn. The stares and smirks turned to glares when my name was called ahead of some of theirs.

I was shown into a room where five or six men greeted me, among them the show's producer, Gene, who was sitting behind a huge desk.

"Why, Mr. R.," I said, truly puzzled and a little shaken, "what are you doing here?" My agent had never mentioned Gene's name in connection with this audition.

"Oh, I've got a little something to do with this," he answered, grinning.

I composed myself as best I could and turned my attention to the men across the room. They included Joe Sargent, who directed the first and several subsequent episodes, Bob Justman, the show's associate producer, Eddie Milkis, and Jeff Peters. We chatted for a bit, and someone asked me about the book I was reading. In discussing the book later, Gene and I hit upon the idea that the character he would formulate for me would hail from Africa. But at that time Uhura had not been conceived. In fact, when it was time to read, I was told, "We haven't quite decided how the character is going to be, so would you read this other character so we can get a feel."

They gave me the script and told me two of them would be reading the parts of Captain Kirk and Bones, and I'd be reading the lines of a character named Spock. Glancing through the script, I was impressed; it looked like a good, rich part, but a lot of the language struck me as highly technical and stilted.

"Before I read, tell me about this character Spock. What is she like?"

"Oh, you're not reading for *that* part. Spock has already been cast."

"Pity," I replied, envying the woman who'd landed this great role. "Well, be that as it may, tell me about her anyway, so I can at least be like her."

"Don't you know anything about the show?" someone asked in apparent disbelief.

"No. I just got in from Europe."

"Oh, that's right. Well, first of all, *she's* not a she, she's a *he,* and he's not from Earth. Actually, he's an alien, with green blood and pointed ears."

"Wait a minute. How am I supposed to play green blood and pointed ears?" Everyone laughed at that. Then I asked, "*Could* this character be female?"

"Well, yes," someone quipped, "but Leonard Nimoy would not like it."

I didn't recognize the name, so I continued, "Okay, so we have a half-alien, half-Earthling male with pointed ears and green blood. What am I supposed to do with this? If the character could be female, what is the character like? Outside of the ears. Just let me read as if I were really going for this part as a female."

As I learned later, despite their having heard over fifty actresses read up until then, I was the first to ask these questions, and, intrigued by the possibilities, they urged me to continue. I frankly but courteously pointed out, "Well, I think that if *you* don't know what the character's like, how can *I* know what the character's like? I can play this part any way from Marilyn Monroe to Sojourner Truth. If I know what the character is like, you can see if I can act and take direction."

Joe Sargent loved my approach, so they explained more about Spock's background, how he never smiles, lacks a sense of humor, is philosophically devoted to logic, and so on. After I had delivered a long scene, everyone sat looking at me in silence. Finally Bob Justman said, "I think we ought to have Penny call down to personnel and see if Leonard Nimoy has signed his contract yet." Even without knowing Leonard, I knew this was a great compliment. They asked me if I would mind waiting, and then Penny showed me into a quiet anteroom. I had no idea what was happening, but I'd been around long enough to appreciate the complexities of casting and not to get my hopes up too high. I soon found myself so deeply reimmersed in the world of *Uhuru,* I lost all track of time. After an hour or more, Joe Sargent looked in. Surprised to see me, he asked, "What are you doing still here?"

"You told me to wait."

"Oh, my God, I'm so sorry. Didn't anybody tell you?"

"No," I replied, bracing myself for the inevitable rejection but consoling myself with thoughts of a first-class return trip to my beloved Paris.

Joe smiled broadly. "Come on, big talent. You got the role when you first walked in the room. Let's go to lunch." And so it began.

As I soon learned, this was the dream to which Gene had alluded so often in the past. Interestingly, though he'd said many times before that there might be something in this for me, that day I won a part that had yet to be created. It was only after I'd been brought on board, and Gene and I conceived and created her, that Uhura was born. Many times through the years I've referred to Uhura as my great-great-great-great-great-great-great-granddaughter of the twenty-third century. Gene and I agreed that she would be a citizen of the United States of Africa. And her name, Uhur*a,* is derived from Uhuru, which is Swahili for "freedom." According to the "biography" Gene and I developed for my character, Uhura was far more than an intergalactic telephone operator. As head of Communications, she commanded a corps of largely unseen communications technicians, linguists, and other specialists who worked in the bowels of the *Enterprise,* in the "comm-center." A linguistics scholar and a top graduate of Starfleet Academy, she was a protégée of Mr. Spock, whom she admired for his daring, his intelligence, his stoicism, and especially his logic. We even had outlined exactly where Uhura had grown up, who her parents were, and why she had been chosen over other candidates for the *Enterprise*'s five-year mission.

In hiring me, the ever-resourceful Gene had begun the process of additional casting, explaining to the network that he wanted to add a little "color" to the bridge. They assumed he was merely redecorating the set, and he was wily enough not to mislead them into learning the truth.

Having experienced my share of ups and downs in the business, I welcomed the security a series offered. Not only did it mean a regular paycheck, but, most important, I could be home more with my son and be there for my mother and family. I could finally replace my dumpy little car with a gorgeous red Jaguar and buy my mother her house. I only wished Dad had lived to see his little "Chicken" strut her stuff.

Once I was officially hired, my agents went to work refining the details of the deal. Due in part to the vicissitudes of show business and thanks to the actors' union, agents and production companies recognize that an oral agreement is as valid and binding as a written one. In other words, if a producer tells your agent that he is hiring you, and you both agree on your salary, he is bound to live up to the deal. Contracts are typically signed later, often quite a while after you have begun work.

I was still basking in my good fortune when one of my agents called to say, "Nichelle, we've got a problem on the contract."

"How could you possibly have a problem?" I asked, stunned. "It's a done deal."

As my agent explained, it was—that is, until the network executives saw in the first script exactly what Gene meant when he said he was recasting one part and wanted to add a little "color" to the bridge. After having triumphed in the banishment of Number One, the network men had a fit when they saw that not only was there now an important woman in the command crew and on the bridge, but a Black one! When they realized that Uhura's involvement would be substantial and her lines went well beyond "Yes, Captain!" they furiously issued Gene an ultimatum: Get rid of her! Gene flatly refused.

Much to Gene's credit, neither he nor anyone who knew of this ever revealed it to me. In fact, the bliss of my ignorance would extend throughout *Star Trek*'s run. I would not discover the truth until nearly seven years beyond its cancellation and then only by accident. Unbeknownst to me, my agents and Gene conspired to concoct a brilliant strategy to save Uhura.

I would have been well within my rights to force the contract. But as my agents wisely pointed out, while the producers could be forced to honor a thirteen-week contract with me, they could not be forced to *use* me. This is the tack the network pressured Gene to take, so that I could be bought out, and he adamantly refused. While Gene and my agents struggled to save my part, they never wanted me to learn the truth of the problem at hand. At one point Gene said of the network's bigotry and his clandestine collaboration with my agents, "I don't want Nichelle to know about this, because she'll feel that she came in on this the way many Black people do—through the back door. I will not do that to Nichelle." God bless him.

My agents presented the situation to me this way: "Look, the network has bought the series, and they will not honor another contract. They're angry about Gene wanting more contracts. It has nothing to do with you." Of course, after they'd repeated "It's not a racial thing" for the twentieth time, I should have realized something was up.

"But it's not a new contract," I argued logically. "I'm just replacing Lloyd Haynes, who is also Black. So why is this a problem?"

Without answering me, my agents quickly set forth the plan: "Here's what's going to happen. You will be on, but you will not be under contract."

"Well, what the hell am I going to be?"

"It'll be on a daily basis," they said, "when they need you, but—"

"Look! I've worked all these years *not* to be a day player," I cried bitterly. "I will not do it!"

Of course, my agents knew that Gene was going to use me exactly as he'd planned, only now even more often. To my agents, this was a winning approach. To me, though, it was a crushing disappointment, a humiliation, and somewhere in my subconscious I knew the race issue played a part. But I bit my tongue and swallowed my pride as my agents, who'd worked so hard on my behalf and were just as hurt as I was, tried to persuade me.

"We know you're going to be great in this. We have the script right here, and you've got a great part. Just go in there and be fabulous.

"Besides, Nichelle, if at any point something better comes along, you're free to go. Let's just take the money and run, establish yourself in television, and see what happens. You'll be working, and we'll have film to show when you're up for other parts."

I knew they were right, and as much as it hurt me to accept what I considered "seconds," I knew this was still a rare opportunity. Knowing the full story as I do today, I've often wondered what would have happened had I fought for the contract on principle, or if the producer had been anyone but Gene. My agent assuaged some of my fears when he added, "You know Gene loves you, and he's promised to look out for you."

Gene more than made good on his promise to use me.

Because of the wage structure, I ended up earning more as a day player than I would have had I been under contract. In addition, Gene helped arrange for me to work on another series when I had down time on *Star Trek*. Few people knew that for a year I (or, rather, my back) appeared on *Peyton Place* in the role of a nurse. Without slighting Gene or anyone else, though, I must be honest: I found the whole situation humiliating. None of the other cast members knew I wasn't hired on the same basis as they were. Every time I had to perform some publicity function and remark about how wonderful the network was, the words all but caught in my throat.

Further, quite frankly, I resented being one of the first actors on the set each day and among the last to leave. Whenever an assistant director remarked late in the day, "Stick around, Nichelle. We may need you for Bill's closeup," I felt like the scullery maid. It was only after endorsing a few paychecks that I began to see the method to Gene's madness. This was Gene's way of getting back at the suits in the front office. Not only did Gene get what he wanted, he made sure they paid—literally and dearly—for it.

CHAPTER SEVEN

While thrilled to be on *Star Trek,* I dreaded the thought of getting up before dawn to make my six o'clock call. Being nocturnal by nature, a regular after-theater and nightclub schedule of two A.M. dinners and afternoon "breakfasts" suited me beautifully. The earliest I'd ever reported to a set was eight o'clock for *Porgy and Bess.* This was going to take some getting used to.

I was living in a little house on Orange Drive, only about a half hour from Desilu Studios, so I'd leave the house around four-thirty or five. This particular morning was simply miserable. It was still dark out, foggy, and pouring rain. Why no one in Southern California knows how to drive in the rain is a mystery. I'd turned onto Melrose Avenue and was mere blocks from the set when a driver behind me began honking incessantly. He overtook me, then cut me off. I slammed on the brake and instinctively jerked the wheel to my left, only to find myself in the oncoming lane with a Grand Prix bearing down on me.

The next few seconds passed in a blur, as the impact of

the larger car forced my little Renault up into the air, landing on top of it. Everything stopped. Opening my eyes, I looked down and saw blood everywhere. Then people started rushing toward me, including the driver of the Grand Prix, who practically screamed, "Are you alive?"

"I'm sorry about your car," I answered.

"My car? It's amazing you're *alive.*" After I was helped out and glimpsed the twisted wreckage, my knees buckled. Many people rushed from their houses when they heard the crash, among them an elderly couple, who invited me inside. Unaware of the extent of my injuries, I asked them to please phone the studio and ask them to send someone for me. Then I asked if they could show me to the bathroom. I'd been pressing ice to my lip, and though it hurt to walk, I figured my cuts and bruises were not life-threatening. Then I saw myself in the mirror.

Oh, my God! There goes my career!

For a moment, I stood transfixed by the horrible sight and began to mourn Uhura. Between my puffy eyes, wet hair, and torn lip, I looked dreadful. I had almost accepted that once the assistant director saw me, Uhura would be recast; after all, business is business. But I'd be damned if I wasn't going to at least give it a try. The couple handed me my jacket and my huge bag, in which I'd packed some things for that evening. I pulled a great orange velvet tam over my soggy hair, put on a pair of elegant gold hoop earrings, and applied some makeup.

"Are you all right?" the woman asked through the bathroom door.

"Fine," I replied. Pulling off my sweat clothes, I nearly gasped at the sight of my badly bruised heel and knee. No wonder I felt as if I couldn't walk. Gingerly I pulled on some clean black pants, a cashmere sweater, and black leather boots.

"They're here to get you," she called a few moments later.

"Be out in a minute!" My head was spinning and my body ached, but I'd managed to remake myself into some semblance of a human being, though I sure didn't feel like one. Through the door I could hear the couple talking to the assistant director, who'd just arrived: ". . . It's amazing she isn't dead! She was bleeding horribly and could hardly walk." When I stepped into the living room, using every ounce of concentration I could summon not to limp, the old couple looked as if they'd seen a ghost. They actually peered around me, as if looking for the dreadful hag who'd gone into their bathroom twenty minutes before.

"Were you in that accident?" the AD asked in amazement. They had passed the wreckage, thinking, *She couldn't have survived that one.*

"Yes." I looked presentable enough. And to the old couple who had seen me in my "before" condition, I looked nothing short of terrific. But there was no getting around the fact that I needed medical attention. The AD phoned Gene. They agreed they would work around me, and the AD would accompany me to the hospital.

In the emergency room, a marvelous doctor, probably somewhere around sixty-five, examined me thoroughly to make sure I had no serious internal injuries. Next he turned his attention to my lip. "Oh, nasty," he remarked. "We're going to have to stitch that. Take about five or six stitches."

Well, that's it for me, I thought, staring up at the ceiling.

"But don't worry," he added, as if reading my mind. By then he'd been told that I was going to be in a television series, and as he started to stitch me up, he inquired about my work, then added, "I've got news for you. You're the luckiest little lady on the planet because you've got me. You're not going to lose your job, and you're not going to lose a day of work! *If* you do everything I tell you."

I nodded.

"I just returned from spending two years in Mexico, and

I've got some wonderful magic that's going to have you up and around in no time. It's still illegal in this country, but I'm going to give it to you anyway because it will reduce the swelling, so you can't even tell it.

"Now listen carefully," he continued. "I'm going to give you a shot that will allow you to function for about eight hours, but no more. I've given you a little bit more than the standard dose, so you're going to feel a little woozy. And I'm also giving you something that will counteract that and make you alert enough to handle your job. Take these pills at the times I've specified, but by all means make sure that you are at home and in bed by six o'clock. This stuff is magic, but it's going to wear off, and when it does, you cannot have any more, and that will be all she wrote. Sort of like Cinderella at the stroke of midnight—except you're going to turn into the pumpkin. Okay?"

"Okay," I mumbled gratefully as the drugs quickly began to take effect.

By the time I got to the soundstage, I felt surprisingly well. Everyone on the set was expecting a basket case, so they were as amazed as I was to find me basically all right. I got through what was left of the morning, rested in my dressing room during lunch, then began work again. Due in part to the drugs, I'd lost track of time, and since I looked and functioned so well, everyone assumed I must be all right. It was around five-thirty and nearing my "witching hour." I was standing by the railing near Uhura's station on the bridge, listening intently as the director ran down the next day's shoot. Suddenly I felt dizzy and off-balance, and felt myself slowly fall forward. What surely took a fraction of a second seemed to pass in an eternity. I remember seeing everyone on the bridge in slow motion as they turned toward me, then Bill Shatner looking at the director, then back at me, and then Captain Kirk leaping across the bridge toward me, screaming, "Uhura!" then catching me in his arms with my head just inches from hitting the floor.

"Is she all right?" the director gasped.

"My God, she could have broken her neck!" Bill exclaimed. Looking down at me in his arms, he asked gently, "Are you all right, Nichelle?"

Still holding the stupid script and fighting to form words, I replied, "Yessssth." I couldn't even raise my head, let alone get up. My fairy godfather had been right: Once this spell was broken, it was gone. And so was I.

Everyone on the set scattered to help, as Bill gallantly gathered me up in his arms and turned to carry me back to my dressing room, when the director yelled, "Someone else help Nichelle! We have to finish this before we wrap for the day!"

"That *is* a wrap for today," Bill replied firmly.

"I didn't call a wrap," the director snapped.

"*Yes, you did!* That's a wrap!" When someone else suggested that a driver be called to take me home, Bill said, "Don't bother. I'll take her."

Limp as a rag doll, I was helped out of my costume and into street clothes. Fortunately, Bill got my address from the files, because by then all I could do was slur. He put me into the passenger seat of his sleek black Stingray sports car, and away we went. By the time we got to my house I couldn't walk at all.

"Have you got your keys?" he asked.

"Yessssth . . ." There was poor Bill, holding me—looking like hell—in one arm, while trying to fish my keys out of my pocket with the other hand. Suddenly my son, Kyle, snatched open the door to see a strange man carrying his mother, who looked like she was drunk.

"What have you done to my mother?!" he demanded. I'll never forget the look on poor Bill's face as he tried to assure my irate son that he was on a mission of mercy and that his mother was safe.

I wasn't required back on the set for a couple of days, so I rested and recuperated. From that moment and for many years to come, Bill Shatner was my hero. His behavior that day was totally in character with the Bill I would come to know and love during the first year of the series: warm, open, fun. That was true of the entire cast and crew. I believe everyone shared a sense that *Star Trek* was special, that the stories we were bringing to life were of value.

Another factor that distinguished the *Star Trek* set was that virtually everyone there had been handpicked by Gene, who had first worked with Leonard Nimoy, Walter Koenig, Majel Barrett, and me on *The Lieutenant.* DeForest Kelley knew Gene from having starred in Gene's failed pilot for *333 Montgomery.* Of the original cast, I believe only Bill, Jimmy Doohan, and George Takei had not worked with Gene before.

By having to report to the studio so ungodly early each day, we got to know one another quite well. Leonard Nimoy and I were always in the makeup chairs first, since our characters required more intricate makeup than the others. Leonard was, and is, a thoroughly charming, ethical, and thoughtful man. Grace Lee Whitney, who played Yeoman Janice Rand during our first season, was warm, vivacious, and hilarious, while DeForest Kelley (whom we called Dee) was every bit the proverbial softspoken Southern gentleman. Jimmy Doohan was jovial and friendly, if a bit blustery at times, and Bill, who has a weird sense of humor, would hold forth and regale us with some stupid story. We'd all laugh because the stories *were* so stupid, but Bill, who thought they were hilarious, laughed the whole way through, sometimes so hard he couldn't finish telling us anyway. Gregarious George Takei, ever the bon vivant, invariably strode in at seven A.M. with an inexcusably cheery "Good morning!" to which we would all growl menacingly, "Shut up, George!"

Except for a few weeks in the spring when we were on hiatus, we worked five days a week on a six-day-per-episode shooting schedule. On a typical day, we started filming at eight, broke for an hour-long lunch around noon, then returned to the set so we could finish by six, though many times we were still there at seven or eight. Because of the stringency of the work rules and the high cost of overtime, however, we could not afford to work more than six days. Each episode had to be wrapped up by then, or heads would roll.

As with most television series, *Star Trek*'s scripts were never truly finished. We each received a copy of the new script sometimes just a day before shooting. Then at least once a day—perhaps several times—you got newly revised script pages, each revision printed on a different color paper to distinguish it from its predecessor. We hardly rehearsed our scenes at all, and we didn't do full read-throughs of the script. A couple of minutes before shooting the scene, we'd block it out with the director. Whatever revisions had been made were usually distributed throughout the workday.

The early versions of those first scripts reflect Gene's intention to build stories around an ensemble of basically equal characters. The troika of Captain Kirk, Mr. Spock, and Dr. McCoy was just taking shape, but Gene intended to expand the roles and participation of Sulu, Uhura, Yeoman Rand, Scotty, Nurse Chapel, and, later, Chekov. This was years before programs such as *The Mary Tyler Moore Show* and *M*A*S*H* broke the "one-star, one costar/sidekick, multiple supporting actors" mold. However, the network saw no reason to deviate from this familiar formula, especially since there were enough story lines to work around Kirk, Spock, and McCoy. Gene confided in me, and it was apparent in the first versions of the early scripts, that he was developing Uhura as a major character, and each first draft of a new script reflected that desire. So seeing my wonderful role being constantly cut with every rewrite was demoralizing. I remember thinking, *Why let me see the original script in the first place?* It was sheer torture.

The hard work aside, my memories of working on the

series are largely happy ones, especially in the early days when we *were* a real team, each of us trying to find his or her place.

Beneath my veneer of sophistication, I still had moments when I felt absolutely green. One occurred between takes just a couple of weeks into shooting. I noticed that Bill, Leonard, and Dee were standing across the set, talking conspiratorially, it seemed, when they all glanced my way. I smiled, they smiled, so I approached them, hoping to get in on what seemed like some good gossip, and said, "Hi." Then I got that strange feeling you get when you sense someone's been talking about you, but you're not really sure. Suddenly their conversation turned bland and guarded. I walked away, then looked back. They were definitely talking and glancing over at me. Now I was completely baffled and not sure what to say or do.

Just then Dee came over and said, "Nichelle, the guys and I were talking about something, and we wondered if you . . . Well, they sort of designated me the one . . . well, they're too chickenshit to do it themselves, so I've been designated to come over and find out: Who does your work?"

"What do you mean, 'Who does your work?' "

"You know, who does your work? Because it's excellent."

"Oh, thank you," I replied, without a clue as to what he was talking about. My bewilderment must have shown, because his voice took on an impatient edge.

"Come on, this is Hollywood. Everybody does it sooner or later. Yours is excellent, so share it."

In total frustration, I finally said, "Dee, I don't know what you're talking about."

"Don't be coy. One actor to another: your dental work. Your caps. Who did them?"

I didn't know whether to laugh or cry. Just a few years before, I'd lost a lucrative contract to do commercials for Colgate toothpaste after some executives complained my teeth looked too perfect to be believable. "We want average-looking teeth," the ad men said. "Not some actor with perfect caps." Even when my agents offered to prove to them that my teeth were real, they refused to believe it, and I didn't get the commercial. I never used Colgate again.

"Is this going to cost me?" I asked Dee.

"What do you mean?"

"Private joke," I answered, shrugging. "I don't *have* any such dental work. I haven't even found a dentist out here yet."

By this time, I was getting pretty animated, and from across the set I saw Leonard and Bill watching closely.

"I don't mean to insult you," Dee replied, "but everybody has dental work. I don't believe you. They just don't look real."

"Examine them for yourself," I replied, never dreaming that Leonard, Bill, and Dee would be taking turns inspecting my teeth, as if I were some kind of horse. "Satisfied?" I asked. Just then my makeup man happened by. Seeing how they'd ruined my makeup, he started screaming, "What have you done to her?"

We shared many warm, happy times together, and being together day in and day out set the stage for several close, enduring friendships. In the beginning, I counted Bill among those friends. I remember one time when he and I were shooting our scenes late in the day. We were just about the last people on the soundstage, and as I finished changing my clothes to leave, he knocked on my dressing-room door. "Have you got a moment?" he asked.

"Sure, come in."

We chatted for a couple of minutes, then he grew very serious. "Can I ask you something personal?"

"Not my teeth again," I kidded.

"No. You have a son."

"Yes."

"He's a lovely child," he said earnestly.

"Thank you."

"I've watched you, Nichelle, and I respect you. You've gone through a divorce. How did you handle it?"

I must admit that while I felt I knew Bill pretty well, his sudden openness and vulnerability came as a surprise.

"My wife wants a divorce, and it's killing me," he confessed. "I have three beautiful little girls, and I don't know how I can live without them."

"You don't have to live without them, Bill."

"But I don't know how to live without seeing them every day."

"Is there no way to reconcile?" I asked.

Bill explained that there was not, not at that stage. "I don't want this divorce," he stressed. Then, alluding to his reputation as a ladies' man, he added, "I know it's my fault, but I never thought it would come to this, and I don't know how to handle it. I don't know how to not see my daughters."

"If it has to be, then the thing you have to do is make up time with those girls more than you would if you were at home every day."

"But you're lucky in a way. You always had your child," he replied.

"No," I corrected him. "I'm lucky I always had my parents. I was a single mother who had to work, and my work often took me out of town. I'm grateful that I was able to be home with my son during those first crucial years, but after that, I had no choice. So, Bill, I do understand your pain."

We sat facing each other, knee to knee, holding hands and softly crying. In rare moments like these, Bill was like a little boy shouldering the problems and emotions of a man. In him that evening I saw love and tenderness, and I felt tremendous compassion for him. And love.

That fall *Star Trek* premiered on NBC to a less than overwhelmingly positive response. The debut episode, "The Man Trap," revolved around a shape-shifting, salt-craving monster with the power to assume a form attractive enough to seduce whomever it encounters. To Bones, she is a youthful version of a long-lost love, for instance. Uhura comes close to being attacked by the monster in the guise of a beautiful Swahili-speaking Black man. Fans do not consider this one of the best episodes, but it had its moments. This and other episodes suggest how Uhura and the other characters might have developed further. At one point Uhura remarks to Mr. Spock, "Sometimes I think if I hear that word *frequency* one more time, I'll cry," a line I'd repeated often enough to Gene to warrant being memorialized in this scene. In others, such as "The Naked Time" and "The Squire of Gothos," Uhura makes it quite plain that she is no damsel in distress. And in "Mirror, Mirror" she proves she can fight, too. Uhura was a new kind of television woman in many ways. Yet even at this early point in the show, it was becoming uncomfortably obvious that whatever ambitious plans Gene had for my character, Uhura's role was constantly being diminished.

Perhaps if all I saw were the final scripts, it might not have been so demoralizing. But to watch as day by day parts and lines were hacked away at until nothing remained hurt me, professionally and personally. One day I confronted D. C. (Dorothy) Fontana, our script consultant and Gene's right-hand woman since before *Star Trek* began, about why my parts were always being cut. She wrote several wonderful scripts that focused on Uhura, and all of them were decimated. As the only woman on the writing staff, Dorothy understood Uhura's importance to the show.

"Why is this happening, Dorothy?" I asked.

"Don't talk to me about it," she answered, almost in tears. "Just leave me alone, Nichelle."

Several forces—from both off and on the set—come into play here, and it's impossible to definitively reconstruct the events. But even in the fictional, enlightened twenty-third century of Gene's imagination, a strong, independent Black woman was not welcome as an equal. This was, after all, still Hollywood, and although Gene basically controlled the show, the network suits approved the scripts.

The first line of resistance was, and would remain, the studio's front office. Chagrined by Gene's having outmaneuvered them when it came to hiring me, they now refused to back down. First they predicted that the network affiliates in the Deep South might not carry the show, but they were wrong. Because of my exotic makeup—which strongly emphasized my almond-shaped eyes and high cheekbones—and the way I was lit, a large number of viewers who saw the show first in black and white wrote to commend the network and *Star Trek* for prominently featuring an *Asian* woman in a leading role! I understand that some of the studio people patted themselves on the back, then asked around to find out just who the two Asian characters were. From the sound of our terribly unauthentic "Asian" surnames, they deduced it must have been Sulu and Uhura. As more people saw the show in color—and realized I was not Asian but Black—viewer response was overwhelmingly positive.

The most painful experiences for me, however, occurred at Desilu (prior to Paramount), where racism—regardless of how subtle—was indisputable. While network executives may have given lip service to the idea of featuring more Black actors in prime time, the tube still reflected an overwhelmingly white world. Except for Bill Cosby's costarring role with Robert Culp in *I Spy* and Greg Morris on *Mission: Impossible,* the majority of Black faces you saw on television belonged to singers and comedians. The program that broke the de-facto color line for leading Black women, *Julia,* would not debut until 1968.

Having grown up as I did, I could not tolerate racist comments and actions. I'd seen enough to know what people really meant, regardless of how they tried to disguise it. And, as always, actions speak louder than words. Blatant racism is obvious and stupid, but the evil of most racist actions and comments is in their veiled insidiousness. One day I arrived at work and was surprised when the security guard at the gate, who had shown a subtle dislike for me and whom I knew by name, refused to let me in.

"What are you talking about?" I asked. "I work here!"

"Sorry, hon, your name isn't on this list. Evidently you don't work here no more."

When I reminded him that I'd been coming through this gate for weeks and reiterated who I was, he snorted, "I don't give a damn who you are."

Furious, I drove down to the next gate and had to walk back some distance to the set.

We were not far into the second season when I was surprised to learn that Grace Lee Whitney had left the show. We'd become friends, and I was very sorry to see her go. Then one day an assistant to someone high up on the Desilu ladder said bluntly to me, "If anyone was let go, it should have been *you,* not Grace Lee. Ten of you could never equal one blue-eyed blonde." He fairly snarled as he walked past me. For a moment I shook with rage. Suddenly I understood the action of the guard. Was this merely one man's opinion or something that had been voiced in the front office? Then an incident occurred that made the feelings of some at the studio painfully clear.

From the first week *Star Trek* aired, we all received fan mail. Naturally Leonard and Bill got the most. Regularly, someone from the mailroom would deliver our fan letters—usually six, a dozen, maybe twenty a week—to the set. I was so thrilled to get fan mail; it's still one of my pleasures. Curiously, every so often, one of the mailroom guys would hand me a much larger pile and explain,

"These were down in the mailroom. We just didn't get them to you before." I would be so grateful it was almost pathetic.

Then near the end of the first season, I'd grown weary of seeing my good scenes and lines being hacked away and enduring the racist insults off the set. I was seriously considering quitting. Everyone *on* the set was so great, why all this animosity off the set? I wondered. I didn't understand, but I kept my own counsel. I thought I could handle it.

One day I was walking across the lot when I recognized two of the guys from the mailroom.

"Hi!" I called out. They smiled and kept walking, then suddenly stopped and turned back. *They must want an autograph,* I thought.

"You're Nichelle Nichols," one said.

"Yes, I am."

He glanced at his coworker, then back at me, as if unsure of what to say. "You know," he began, "we work in the mailroom, and we've got all your fan mail—"

"We think it's such a dirty damn thing that's happening to you," the second guy blurted. "We just think it's so low."

"What are you talking about?"

"We've been ordered not to give you your fan mail," he explained.

"What are you talking about? I get fan mail."

"No," he insisted. "You *don't* get your fan mail. We have stacks—bags!—of letters for you. Yours is the only fan mail that matches Shatner's or Nimoy's."

I stood there frozen in amazement. I had no idea. The two men surely appreciated the impact of their revelation, because the other quickly added, "But if you ever tell anybody we told you this, we're history."

I didn't know what to say. I was grateful for them having told me, but furious at whoever pressed them to keep this secret. Aware that studio careers often do start in the mailroom, I nodded a promise not to tell.

"You know," one suggested slyly, "nobody can stop you from coming to the mailroom to collect your mail. And we'll show you."

Days later I saw for myself the boxes and bags of mail from all over the country, from adults and children, all colors, all races. To say I was stunned does not even begin to convey how I felt. It was "just" fan mail, but to those who had ensured that I worked without a contract, who seemed at every turn to remind me that I was dispensable, this was the ultimate humiliation. I left the mailroom and headed back to the set, where I locked myself in my dressing room.

There were so many good things about working on *Star Trek*—the money, the exposure, my coworkers—that it was with great difficulty that I resolved to leave after the first season. After we wrapped up the last show, I walked into Gene's office and resigned.

"There's too much here that I just can't take," I explained. "I've put up with the cuts and the racism, but I just can't do it anymore."

Gene listened attentively, then said, "Nichelle, please think about it."

"Gene, you've been wonderful, but there's too much wrong here, and I can't fix it." We talked a while longer, and before I left, we hugged warmly. Then he said, "I don't want you to do this. I can make things better. I do have a problem, and I am fighting a hard battle."

I sensed what Gene had alluded to, but I didn't really know what he was trying to communicate. Remember, at this time, I had no idea how far he'd gone to protect me.

"If you leave, they win," he said intently. "And if they chase you away, they win double."

I said goodbye to Gene, thinking to myself that if I stayed and allowed myself to be treated as less of a person than my coworkers, the ubiquitous "they" were winning, too. It simply wasn't worth it to me anymore.

The following evening I attended an important NAACP fund-raising event. I was chatting with someone when a man approached and said, "Nichelle, there is someone who would like to meet you. He's a big fan of *Star Trek* and of Uhura."

I turned to greet this "fan" and found myself gazing upon the face of Dr. Martin Luther King, Jr. I was stunned, and I remember thinking, *Whoever that fan is, he'll just have to wait.*

The man introduced us. Imagine my surprise when the first words Dr. King uttered were, "Yes, I am that fan, and I wanted to tell you how important your role is."

He began speaking of how he and his children watched *Star Trek* faithfully and how much they adored Uhura. At that moment the impact of my decision really struck me. Nevertheless, I replied, "Thank you, Dr. King, but I plan to leave *Star Trek.*"

"You *cannot,*" he replied firmly, "and you *must* not. Don't you realize how important your presence, your character is?" he went on. "Don't you realize this gift this man has given the world? Men and women of all races going forth in peaceful exploration, living as equals. You listen to me: Don't you see? This is not a Black role, and this is not a female role. You have the first nonstereotypical role on television, male or female. You have broken ground—"

"There have been other Black stars," I countered.

"In TV?" he replied. "Yes, Beulah, Amos and Andy. Do I need to go further?"

"No," I answered softly.

"You must not leave. You have opened a door that must not be allowed to close. I'm sure you have taken a lot of grief, or probably will for what you're doing. But you changed the face of television forever. You have created a character of dignity and grace and beauty and intelligence. Don't you see that you're not just a role model for little Black children? You're more important for people who *don't* look like us. For the first time, the world sees us as we should be seen, as equals, as intelligent people—as we *should* be. There will always be role models for Black children; you are a role model for everyone.

"Remember, you are not important there in spite of your color. You are important there *because* of your color. This is what Gene Roddenberry has given us."

All that weekend Dr. King's words echoed in my mind as I weighed every factor. Perhaps he was right: Perhaps Uhura was a symbol of hope, a role model. And if that were the case, did I not owe it another chance? Granted, Uhura's full potential had not been realized, and, sadly, probably wouldn't be. But she was there, wasn't she? And that had to count for something.

When I returned to work on Monday, I went to Gene's office first thing and told him about my conversation with Dr. King and my decision to stay.

A tear came to Gene's eye, and he said, "God bless that man. At least someone sees what I'm trying to achieve."

How interesting that the person most responsible for keeping me on board the *Enterprise* was, among many other things, a fan. In the *Star Trek* universe, no culture or empire we encountered while boldly going where no *one* et cetera, et cetera . . . ever waged a battle as loyal, as brave, and as lonely as did fandom on our behalf. In the "real world" side of the parallel universe—where the people who are counted in the almighty Nielsen ratings are as faceless as Vaal and the powers that be as cunning as Klingons—Vulcan-type logic was conspicuously absent.

Case in point: the Nielsen ratings. The critics dismissed *Star Trek* out of hand at the start. But network executives and program chiefs rarely pay attention to critics, so they really don't matter. The Nielsen ratings, however, ruled, and our Nielsens were not good. Given their tremendous significance and power, you might assume that they represent a scientific survey of hundreds of thousands of American viewers. You would be wrong: then it was about 1200. I never understood how a multibillion-dollar industry voluntarily submitted to being ruled by a mere 1200 families in Middle America, about the population of a very small university or a single large office building. If the networks wanted a real idea of who watched what, they should have surveyed at least 100,000 families. Or how about 2 million people, which still would have been less than one percent of the national population? As for the Nielsens representing some scientific statistical analysis, no self-respecting scientist, statistician, or mathematician would agree. It's funny how many programs now regarded as thought-provoking TV classics—such as *Star Trek* and, from that period, *The Prisoner*—have found massive audiences and/or critical acclaim in syndication, on cable, or (in the recent case of *I'll Fly Away*), under the nurturing wing of the Public Broadcasting System. Unfortunately for *Star Trek,* there was no other possible home.

The midseason call for our cancellation resulted from the fact that the majority of those 1200 Nielsen families preferred to watch the two half-hour perennial favorites that ran against us: *My Three Sons* and *Bewitched* (that season's eighth most popular show). Our second season would pit our first half-hour against the year's third most popular show, *Gomer Pyle U.S.M.C.,* which was followed by *The CBS Friday Night Movie.*

The Nielsens, like any other comparative rating system, is really just a horse race. Simply because your horse doesn't come in first doesn't mean it didn't run. So it was with *Star Trek.* In fact, tens of millions of people were watching us. When rumors of our cancellation began to circulate, leading science-fiction writers and viewers launched the first letter-writing campaign. Imagine NBC's surprise when tens of thousands of letters poured in, and fans held a newsmaking candlelight march in support of a supposedly "unpopular" show. Not only did the fans save the show, but more important, the integrity of the show, since one way that the network had considered making *Star Trek* more popular was to "dumb" it down. It was not the last time fandom answered our distress call.

By now you know that Gene Roddenberry was, in his way, a rebel, a thorn in the side of the television establishment. In hindsight the battles he joined are the nobler ones: The integration of the Starship, the Starfleet mandates of noninterference, the preference of nonviolence over violent solutions, and IDIC—Infinite Diversity in Infinite Combinations—all called to arms the best of human nature. Yes, Gene and those he surrounded himself with fought those good fights, and they certainly took their toll. But what made the making of *Star Trek* so arduous were the petty, silly things Gene was forced to defend. As Mr. Spock might say, that's because the suits were human. Sometimes, though, I wasn't so sure.

Shortly after I'd first met Gene, he came to hear me sing at Ye Little Club in Beverly Hills and went away so impressed that he helped arrange for the MGM screen test that led to the casting couch debacle. The first-season episode "Charlie X" concerned a teenaged orphan named Charlie, whose telekinetic abilities far exceed his power to control them, making his existence among humans potentially dangerous. It's a powerful, provocative story, and Gene felt the episode could use a few lighter moments, so he proposed having me sing in the crew recreation room. Somebody upstairs told him he couldn't have singing on the show.

"Of course we can!" Gene argued. "We can produce anything we want to, and the public will accept it or reject it according to how good it is." In network television, this view was heresy.

"This isn't a space musical," the network boys reminded him, as if Gene didn't know. "Look, they're ordinary human beings," Gene countered. "Uhura certainly wouldn't break out into song and dance on duty at her console, but this is in the recreation room, where the crew is relaxing. Hell, when I was in the air force, we had people who were musicians and entertainers. If someone could sing or play a guitar, they did, and we welcomed those times."

Well, okay, they conceded, we'll try it. But only once. And it can't be too dramatic. And then I was informed, "It can't be too good singing."

"You're going to have to argue with my voice about that," I answered, laughing to myself. The song I performed was a parody of an old English madrigal, and in singing it, I sort of tease Mr. Spock. It came out beautifully, but the network at first did not officially okay its inclusion and seemed ready to cut it at any time, though thank goodness they didn't. Much to NBC's surprise, the fan response was extremely positive, so much so that I would sing "Beyond Antares" in two future episodes: "The Conscience of the King" and "The Changeling." Naturally, in the revisionistic hindsight network execs mistake for foresight, my singing had been a fantastic idea. "Let's do it again, since it reveals the crew's human side," they enthused, and made a point of telling Gene, as if they'd forgotten whose idea it was in the first place.

Many of these skirmishes were more amusing than anything else. One of the banes of the cast's existence—and the subject of countless comedians' barbs in the years since—was our uniforms, especially the guys'. Careful viewers were not alone in wondering, *If they can put a man on Cestus III (or Janus VI or Gamma Hydra IV), why can't they come up with a velour fabric that doesn't cling, shrink, crawl, or form unattractive rolls?* The fluctuating midriffs of some of the guys only exacerbated costume designer Bill Theiss's neverending struggle to fit everyone properly. Even Leonard's lean, lanky body could not overcome the curse of those hideous suits, whose alternately gaping and hugging fabric made almost everyone look sorely out of shape. I must say, the crew women's one-piece suits fared much better than the guys'.

Theiss had a fit whenever the script called for a curvaceous actress, especially when that meant fitting her into something appropriately sexy. Judging by some of those revealing outfits, you might deduce that Bill Theiss enjoyed working with the female form. Hardly. He could be seen wandering about the set, muttering, "All those curves! All those bulges! Oh, God . . ." In fact, Bill Theiss preferred girls who looked like boys. Periodically he would tell me that he wanted me to lose weight, even though I was a perfect size 8 and in excellent shape. "It's impossible. No matter how much weight you lose, you'll never lose *those.*" I came to suspect that Bill Theiss considered having a butt and breasts signs of genetic inferiority.

Well, obviously, I had both, and I teased him mercilessly about it. At the time I would laugh, even though sometimes my feelings were hurt. Besides, even if I say so myself, I think I wore my uniform quite well, thank you. One time Bill Theiss complained to Gene that I was just too darn zaftig and that my curves wrinkled the fabric. Gene, an avowed admirer of the female form, replied, "Bill, I like it. She looks like a *woman.*"

In later years, especially as the women's movement took hold in the seventies, people began to ask me about my costume. Some thought it "demeaning" for a woman in the command crew to be dressed so sexily. It always surprised me because I never saw it that way. After all, the show was created in the age of the miniskirt, and the crew women's uniforms were very comfortable. Contrary to what many may think today, no one really saw it as demeaning back then. In fact, the miniskirt was a symbol of sexual liberation. More to the point, though, in the twenty-third century, you are respected for your abilities regardless of what you do or do not wear. I'll tell you one thing: I would not have worn those silly high-water bell-bottoms with the ruffle at the calf the guys had to wear for anything. Several times I offered Bill Theiss some unsolicited advice: "Why can't you just cut those goddamn things longer and preshrink them?"

There was a great deal of fun, camaraderie, and laughter on the set. And, of course, Gene's infamous practical jokes. Bill Theiss had just designed another uniform for me in a new red color Gene ordered, which was different from the pea-green one I wore in the first show. We stopped by Gene's office for his approval. As we were sitting and talking in his office, the phone rang. It was Eddie Milkis, one of Gene's key right-hand men. Eddie was the problem-solver, so Gene knew that if he was calling, there must be a problem, and he just wasn't in the mood for it right then, but Eddie was insistent. After relenting and telling him to come on over, Gene devilishly instructed his secretary to let him know when Eddie arrived, and busily set up the prank.

Gene's "office" was actually a large suite, with an outer office, where his secretary sat, his own huge inner office, and a smaller kitchenette, where he kept a refrigerator full of champagne, a bar, a coffeemaker, and other amenities.

"They're driving me crazy," Gene said. "Nichelle, would you do me a favor and be in on this? Eddie does a great job, but he's such a worrywart about everything, I'd like to teach him a lesson."

Gene, being a very large man, often wore oversized cardigans. Pulling his off, he handed it to me and said, "You and Bill go inside and put this on so it looks like you have nothing on underneath. Then when I say, 'Eddie, Eddie, you worry too much,' you just walk in like you don't know somebody's in here."

"Got it," I replied. Bill and I went into the inner office, giggling like schoolkids, and he helped me get ready. I stood with my ear pressed against the closed door, waiting. Eddie was complaining about something or other, and

Gene was trying to console him. He let this go on for a few minutes before he gave me my cue, and I sauntered casually into the room. There I stood, my hair a little mussed, Gene's cardigan barely covering the red panty bottoms I always wore under my costume, and a bottle of champagne in hand.

"Oh, Gene," I cried with the proper hint of embarrassment. "Oh, I'm sooo sorry." *Gulp.* "Oh, hi, Eddie!"

Without missing a beat, Gene nonchalantly remarked, "Eddie, you know Nichelle, don't you? Come on in, Nichelle."

Eddie was mortified. "Um . . . um . . ." was the best he could do.

I walked over to the sofa, deliberately avoiding eye contact with Eddie, and made a coy show of sitting down with my legs curled under me so that my (Eddie thought) nude bottom would not show. The whole time I cast seductive, knowing glances Gene's way, smiling constantly like a cat with a bowl of cream.

"I'll be with you in a minute, Nichelle," Gene said casually. "Just relax."

"Okay, Gene," I purred as I sipped champagne.

"Oh my—" was the closest thing to a sentence Eddie could come up with as he gamely tried to carry on with the business at hand. I must say, Gene deserved an Oscar for his performance. When he finally couldn't hold back any longer, a great guffaw burst from his throat, and we all came unglued.

"You guys are awful!" Eddie sputtered.

Eddie was almost as upset at being had as he was about the "delicate situation" he thought he'd stumbled into. He was livid. By then Bill Theiss had emerged from hiding, and the three of us laughed until we could barely stand.

Gene could construct a practical joke out of almost any situation, as I soon learned. One of the more problematic aspects of working on *Star Trek* was that while the in-house staff remained the same, we worked with a different director each week. While a number of directors worked on several episodes over the show's three-year run (among the best were Vince McEveety, who'd rescued me during *The Lieutenant;* Marc Daniels, Joe Sargent, and Joseph Pevney, who separately directed the majority of second-season shows), others directed just one, two, maybe three episodes. Considering that we shot seventy-nine original shows, you can imagine how many different directors we had.

In order to present an episode effectively, a director, like a writer, had to understand not just the script and characters, but centuries of fictional history and the limitations and capabilities of technology, and alien cultures.

This is not to say that a few inconsistencies did not creep in here and there over the years. But overall, each script stayed fairly true to the show's "Bible," the book that spells out for writers and directors the rules of the show. This consistency further supported the idea of each episode belonging to the history of the whole mission. It also made our characters all the more real. So it was that Mr. Spock did not smile or laugh (unless under the influence of nefarious forces); Bones epitomized an old-fashioned cynicism about the value of "progress" (as evidenced in his undying suspicion of the transporter); and Chekov maintained his Soviet chauvinism (although isn't it funny that we haven't even left the twentieth century, and his beloved Leningrad is no longer so named?). And, according to the book, Uhura was, among other things, a no-nonsense professional. Not cute, not coy, not mere female decoration. She meant business.

Every actor on the show took his or her role seriously. The integrity of our respective characters always came first, and it was not unusual for any of us to question a line or action that struck us as innately wrong. Most directors respected our insights and relied on us for our input.

We were shooting one day with a new director, and everything was clipping along beautifully until he told me to do something cutesy that Uhura simply would not do. Everyone on the set fell silent. With all eyes on me, I replied firmly, "I'm sorry, but Uhura can't do that."

"What are you talking about?" he demanded.

"Uhura the character just wouldn't do that."

"That's ridiculous!" he scoffed. "Now, let's take it from the top. Action!"

Then: "Cut!"

"Nichelle, what is the problem?" he asked heatedly.

"I don't have a problem."

"But you didn't do what I told you to do."

"That's right. And I told you, Uhura can't do that."

"Look, *Miss* Nichols: When the director asks you to do something, that's what I want done. Let's take it from the top again."

And of course the same thing happened. When several of the cast members came to my rescue and tried to explain to the director why I was right, he nearly lost it. "I don't want to hear these excuses for her!" he shouted. "No actress is going to tell me she's not going to do something I tell her to do."

"I do not need a lesson in proper decorum on a set," I informed him. "I know what the job of an actor is, and what the job of a director is. And as far as I'm concerned, the director is God. If you want something done, I, the actress, will do it."

"Fine," he replied, obviously relieved and pretty sure he'd won.

"But Uhura can't do that. If you want me to explain to you why—"

"I don't want to hear it!" he shouted as he flung his script to the floor. "I won't have it! I'll have you thrown off the set."

"You don't have to bother," I answered, turning toward

my dressing room. I heard murmuring and him yelling, "Take five!" Then from my dressing room, I saw him talking on the telephone, and while I couldn't make out every word of his rant, the terms "uncooperative actress" and "I told her" cut through. I stood there shaking. At one point Bill stuck his head in the door and said, "Hang in there, Nichelle, it's not that big a deal." I was pretty well convinced, though, that a head was going to roll: mine.

The director slammed down the receiver and shouted, "Go to lunch! Go to fucking lunch!" So that gave me a whole hour to worry and wonder about what would happen. We returned to the set, only they didn't need me, because the director decided to do a couple of other scenes instead. I was sitting around with Bill, Leonard, Dee, and the rest of the gang, uneasily making small talk, when the assistant director said, "Nichelle, Gene wants to see you in his office right away."

I rose from my chair, and as I started walking across to the door, I heard the guys saying, "Ooooooh," "Uh, oh," "Now she's gonna get it," and giggling, just like a classroom full of third-graders.

I stopped and glared at them: Bill, Leonard, Dee, Jimmy, George, the whole bunch of them acting like bad little boys. "Oh, shut up!" I said, marching out the door. I made my way across the lot to Gene's office, thinking nothing of it. Yet when my casual hello to Gene's secretary elicited a funereal, "Oh. Hello, Miss Nichols. You may go right in. Mr. Roddenberry is expecting you," I started to wonder.

"Hi, Gene."

He peered up at me with those big hawk eyes. "Oh, hello, Nichelle," he said distantly. "Have a seat, please," then proceeded writing. "I'll be right with you."

I could see he wasn't really writing anything, just going through the motions. And so I sat. And sat. As Gene made phone calls and wrote notes, my determination just hardened. I reminded myself that I was right, and I wasn't letting anybody compromise my character, even if it cost me my job. Well, maybe not. Then I started composing my defense: Sure, I would do it, but it would be on Gene's head when all the fans noticed something wrong. And so on and so forth until I had myself pretty worked up.

Finally Gene looked up. "I got a call from the director."

"Yes, I am aware that you did."

"Nichelle, he was complaining about having an uncooperative actress on my set and as you know, I will not tolerate an uncooperative actress on my set."

Gene had never spoken to me like this, and I sat in stunned silence as he continued. "I explained to him that I was shocked at his telling me that you were that uncooperative actress. I told him that Nichelle Nichols is the most cooperative actress in the business."

"Thank you, Gene."

Gene then repeated the whole conversation, practically verbatim, and asked me to confirm that it was correct. "I was looking out for the show," I added defensively.

"I just asked you, 'Is that correct?' " Gene snapped.

"Yes, that's correct," I answered, tight-lipped.

"Well, that's why I told him that Nichelle Nichols was a cooperative actress and that you, the actress, will do anything that a director directs her to do." Gene paused for a second, then stared straight into my eyes. "But I explained to him: Uhura can't do that."

First I thought I heard one snicker, then another, then loud giggles, and finally huge laughs as one by one the producer, the associate producer, and other staffers came out from behind the sofa, the inner and outer offices, everywhere.

"You really stick to your guns, don't you?" someone asked me, as Gene howled with laughter. In that moment, I was furious. "Gene, dammit, you got me again. I swear to God, I will get you for this!"

"Oh, I hope so!" he replied, smirking proudly. "Is that a promise?"

I returned to the set, my makeup streaked with tears of

laughter. Of course, everyone there had been in on the joke, and as I headed across to makeup, one by one everyone started clapping. The scene in question had been rewritten, and everything was fine. I don't think the director ever fully recovered, though.

We in the cast played our own practical jokes. Even considering how seriously everyone on the set took his job, there were plenty of things to laugh about. The *Star Trek* blooper reels are full of us dashing into doors that failed to open on cue, missteps, and mistakes. Sometimes we would get so punchy that, for no logical reason, my just saying, "Hailing frequencies open, Captain," made us crack up. Or Jimmy, a master of many voices, would deliver his trademark "I need those dilithium crystals, Cap'n, or I can't promise you she'll hold" in the voice of José Jimenez or Marilyn Monroe.

The worst offender, however, was George Takei, who, despite his deep intellect and acute social awareness, had a habit of making up silly singsongy ditties on the spot. We would all laugh at them, but George, like a rambunctious little boy, simply would not give up on it once he got going. We cajoled, begged, pleaded: "Okay, George. Enough! Enough!"

"Okay, okay, fine," he'd answer, trying to contain himself. A second later, he'd burst out laughing again. I was able to imitate him perfectly, so whenever he got out of hand, I'd wait until George began to wind down, then I'd start laughing just like he did: a deep, loud "Angh-angh-angh-angh" that can only be described most charitably as the cry of a very sick goose. With each *angh,* my voice rose an octave until George would nearly scream, "Oh, oh, oh, okay, stop it, Nichelle! Please," by which time he was doubled over in pain and laughter as we "duetted" on "The Ballad of the Constipated Goose." Many times when George couldn't stop laughing, we would just walk away from him, one by one, leaving poor George there until we heard the director scream, "Cut!"

The cast's revenge on George came to us in the second season in the person of Walter Koenig (Chekov). Like George, Walter is a very gifted, intelligent, sensitive man, and a fine and serious writer. He is also quite a prankster. Walter's idea of a great practical joke was to nonchalantly mention that something horrible had occurred on the set or at the studio. George's Achilles' heel is his gullibility, and within a couple of sentences, Walter would have George hanging breathlessly on every word, speechless except for the occasional, incredulous "Really? Really, Walter?"

Walter would nod seriously, then once he was sure George had swallowed the last piece of the bait, throw out a little more. "But wait! That's not all . . ." Finally after several minutes of hearing this tale—which seemed to be growing like Pinocchio's nose—George would exclaim, "You've got to be kidding! You're lying."

When he finally had enough, Walter would calmly and innocently say, "Of course, George. Of course, I'm lying. You really didn't believe that, did you?" You'd think that by now, George would be wise to Walter, but as you'll read later, such is not the case.

One of our favorite targets was Leonard, simply because, unlike Bill, among others, he was even-tempered to the point of sometimes being inscrutable. Off the set, he could be absolutely hilarious, with his dry wit and infectious laughter. I recall so many happy times with him. We both participated in many worthy causes and were involved in innumerable political and social events, so we saw each other often. Although I do admit that even in my mind Leonard and Mr. Spock are so enmeshed that I find myself momentarily shocked whenever I see him laughing.

It is not easy to ruffle Leonard's feathers, which I suppose makes trying to all the more fun. The lot where we filmed was pretty large, so Leonard, taking a cue from the security and staff people there, bought a bicycle, which he parked outside the soundstage. Every day at lunch, he would hop on his bike and speed across to the commissary in a matter of minutes, while Grace Lee, George, Jimmy, Dee, and the rest of us trudged across the lot, talking about Leonard like a dog. We were all so jealous of him for having a bike, yet none of us ran out and got one of our own. We didn't want to be copycats. Besides, it was more fun to trash Leonard for being smart enough to have a bike than it would have been to join him.

One day Bill got together with us and the crew and decided to string Leonard's bike up from the soundstage rafters. Who would ever think to look for it there?

For several days Leonard stalked the set in a snit of righteous indignation. "Can you imagine?" he'd ask anyone who would listen, "My bike! Somebody stole my bike!" What Leonard failed to notice was that every time he mentioned it, we would glance up at the ceiling, scratching our heads, while commiserating with him.

"Wow, that's just terrible," I'd answer, looking up. "Leonard, I just can't imagine." George, Walter, and Jimmy, who were always game for a good practical joke, really got into it. Bill made it his daily business to inquire of Leonard, "Any news on your bike, old buddy?" One time we were all standing with Leonard, all looking straight up, when it finally struck him: Why were we all looking up? Slowly, Leonard's gaze drifted upward.

Spotting his beloved bicycle dangling from cables overhead, Leonard spluttered, "I can't believe this! I really cannot believe this!" We all cracked up. I'm not sure Leonard ever truly forgave us. Years later, when we started shooting the first *Star Trek* movie, Leonard had his new bike outfitted with a metal panel bearing his name and the plea: "Please Do Not Steal My Bike." The temptation was almost irresistible. But then we were afraid that Leonard might have really made good on his implied threats to hire private detectives and install security cameras to protect his precious bike.

Usually, though, Leonard remained Vulcan-cool. Perhaps the most elaborate hoax involved his son, Adam, who was about eight years old while we were filming the original series. A great deal of planning went into this prank, because it required that Adam be fitted in a child-size Starfleet uniform and be made up—ears and all—to look just like his daddy.

The script called for a scene on the bridge in which Spock would be sitting in the captain's chair with his back to the elevator door. A yeoman was supposed to enter and say some lines, at which point Spock was to spin around in his chair, so he was facing the yeoman, and continue their brief exchange. They had Leonard's son, in his Vulcan disguise, waiting in the elevator. The door opened, Adam delivered the yeoman's lines, then Leonard turned to him and answered without breaking a smile or missing a beat. We couldn't get so much as a Spockian arched eyebrow out of Leonard. The real kicker came when Adam "stepped out of character," so to speak, to say, "But, Daddy, I love you."

"Thank you, Adam," Leonard said evenly. As the whole cast and crew stood around in breathless anticipation of Leonard's big crack-up—which never came, by the way—the joke was on us.

CHAPTER EIGHT

Overall, it was smooth sailing on the good ship *Enterprise.* Whatever turbulence we encountered usually emanated from "out there," somewhere off the set. While we happily worked away bringing Gene's vision to reality, Gene suited up and did battle with the assorted real-life monsters that sought to compromise, control, or end our mission. Throughout the years, Gene came to cast the whole *Star Trek* offscreen drama as a battle pitting the forces of good against those of evil, and in many ways it was. In creating and producing *Star Trek,* Gene set out to change the face of American television. The time, energy, and commitment that goal extracted were staggering. Gene knew he needed help. Most people didn't realize it, but his health was in great jeopardy.

Not long into the production of the first season, he brought his friend Gene Coon aboard to act as producer, so he could devote himself full-time to being executive producer. Coon, who'd had a hand in creating *McHale's Navy* and *The Munsters,* and had written for many popular programs, including the sci-fi Western *The Wild Wild West,* refined Gene's original vision. He conceived and/or wrote many of our most important episodes: "Arena," "Space Seed" (which became the "prequel" to *Star Trek II: The Wrath of Khan*), "Metamorphosis," "A Taste of Armageddon," and "Errand of Mercy," among them. In some cases, when another writer had conceived the story (as is typical in television, where scripts often reflect the work of several writers), Gene Coon shaped it into its final form.

Gene Roddenberry's goals for *Star Trek* were extremely ambitious; he even referred to his stories as "morality plays." He understood that it took great story lines, compelling characterizations, and believable dialogue to bring those complex philosophical issues to life, and he knew that Gene Coon could do that. Coon's unique talent was his ability to render characters—even the alien villains—so that they were emotionally true. He easily struck a balance between the story's action and its "message." Without him, the *Star Trek* universe would be a far different place; there would be no Klingons, for example, which he and Gene Roddenberry created.

Speaking as his friend, however, I feel Gene Coon brought something else to the set, something intangible and equally precious. First and foremost, he relieved Gene Roddenberry of the day-to-day running of the show, leaving him free to fight other, bigger battles, and nurture his fragile health, which he had kept a secret. Gene Coon also understood *Star Trek*. He not only respected Roddenberry's vision but actually improved upon it. Coon and Roddenberry also enjoyed a very warm and close friendship, the value of which cannot be underestimated. From their respective offices, situated across a hall from each other, they would shout ideas back and forth or walk into each other's offices, bouncing around ideas and making decisions about the show. When the day ended, they would both wind up in one or the other's office, where I usually found them discussing the day's events. I passed a few evenings after work with the two of them, sharing a drink and laughing, as they wrote, dissected, and rewrote future episodes. Their collaborations were seamless: Sometimes I couldn't tell where one started an idea and the other finished.

These two Genes loved and respected each other like brothers. They were on a mission together, bound for glory. In Gene Coon, Gene Roddenberry found a kindred spirit who could express in a script his feelings as well as, if not better than, he could. For this, Gene Roddenberry loved him.

Gene Coon had an incredible sense of humor. Almost every time I ran into him, he'd say, "C'mon, Nichelle, when are you gonna break down and be my girlfriend? You know I love you."

One day in his office, when I mentioned something about the painting hanging over Gene Coon's desk being powerful but morbid, he said, "That's why I keep it where I can't see it! It's a gift from my wife."

"Oh, she bought you that?"

"No, she painted it. I like to have people sit before me and have to look up at it. It makes them squirm, and, even better, *I* don't have to look at it."

His executive secretary was a beautiful Black woman named Andrea Richardson, who I believe was the first Black executive secretary on the lot, and whose miniskirts revealed long, shapely legs even Tina Turner would envy. She shared Gene Coon's wild, sardonic sense of humor. Long before Black comedians made it "hip" to defuse racially offensive terms by using them themselves, "Andi" could stop you in your tracks. In a low, sultry voice she would answer Gene Coon's phone, "Coon's coon!" If you didn't catch it the first time, she would not repeat it. While you were still asking yourself, *Did she just say what I thought she just said?*, Andi would politely say, "Yes, this is Mr. Coon's office. May I help you?"

Unfortunately, one of the many things Gene Coon and Roddenberry had in common was a less than perfect marriage. One evening, at an awards dinner, I happened to be seated at a table with the two Genes and their wives. You know that men often complain to you that their wives don't understand them or respect them, but in their cases, it seemed to be true. I had the bad luck to witness the two (soon to be ex-) wives insulting their respective husbands for all the world—and their husbands—to hear. Everyone at the table was obviously uncomfortable witnessing the wives' withering putdowns while Gene and Gene sat silently, smoking their cigarettes, staring off into the distance. Then the two Genes quietly and politely excused themselves from the table and did not return until the very end of the evening. The next week, Gene Coon left his wife, and soon thereafter, Gene Roddenberry left his.

They were the Gene and Gene, the two Genes, the Geneiuses. Knowing them as well as I did, I came to think of them not as two separate people, but as two complementary sides of the same coin.

Unfortunately, Gene Coon left after our second season, partially because he began to suffer the same exhaustion and burnout Roddenberry had hired him to escape from himself. But another factor in Gene Coon's decision to quit as producer was more personal. After enduring a long and unhappy marriage, quite by chance he had rediscovered his first true love, Jackie. Joyfully married to Jackie, Gene Coon continued to contribute stories to *Star Trek* and lived an unbelievably happy life until he passed away just five years later. He is greatly missed, but I am sure that wherever he is, he knows what an enduring legacy he left behind.

One of Gene Coon's great contributions was to loosen up our characters and bring more universal, human experience to the *Enterprise*. The three-way interplay among Kirk, Spock, and Bones was Coon's idea, for example. He, like Gene, also felt strongly about building episodes around other characters. For the network and the studio, who were loath to encourage an ensemble cast, the popularity of Kirk and Spock was welcome. It meant that like most other popular TV series of the time, you had your one or two heroes, and everyone else functioned as satellites around them. Gene Roddenberry still fought hard to bring the rest of us to the forefront, but he was continually thwarted. At the start, our set was like a small, private fort, surrounded by unfriendly forces. But by the second season, as Bill Shatner's temperament began to change, Gene found he had a problem within the fold: his own Captain Kirk.

Gene's bumpy relationship with Bill and, perhaps to an equal extent, with Leonard was quite complex. Some would say that the fact that Gene created characters with whom the actors (including the rest of the cast) were so closely associated lies at the heart of the friction. Having suffered for it myself, I can certainly empathize with their unhappiness at being typecast. At different points in their careers, both Bill and Leonard have made it abundantly clear that they were "divorcing" their characters. Leonard even titled his autobiography *I Am Not Spock,* while Bill has often been disdainful of fans who love him as Captain Kirk. But the fans would not allow them to leave their characters behind, and over time each has had to make peace with the fact that regardless of whatever else they may achieve in their careers, they will always be Captain Kirk and Mr. Spock, just as we will always be Uhura, Bones, Scotty, Sulu, and Chekov. At the same time, any self-respecting actor puts enough of himself into any role that it's impossible not to feel somewhat proprietary. Sure, someone else may have dreamed up your character and sketched it out on paper, but you the actor have given it life, and in doing so, you forge a bond with your fictional alter ego.

I don't think that people then fully appreciated how

much of himself Gene invested in *Star Trek,* and I'm not talking about the long hours and the arguments with the studio and the network. In his mind, Gene wrote himself when he created Captain Kirk: volatile, emotional, committed. But he was also Mr. Spock: a man governed by reason. As much as I loved Gene, I will be the first to admit that he could be difficult and infuriating. Gene, Bill, and Leonard possessed three of the strongest egos on this planet, and for whatever reason, over time they grew apart. Leonard has spoken of feeling underappreciated, for example. Bill has made it clear that he felt Gene "jumped ship" after the second season. What I do know is that once Gene hired Gene Coon, he focused on being the executive producer and was no longer a constant daily presence on the set. Unwittingly, he left a vacuum begging to be filled. Without anyone's consent, Bill Shatner stepped into the role, bossing around and intimidating the directors and guest stars, cutting other actors' lines and scenes, and generally taking enough control to disrupt the sense of family we had shared during the first season.

In his first volume of memoirs, Bill confessed to not having been aware of how everyone else on the set truly felt about him. I for one was not surprised he hadn't noticed, since Bill began to make it plain to anyone on the set that he was the Big Picture and the rest of us were no more important than the props. Anything that didn't focus exclusively on him threatened his turf, and he never failed to make his displeasure known. I was especially hurt and offended years later to read him describing us as "the dysfunctional family." In fact, the rest of us were and still are a family, the very one he chose early on to distance himself from. Then and for many years afterward, I attributed his attitude to insecurity. He always got along well enough with female guest stars, at least with those who succumbed to his initial charm. I pitied those who didn't, though, and had great respect for those, like Lee Meriwether and

Mariette Hartley, who were strong enough to tell him where to go. But male guest stars seemed to truly bother him. When Ricardo Montalban made his first appearance as Khan in "Space Seed," he was completely baffled by Bill's animosity toward him. True, they were adversaries in the script, but Ricardo, one of the sweetest men on this planet, didn't understand why Bill continued to express that attitude after the director yelled "Cut." At the same time, Bill is an incredibly charming man. My impressions of him from my first weeks on the show have always stayed with me. Whenever Bill did something that bothered me, I'd dismiss it, thinking that his lapses resulted from thoughtlessness. That, however, would change.

As I've said, our scripts were being revised constantly. One day, just as we were setting up to shoot a scene in which Uhura had an important part, Bill refused to do it. "Somehow, it's just not right!" he kept saying, and as he, the director, and some other production people went off to discuss it, I became perplexed. This wasn't the first time this had happened, but since in this case Uhura's lines concerned her communications expertise, I didn't see how they could be cut. We went on to shoot another scene while they rewrote the "offending" segment to Bill's satisfaction. Later when I scanned the revised script, my lines had been cut down to "I have Starfleet Command, sir," before he and Spock took over.

"Just a minute," I said. "What is this about?"

Caught totally off-guard, Bill stammered, "Uh, Nichelle. Baby, it's nothing personal. This is for the good of the scene. There's no reason for you to say this. If it's going to come from anybody, it ought to come from Leonard!"

"Since when is Spock a communications expert?" I demanded.

I was furious, but I was not alone. The entire cast knew how I felt, because Bill was doing it increasingly often, and to them, too. Even Leonard was embarrassed and refused to cooperate. The result was that the whole scene was totally rewritten. Once again, Bill got his way.

Somehow humor helped us get through it. George Takei often stated, "Bill is not going to be satisfied until we're all gone and he gets to do all our parts," then proceeded to imitate Captain Kirk delivering all of our trademark lines: "Hail! Ing! Fre! Quencies! O! Pen! Cap! Tain!," "Fas! Cin! A! Ting!," or "He's! Dead! Jim!" We would all squeal in painful laughter until tears rolled down our cheeks.

We all stuck together and learned to live with Bill. We discovered early on that the day went much easier if we shook our heads and let it go.

How or when Gene got wind of this, I'll never know. But soon I began to notice that the directors would set up shots so that whenever George, Walter, Jimmy, or I had "insignificant" lines, we were onscreen. If the script called for a closeup on Bill, they'd use a two-shot, so you would see me in the background. Or they'd suggest, "When we do that shot, Bill, why don't you throw that line to Nichelle?" None of us knew until later that Gene had demanded this.

To Bill's way of thinking, however, he wasn't being circumvented but indulged. In the absence of noisy arguments to the contrary, I think he concluded that whatever he did was all right with us. It wouldn't be until over twenty-five years later that he finally learned otherwise. Even now, I'm not so sure he is convinced or really understands how we felt or what we suffered.

Even the most devoted *Star Trek* fan will concede that our third season was our weakest. While the last leg of our network voyage did have its highlights—"Let That Be Your Last Battlefield," "The Tholian Web," "The Day of the Dove"—the specter of "Spock's Brain" (written by Gene Coon under the pen name Lee Cronin) cannot be denied. Not surprisingly, Leonard, who felt very protective of

Mr. Spock, was particularly vocal about what he believed were assaults on his character's dignity. Unfortunately, without the two Genes' close guidance, writers often opted for the obvious. How else to explain the third season's seeming obsession with showing Spock "out of character" and making a fool of himself? Most of the time these antics were gratuitous, and while fans are forgiving, Leonard felt hurt and upset that no one in charge seemed to care about the integrity of his character. He was not alone. The strained relations between him and Bill, and the two of them and Gene, seemed to have reached an impasse. I'm fairly sure that until the day Gene died, these issues were never fully resolved.

The million-plus fan letters that bought the show one last reprieve boosted morale temporarily but could not stem the tide. *Star Trek* was being eroded from within. NBC promised Gene to move the show to a better time period, early on Monday nights. He agreed then to return to the series in a more hands-on role. When NBC reneged and gave us the ten o'clock Friday night slot—when, as everyone knows, our viewers were out of the house or the dorm on dates—Gene played the only card he had. Thinking his refusal to produce would move NBC to make good on its earlier promise, he gambled. And lost. If we had been scheduled for any other night, we might have stood a fighting chance.

Star Trek's popularity and its fans' devotion were no secret, least of all to NBC. In just our first season, *Star Trek* received over six thousand fan letters a week, second only to *The Monkees*. In the promotional literature NBC distributed to potential sponsors before the second season, the network trumpeted research that indicated that among younger, middle- and upper-income, well-educated viewers, *Star Trek* was a hit. It also quoted Isaac Asimov, who said that our show was "the first good television science fiction." Students from Cal Tech had demonstrated at NBC's Burbank headquarters.

While NBC paid lip service to expanding *Star Trek*'s audience, it slashed our production budget until it was actually ten percent lower than it had been in our first season. Ten percent probably does not sound like much, but rising costs and escalating salaries ate up enough of the budget that in real production terms, we were probably actually working with significantly less money than that. This is why in the third season you saw fewer outdoor location shots, for example. Top writers, top guest stars, top anything you needed was harder to come by. Thus, *Star Trek*'s demise became a self-fulfilling prophecy. And I can assure you, that is exactly as it was meant to be.

In the third season new producer Fred Freiberger did everything he could to shore up the show. I know that some fans hold him responsible for the show's decline, but that is not fair. *Star Trek* was in a disintegrating orbit before Fred came aboard. That we were able to do even what we did is a miracle and a credit to him. One day Fred and I had an exchange, and he snapped at me. Even then, though, I knew he wasn't angry with me but with his unenviable situation. He was a producer who had nothing to produce with.

Still, as time passed, the experience grew draining, and many of us, including Gene, began making plans for the future. I read the handwriting on the wall toward the end of the second season. Perhaps because I had worked so closely with Gene creating Uhura, the constant diminution of her character pained me. The writers had managed to get in some wonderful parts for me—in "I, Mudd," "The Man Trap," "The Squire of Gothos," "Mirror, Mirror" and, of course, "The Trouble with Tribbles"—but it was always a fight that didn't end until Uhura's role was cut back considerably.

In television's conventional wisdom at the time, you needed to have at least five seasons' worth of shows before you could dream of seeing the series syndicated. Although Gene knew it was probably futile, he thought that one way to renew interest in the series was to introduce more story lines that concentrated on the other characters. And in fact, in an NBC press notice announcing the second season, a full paragraph promises that four of us—Sulu, Bones, Scotty, and Uhura—would each have at least one chance to "play the central character role." It never happened, and instead guest stars were routinely involved in plot lines that could just as easily have been handed to any of us. One of my particular complaints revolved around who got to "beam down" onto the planet. Considering that the communications officer was the sole crew member with a vast knowledge of alien languages and communications technology, you would think Uhura might be useful. Besides, with the captain, his first officer, and our medical officer running around down there, who was minding the ship? Being fourth in command, it should have been Uhura. Then again, I suppose, this was fiction.

Reading through comments my costars and others involved with the show have made over the years, I sometimes detect a hint of resentment, of feeling betrayed by Gene. After all, you might argue, he could have stayed more directly involved with the show. But, in Gene's defense, I must say that even if he'd stuck by the show, the outcome would have been the same. I don't fault him for that. However, toward the end of the second season Gene did one thing that I don't believe I will ever quite forgive.

Gene had many wonderful qualities, but he was not someone you wanted to have as an enemy. In his darker moments he was prone to a tenacious jealousy and possessiveness that could not be reasoned away. I know that throughout our friendship Gene sought to do the best for me. Once when we discussed my leaving he said, "I want you to stay with this because I believe it will turn into something that will benefit you for many years to come." And he was right. But while there was never any doubt that our romantic relationship was over long before *Star Trek* began—and it was never rekindled—Gene still could act like a jilted lover whenever he felt me moving away.

During *Star Trek*'s first year, *Mission: Impossible* began filming on a nearby set. Gene knew the show's producer, Bruce Geller, and Bruce respected Gene. In fact, Bruce's office suites were upstairs over Gene's, and the two became good friends. The year after Bruce launched *Mission: Impossible,* he premiered another hit, the long-running detective drama *Mannix.* In its first season Joe Mannix (played by Mike Connors) worked for a private detective agency. In the second season Bruce decided Mannix should be out on his own, and so he created Peggy Fair, a Black woman whose policeman husband—a friend of Mannix's—had been killed in the line of duty. Peggy would be Mannix's indispensable secretary and much more.

Bruce told me he had written the part for me. Knowing, as everyone else did, that *Star Trek* was in its third and last season, Bruce offered it to me through my agent, and of course I accepted, thrilled at the prospect of going from one series to another, and in a starring role. Since I was under contract to Gene, however, I needed for him to release me from my contract. Unwisely, perhaps, Bruce felt that his relationship with Gene was such that he could approach him directly. But at the time, Bruce was getting along quite well with the studio heads, while Gene was not, and I think this caused some resentment on Gene's part.

When Bruce asked Gene if he would cancel the remainder of my contract, Gene caustically replied, "Over my dead body." Stunned, Bruce backed off at once rather than risk incurring Gene's wrath. When I heard about Gene's refusal, I was incredulous, and called Bruce. He described Gene's reaction when he broached the subject: "I saw the hurt in his face. It was like, 'You're trying to steal her from me.' " My first impulse was to confront Gene, but Bruce made it clear that he didn't want any bad blood between him and Gene, and there was no point in pursuing it. I was crushed.

Gene's decision hurt me deeply on a professional level, too. To be a Black actress even now is to be in the minority of a minority. There simply are not enough roles to go around, and those that exist are understandably coveted and hard-won. By then I'd had my share of "almost"s, having lost to turns of fate roles in the Debbie Reynolds film *The Singing Nun* and the film version of *Sweet Charity,* among other plum projects. But to lose a part that was written especially for me, and for no good reason, was more than I could bear. I had maintained a high profile as a singer even during *Star Trek*'s run, but the reality of a working actress is: You've got to work. I was a single mother with a teenage son. Gene knew I was in no position to take my show on the road again, as it were, and that a role in another series would be a godsend to me and to Kyle.

I was desolate. Everyone knew *Star Trek* was a dead issue; Gene had even told me so as long ago as the second season. He said, "Look, there's no sense in your leaving now unless you have something major to go to. Because they've made it very clear—and this is confidential information—that this show won't go past three seasons. You might as well stay and not leave it for somebody else to come in and be remembered." So here I did have "something major to go to." Why did Gene hold me back?

As it happened, *Mannix* ran for another seven seasons. Gail Fisher got the role of Peggy Fair after Geller instructed his casting people to "get me a Nichelle Nichols." She played it beautifully and won an Emmy for best supporting actress. Through the years Gene and I talked about this, and while he acknowledged my disappointment and hurt, he never apologized. This was not the last time Gene would let me know that I could never really leave him.

For me, the most memorable episode of our last season was "Plato's Stepchildren." In *Star Trek* terms, the story line involved a routine visit to a heretofore unknown planet. There the crew discovers thirty-eight members of a eugenically near-perfect race that settled on Earth during the time of Plato and landed on the planet after ancient Greek civilization collapsed. As Kirk, Spock, and Bones later deduce, the Platonians, as they call themselves, discovered on their new planet food that gave them incredible psychokinetic powers. But, as so often seems to happen when beings are granted the powers of gods or get to live too long (in this case, about 2,500 years), they become jaded and starved for amusement.

Of course, the Platonians suffer one potentially fatal flaw: in their case, no immune system. Having lost the art of medicine through disuse, King Parmen commands Bones to stay behind. When he refuses, Parmen devises a series of physically and emotionally cruel methods of torturing Kirk and Spock. Bones still doesn't change his mind, so Parmen ups the ante, by forcing Uhura and Nurse Chapel down to the planet, in the hope that once Bones sees them endure degrading humiliations, the doctor will succumb.

The episode's blatant antiracist sentiment was expressed in exchanges between the crew and a dwarf jester/servant—the only one of his type on the planet—named Alexander, played by Michael Dunn. Initially self-conscious about his diminutive size, Alexander opens up to and aids the crew after Kirk tells him, "Where I come from, size, shape, or color makes no difference." Later Alexander realizes that despite all the abuse he's suffered from the Platonians (because they consider him "a throwback"), there is nothing inherently wrong with him. "It's them, not me," he announces in a moment of revelation. The rest of the story involves how we outsmart the Platonians and escape back to the *Enterprise*.

The episode's climax comes when Parmen forces Spock

and Nurse Chapel, and Uhura and Kirk, to pair off on chaise longues in a Greek arena, presumably to make love against their will in front of Bones and the Platonians. The combination of sex and humiliation, with Kirk cracking a whip near a quivering Uhura and the Platonians appearing titillated at the proceedings, probably marked this as an early television foray into S&M. But what "Plato's Stepchildren" will always be remembered for is the first interracial kiss ever shown on network television.

In the original script, Uhura was to have been kissed by Mr. Spock. But when Bill Shatner surmised that this kiss was historic and could generate a lot of publicity, he demanded that the script be changed. "If anybody's going to get to kiss Uhura," he said, semijokingly, "it's going to be me—I mean, Captain Kirk."

I was so used to the daily rewrites, I didn't give it a second thought. Interestingly, the fact that this interracial kiss was going to take place at all didn't make much of an impression on me at the time. It's not as if Gene announced that we were about to commit this provocative act, although he certainly knew it would be the first. Given the fact that we were in the twenty-third century and that it was quite clear from the story that Kirk and Uhura are kissing against their will, I didn't see a problem.

It was the last day of shooting, and we knew the scene was scheduled. "At last!" Bill exclaimed lecherously, laughing and winking. Regardless of everything else, I always loved Bill's playful charm. I had remarried that year, and every day I pinned my wedding ring and a diamond and platinum ring that belonged to my mother inside my bra. However, because the gown I wore for the "seduction" scene was low cut, I carelessly left the rings in a drawer in my dressing room. During a break early in the day I returned to my room to find the rings gone. The door was always locked, and only two other people had a key. I felt fairly certain I knew who the thief was, but I couldn't prove it. The betrayal of trust upset me almost as much as the loss of the rings. The police were called, and for the rest of the day I was too upset over the theft to worry about the scene.

Finally, we were back on the set, ready to shoot the scene when suddenly the director realized that this would be an interracial kiss. He panicked and said he wasn't sure that we should do it. Bill was livid. "What the hell is the difference?" he demanded of the director. "What does it matter?"

The director scurried to the front office to clear it with the big guys. The network suits, who probably would not have noticed it otherwise, began to get cold feet, since the director was concerned. Yes, they thought, What would the viewers say? What about the Southern affiliates? Gene told them, "When you actually see the scene, you'll see it's quite harmless. It's not a 'love scene' Kirk and Uhura are voluntarily involved in. It's being forced on them. Obviously there's always been some attraction between the two of them, but they have too much dignity. And I do *not* think the South is going to rise up in arms or fall apart.

"But, okay," he continued, "I'll tell you what: We'll shoot it both ways. We'll go right up to the kiss in one take, and then they'll fight it; then we'll do the kiss in the other take, and then we'll see which one we use." Of course, Gene knew exactly which one he was going to use, and Bill did, too.

This being the last day of shooting, anything that took us into overtime would blow the budget and had to be avoided at all costs. Wisely, the kiss was left for last. We shot the scene several times from several angles. I always get a laugh at the *Star Trek* conventions when asked about the kiss, because I say that Bill and I were so professional neither of us complained once through thirty-six takes. After the first few I could not stop laughing at Bill's silly antics, so we had to do some more. Essentially all we did by making all these "mistakes" was run out the clock.

"Okay," the director said, "let's go for the take without the kiss."

The assistant director, who worked for Gene, interjected, "But we'll soon be in golden time," he warned. "We don't have time."

"Okay, let's shoot it."

Knowing that Gene was determined to air the real kiss, Bill shook me and hissed menacingly in his best ham-fisted Kirkian staccato delivery, "I! WON'T! KISS! YOU! I! WON'T! KISS! YOU!"

It was absolutely awful, and we were hysterical and ecstatic. The director was beside himself, and still determined to get the kissless shot. So we did it again, and it seemed to be fine. "Cut! Print! That's a wrap!"

The next day they screened the dailies, and although I rarely attended them, I couldn't miss this one. Everyone watched quietly as Kirk and Uhura kissed and kissed and kissed. And I'd like to set the record straight: Although Kirk and Uhura fought it, they did kiss in every single scene. When the non-kissing scene came on, everyone in the room cracked up. The last shot, which looked okay on the set, actually had Bill wildly crossing his eyes. It was so corny and just plain bad it was unusable. The only alternative was to cut out the scene altogether, but that was impossible to do without ruining the entire episode. Finally, the guys in charge relented: "To hell with it. Let's go with the kiss." I guess they figured we were going to be canceled in a few months anyway. And so the kiss stayed.

"Plato's Stepchildren" first aired in November 1968 and provoked a huge response. We received one of the largest batches of fan mail ever, all of it very positive, with many addressed to me from girls wondering how it felt to kiss Captain Kirk, and many to him from guys wondering the same thing about me. Interestingly, however, almost no one found the kiss offensive. Shortly thereafter, I received a note from Gene that read: "Thought you'd be interested. This is the only "negative" fan mail we got." Attached was a photocopy of this letter:

> "I'm a white Southern gentleman, and I like *Star Trek*. I am totally opposed to the mixing of the races. However, any time a red-blooded American boy like Captain Kirk gets a beautiful dame in his arms that looks like Uhura, he ain't gonna fight it."

It only took a few days before some of the front-office executives—the very same who had made sure to be on the set while we filmed the kiss, just to make sure we didn't make it any "worse" than it was—began boasting of their support for this brave step in television history.

Our last day of shooting was an extremely emotional time for all of us. We had poured our souls into Gene's futuristic vision, but, as Bill said, "Alas, it was not to be." Well, let's see. In the twenty-five-plus years since *Star Trek* left the air for the first time, the history of network television has been strewn with good programs that are canceled for lack of ratings. Still, *Star Trek* made its mark on television in so many ways, as did our fans. Because of the fans' love and determination, *Star Trek* lives! Their letter-writing campaigns were the first, and in the following years, several other programs destined for cancellation—among them *Cagney & Lacey* and *Designing Women*—were spared only after fans made their voices heard. Despite the pressures and the little quarrels, *Star Trek* had been a wonderful and rewarding if sometimes disappointing experience. I'd made some lifelong friends in George, Walter, Jimmy, Dee, Leonard, Grace Lee, Gene, Majel, and (I thought until recently) Bill. I'd helped create and had portrayed a character who was loved and respected.

Everyone has her own idea about why *Star Trek* has endured; you probably do, too. I firmly believe in the power of vision, and Gene Roddenberry's *Star Trek* raised the prospect that space offered humankind the opportunity to start anew. The show's ethical premises certainly formed a new foundation upon which the classic elements of television drama could be redesigned. But to Gene, it all meant so much more. He believed, as do I and many others, that this was not simply one possible version of the future, but the only viable one.

As Trekkers know, the *Enterprise* crew's mature, egalitarian-universe view is not the result of a sudden enlightenment but centuries of bitter lessons. The late twentieth century's Eugenics Wars, where a small race of superhumans ruled as dictators over approximately forty Earth nations and killed millions, was followed less than a century later by a global nuclear war. Then, sometime in the mid-twenty-second century, intergalactic nuclear war broke out between the people of Earth and the Romulans. That led to the creation of the United Federation of Planets, under whose seal the United Starship *Enterprise* flew.

In countless episodes Gene and the writers addressed the wages of war and aggression, the sacredness of free will and individual rights. As the show so often made clear, we are a contradictory species. What made *Star Trek* so special was that even in the twenty-third century we were only human—Mr. Spock included. While we had learned from the past to temper our emotions with logic and reason, even as late as the last classic crew feature film, Captain Kirk cannot give up hating and mistrusting the Klingons, and so embarks on a pivotal peace mission convinced it is doomed to fail. One of *Star Trek*'s enduring qualities is that with the exception of a few great technological tricks, nothing came easy for the crew. In a world of phasers, transporters, dilithium crystals, and Dr. McCoy's amazing arrays of instant antidotes, ultimately the outcome relied on human beings doing the right thing.

Some people view Gene as a man with a wild futuristic utopian fantasy, but that's too simple. *Star Trek* did not promise that people would magically become inherently "better," but that they would progress, always reaching for their highest potential and noblest goals, even if it took centuries of taking two steps forward and one step back. Ideally, humankind would be guided in its quest by reason and justice. The ultimate futility of armed conflict, terrorism, dictatorial rule, prejudice, disregard for the environment, and exercising power for its own sake was demonstrated time and again. Even our most humorous episode, "The Trouble with Tribbles," illustrated the risks of removing a species from its natural habitat.

Certainly one reason *Star Trek* drew so many young people, especially high school and college students, was that it addressed the problems they faced: the Vietnam War, the Civil Rights struggle, and the seemingly interminable Cold War. The fight for equal rights and protection still has a long way to go, but it's stunning to review some of the major events in recent history: the fall of the Communist bloc, the dismantling of the Berlin Wall, the free elections in South Africa. In 1968 no one ever would have imagined such things were possible, and yet they came to pass, not through war or force, but a collective realization that some ideas and behaviors no longer serve us.

Every time I sat down at my console on the bridge of the *Enterprise,* I felt that I *was* in the twenty-third century, that I *was* Uhura. The promise of that imaginary universe was real to me. I am still very proud of Uhura: proud of who she was (or will be) and what she represented, not only in her time but in ours, and in those of people who will discover *Star Trek* decades from now. As we inch closer to that *Star Trek* universe we revere from afar, I've often thought of what my paternal grandparents would say if they saw me there, and I know that despite all the technical jargon and space-age trappings, they would understand.

After all, they, too, boldly went where no one had gone before, shaping their little piece of the world to conform to their vision of what was right. By doing so, they made the world we live in today a better place than the one they were born into. I believe that we all have the power to change our world. And I believe *Star Trek* offered viewers a valuable sense of mission. Man can change if he wants to, Gene believed. From my own personal experience I knew that to be true: Years later, the studio guard and the executive assistant who had harassed me mercilessly each apologized for his racist behavior. All in all, I'd call our three-year mission a success.

Back on Earth, on a January day in 1969, I packed up my dressing room for the last time, comfortable though a little sad to hang up Uhura's red uniform. *Star Trek*'s hopes for an extended life in syndication were pretty slim, after all, and while television cannibalized feature films for the premises of series, with a handful of recent exceptions, no major film studio was rushing to recycle a dead TV program into a feature. Without syndication, in the pre-VCR, pre-cable dark ages, *Star Trek* appeared destined to live on only as a fond memory.

In show business, everything ends sooner or later. You learn to say goodbye with your chin up and look to the future. After all, you never know what's around the corner, and I relish a challenge. In my personal life, much had changed, too. Toward the end of *Star Trek,* I married my second husband, Duke Mondy, a songwriter and arranger. We had met through friends at a time when I needed a friend. I was still in pain from losing *Mannix,* and he seemed to care genuinely about me and my son. Somewhere deep inside me, however, I sensed that all was not right, that our mutual interest in music would not be enough to overcome our personal differences. Today I can admit that one reason I married Duke was partly because I felt somewhat disjointed. Subconsciously perhaps, I thought that being married would center me, that the fact that I didn't love him deeply would somehow make it better. Whatever my reasoning, I made a mistake. And although we had a few bright moments together, I was relieved when it ended in divorce several years later.

In August 1969, after *Star Trek* died, Gene and Majel were married in a formal Shinto ceremony in Japan. Gene had tried to launch a second science-fiction series without success, and his first foray into feature-film writing, *Pretty Maids All in a Row* (in which my son Kyle had a small part), was not well received. We stayed in touch, naturally, but like everyone else, we were scattering our separate ways, sure that *Star Trek* was behind us.

CHAPTER NINE

What later became known as the Star Trek phenomenon began after the series ended. Despite our poor Nielsens, television affiliates knew the show had a following—Trekkies, a term fans bristled at and considered less favorable than Trekkers—and within a year of our last network broadcast, *Star Trek* reappeared in syndication. From then until now, not a day has passed without the *Enterprise* soaring across millions of television screens. Many times when I'm traveling, the bellman will turn on the television after he delivers my bags, and I'll hear, "Captain, I have reached Starfleet Command." Depending on how jet-lagged I am, it sometimes takes me a minute to realize I'm not hearing things. Gene's vision and *Star Trek*'s message proved to have, literally, universal appeal. By my last count, it had been shown in sixty-six countries, and is most popular in England, Japan, and Germany. In fact, I still receive fan mail daily from England and Germany.

Where the Trekkers showed their force most prominently, however, was at the conventions. The first of them started out modestly enough, but all demonstrated an odd Tribble-like phenomenon: No matter how many attendees were expected, double, triple, quadruple the number actually showed. An early *Star Trek* seminar at Brooklyn College attracted seven hundred fans. The first major convention, held in New York City and designed to accommodate a few hundred, attracted over three thousand. From that point on, attendance numbers grew exponentially, until by 1975 the New York convention stopped accepting registrations at eight thousand.

I attended that first convention in 1970, and never plan to stop. The Trek conventions are unlike any other fan gathering, perhaps because a Trekker is unlike any other fan in the world. One would be hard-pressed to find such a large group of intelligent, sensitive, aware people. Certainly their love of *Star Trek* brought them together, but it is their ongoing devotion to the ideas and principles the show espoused that keeps them there.

The conventions also served to keep most of us together. Without them, I'm not sure that George, Jimmy, Walter, and, to a lesser extent, Leonard and Bill, would have stayed so close. Naturally, Gene was the star of the conventions, the Great Bird of the Galaxy; Majel often came with him, and I passed many happy hours with the two of them.

As guest speakers, I and the other classic crew usually give a speech and then answer questions about the show. Over time we have moved from discussing the episodes to sharing our personal lives. My story of Kyle and his brown shoes became such a favorite that at one convention, some fans went to the trouble of sneaking Kyle in and hiding him among a coterie of fans dressed as the green dancing slave girls of Orion. After they performed their dance, Kyle emerged from the group—wearing a veil, no less—and presented me with a "brown shoe award." My "trophy" consisted of a pair of little brown shoes attached to a plaque.

Naturally, Kyle could not resist saying, "Mommy! I know what color my shoes are: They're orange!" As I screamed at him in mock exasperation, the crowd cracked up.

Conventions are a lot of fun, but they also provide a forum for serious discussion of real-life twentieth-century Earth issues. When I first began appearing at conventions I would really get up on my soapbox, talking about self-respect, love for humankind, individual responsibility, and tolerance. Since 1975 my speeches have also concerned the future of the space program. Often, by the end of my speech, the fans would be crying, and I would be crying. Then we'd all be laughing.

Through the conventions I have met many wonderful fans and made some great friends, among them Allen Crowe, one of the most devoted and knowledgeable *Star Trek* fans in the universe. We met at a convention in the early eighties, after I had received many letters from him. He started the first Star Trek fan club in his native Georgia and has been a devoted Uhura fan from day one.

At the time we met, Allen was an English teacher in Stone Mountain, Georgia, who dreamed of becoming a writer. My business partner and I convinced him to move to Los Angeles, take a teaching position in the San Fernando Valley, and work with us part-time. Eventually we pushed him out of the nest, so to speak, and encouraged him to pursue the real dream he'd come to California for. In short order, Allen became a very successful comedy writer, first for the long-running *Designing Women* and later the highly acclaimed *Evening Shade.*

I derive great personal satisfaction from getting to know some of the fans. I've heard women say, "I came to this convention just to tell you that because of Uhura, I'm a physicist," or "Thanks to Uhura's inspiration, I was able to handle the military," and so on. Having met and spoken to tens of thousands of them, I can attest that none need to "get a life." Performers are so often quoted saying that they owe everything to their fans, that it's become a hollow cliché. But for those of us from *Star Trek*, it is absolutely true. In the absence of any new *Star Trek* adventures during the seventies, fans busied themselves publishing fanzines and their own novels, organizing chapters of fan clubs (some devoted to the entire *Star Trek* universe, others to one character or group), and lobbying for *Star Trek*'s return. Perhaps naively, they believed that if they stuck together and made enough noise, someone would listen eventually. But to people whose faith in the future extends to the twenty-third century, what's a few years?

Everyone who loved the show wanted to see *Star Trek* revived in some form. Except for the reruns in syndication, the only official new *Trek* products were novelizations of episodes or original novels based on our characters. These found a tremendous audience, so it's not surprising that rumors of a new television series took hold and spread.

Gene was approached about bringing *Star Trek* back to television as a Saturday morning animated program. Far from a "kiddie" show, the animated series was quite good, with many of the scripts written by the same writers who had worked on the original series, all under the supervision of Gene and D. C. Fontana. The producers immediately signed up Bill and Leonard to voice their characters but planned to hire other voiceover actors to provide everyone else's. This was not intended as a slight to any of us; it was just cheaper and made the most business sense.

Bill saw nothing wrong with this plan and agreed to do it. Leonard, however, asked, "Where are George and Nichelle and the others?" When he was told that they did not have us, he replied, "Well, then you don't get me." It was only Leonard's deep sense of fairness that kept the classic crew together for that show. In June 1973 we reunited once again, and it was great to be working together as a team. I thought some of the scripts were quite good, and in one—at last!—Uhura got to take command of the ship.

When the show premiered that fall—on the seventh anniversary of *Star Trek*'s debut—fandom went wild. The series lasted two years, and in 1975 won an Emmy for best children's series. By then the fans were hungry for more, and Gene had entered serious talks with Paramount about creating a second *Star Trek* television series. The Trekker boom could not be ignored, and despite Gene's many conflicts with the studio, Paramount knew better than to try to do any *Star Trek*-related project without him—though, legally, it could have produced something without his collaboration. As Gene mentioned so many times during his life, relations between him and the studio were never very good, but because Paramount controlled the rights to the characters, and because fandom recognized and respected Gene as our creator, the two had to work together. Everyone wisely acknowledged that the fans were a force to be reckoned with, and that their loyalty lay with Gene. Soon Gene moved back into his old office on the lot and began work. Given the cumbersome, byzantine process a concept must endure to survive between imagination and film, it's amazing that we have any movies or television programs at all.

In the meantime, we had more conventions. The granddaddy of all the conventions was held in my hometown of Chicago in 1975 and attended by over thirty thousand people. It was the first time the entire cast and Gene were together. Some of us, including George, Walter, Jimmy, Dee, Grace Lee, as well as some writers, directors, and several actors who guest-starred on the series, began appearing at conventions from the beginning. Others, like Bill and Leonard, chose to distance themselves from them, and, by extension, from the fans. Of course, whenever they did appear, the fans loved it.

The Chicago convention was also the first time NASA

permitted a representative to attend in an official capacity. I knew from reading fan letters and talking to conventioneers that many professionals from the aerospace and computer industries were amply represented among the doctors, lawyers, teachers, scientists, businesspeople, and just plain folks who comprised a large segment of fandom.

The day before the convention began, we held a press conference where we answered questions from the fans and the media people. One reporter made a somewhat disparaging remark about the "Trekkies," and I replied, "Just a minute, guys. If it weren't for these people, you wouldn't be sitting here interviewing us. If you want to know what makes the show so popular, go and ask those fans. And, oh, by the way, it's *Trekkers.*"

That drew a nice round of applause. On the other end of the stage I had noticed a tall, handsome, fortyish gentleman with a shock of white hair, sitting on our panel, and I wondered who he was. I remember thinking, *Boy, he's handsome.* When several reporters started asking him questions about *Star Trek,* I discovered he was Dr. Jesco von Puttkamer, NASA's director of science.

"Dr. von Puttkamer, you are an eminent scientist. What would cause a man of your stature to lend his presence to this extravaganza? To a television series?"

Silence descended over the room; the gauntlet had been thrown down. Several reporters who were Trekkers and knew of von Puttkamer's distinguished reputation muttered that the question didn't even deserve an answer, but Dr. von Puttkamer responded thoughtfully, as if he were answering the most important question of the day.

"Well," he began in a warm Prussian accent that recalled a younger Henry Kissinger, "it's not just that *Star Trek* projects into the future a sense of hope for the human species. It's not just that *Star Trek* instills a sense of adventure. Or that it opens the eyes of young people to the possibility of liftoff from this planet. It's not just that it glorifies space travel and that human beings are going forth in peaceful exploration, or that this Gene Roddenberry has given us a reason to hope in that peaceful exploration, in noninterference with other cultures that we can live as intelligent life-forms in the universe. That someday we will make contact and have peace with them. Perhaps there are intelligent people who do not want to be like the Klingons. That we will face these things that are not understandable for us not with militance but with a sense of wonder in our hearts.

"That is not the only reason that I am a fan myself of this beautiful show that gave us IDIC—Infinite Diversity in Infinite Combinations," Dr. von Puttkamer continued. "That makes this work so critical: the universe worth living in, and the equality for men and women in peaceful exploration, knowing we are better than what we think we are. It is not *even* that.

"What I have come here for today is to find out for myself if Miss Uhura's legs are as beautiful in person as they appear on the TV screen."

The room erupted in laughter, and the reporter who'd posed the question blushed furiously. I turned to my friend sitting next to me, the author Harlan Ellison, and asked, "*What* did he say just then?"

"He says he likes your gams," Harlan replied.

When I heard that Dr. von Puttkamer was going to give a presentation that night, I couldn't miss it. The hotel managers were going crazy because of the overcrowding: It was literally wall-to-wall people. Those same managers had dismissed convention organizers' warnings that a huge crowd would descend, and now they found themselves unprepared and, apparently, scared to death. Although *Star Trek* fans are among the most polite and considerate I know, whenever any of us had to walk through the hotel, it was pandemonium as they approached to request autographs or say hello. For that reason each of us were assigned a detail of four to six security people dressed as

"Klingons." When I told my Klingons I wanted to attend Dr. von Puttkamer's speech in a hotel ballroom, they pleaded with me not to go. "You have no idea what it's like down there," one of them said.

From the second I stepped outside the elevator, we were swarmed. The Klingons in front of me and the two at my side, all non-Trekkers, tensed.

"Here's Nichelle!"

"Here's Uhura!"

"Hi, Uhura!"

A sea of fans washed toward us.

"Get her out of here!" one of the Klingons exclaimed nervously.

"No, stop," I commanded gently. And the wave stopped. The Klingons, who didn't know a thing about *Star Trek* fans, stood in dumb amazement.

"Listen, my friends," I said. "I know you love me, and I love you. But I don't really start 'working' until tomorrow. Tonight, I'm just a fan, just like you. I can stay in my suite, and you can give these guys a hard time. But I understand there is a scientist from NASA here and he's giving a presentation tonight. I want to go and see what NASA has to offer, what NASA is up to. Tomorrow I'm yours, but tonight I'm not Uhura; I'm not even Nichelle Nichols. I'm just one of you."

The sea parted, and I walked briskly through the crowd with my stunned Klingons trailing behind me.

I sat through Dr. von Puttkamer's presentation in awe. I admit that until then I had not been fully aware of exactly what our national space program was about. Like most Americans I'd marveled at the program's historic accomplishments: Alan Shepard's first manned suborbital flight in 1961, John Glenn's first manned orbital flight in 1962, and Edward White's first space walk in 1965. For man's first steps on the moon on July 20, 1969, I had sat watching the television, utterly amazed, celebrating with champagne. I'd admired those real-life American heroes of the new, and final, frontier: Shepard, Glenn, White, Bean, Borman, Schirra, Armstrong, and Aldrin, and Collins. But like most Americans, my interest began to wane as the space program seemed to have become a protracted, expensive, high-tech experiment. NASA fulfilled President John F. Kennedy's 1961 edict to put a man on the moon and return him to Earth by the decade's end. From its inception in 1958, NASA pursued its lavishly funded, politically popular mission. But it was not purely scientific desire to explore space that made that possible but the Cold War political necessity to claim and control space. In a nation still sold on the domino theory of possible Communist domination, the sky above loomed as the biggest, the ultimate threat to peace.

Paradoxically, as the hope and tumult of the sixties receded, success crippled the space program. It was easy for us to rally behind NASA when it was going head-to-head with the Soviets in a race for space. But as soon as we broke the tape at the finish line, the race was over. Without a symbolic goal as clear and definite as an American flag on the moon, NASA and its supporters found the country's romance with space cooling. The programs dedicated solely to unmanned exploration were vaguely familiar, but by then public attention had returned to Earth, where issues such as the war on poverty, Vietnam, and civil rights remained unsettled. Not long after man walked on the moon, we began alluding to that historic, awe-inspiring moment with cynicism, as in, "If they can put a man on the moon, why can't they . . ." Fill in your pet peeve.

Listening to Dr. von Puttkamer was a revelation to me. He put the space program in perspective and opened my eyes to its purpose and promise. *This is our future,* I thought. *This is me.* Then it hit me: Where the hell is "me"? There was no one in the astronaut corps who looked anything like me. There were no women, no Blacks, no Asians, no Latinos. I could not reconcile the term "United States space program" with an endeavor that did not involve anyone except white males. No offense to those fine, brave men, but if we in America tell our children they can be all that they dream, why weren't there women and minority astronauts? Thousands of fans wrote thanking me for Uhura's inspiration. Little Black girls and boys, Latino and Asian children had a legitimate right to share in that dream. Things had to change.

Without the time constraints of the weekly series, I was free to pursue other interests, my pet project being Kwanza, a charitable organization founded by ten Black women performers during the Christmas season of 1973. We now number about twenty, and strong among our membership are Judy Pace, Isabel Sanford, Esther Rolle, Vonetta McGee, Denise Nicholas, Marilyn McCoo, Lillian Lehman, Beverly Todd, Sheryl Lee Ralph, Debbie Allen, Margaret Avery, Telma Hopkins, and my sister Marian Smothers. "Kwanza" is Swahili for "first" and signifies the African holiday tradition of celebration and thanks in the spirit of giving, from December 26 to early January. Each year we raise funds to provide food, toys, clothing, and other necessities to disadvantaged families. Because of our positions in the business, we were also able to help in other ways, such as raising money from a special premiere of *Truck Turner,* in which I costarred, to purchase a desperately needed $10,000 fetal monitor for a Black hospital. We have supported the United Negro College Fund as well as Genesee, a battered women's home. Among the many other celebrities who have been unstinting in their gifts of time and money to support Kwanza are Richard Pryor, Oprah Winfrey, former baseball player Curt Flood, Sidney Poitier, and Paul Mooney.

Naturally, I would not trade my experience being in *Star*

Trek for anything. But at one time or another the series' enduring popularity proved a double-edged sword for everyone in the cast. Perhaps because our characters were so distinct, or because the seventy-nine episodes were seen so many times, our personal identities as actors and the characters in the Starfleet uniforms became irrevocably intertwined. Not that we were the only actors in town to suffer from typecasting; it's one of the hazards of the trade. Everyone knows someone who turned in one great, memorable performance that proved too memorable for his own good and has barely been heard from since. Casting agents, directors, and producers are often reluctant to hire someone they consider typecast, thinking—wrongly, I believe—that an audience can't be trusted to look at me in another role without seeing Uhura.

Following the cancellation of *Star Trek,* I began a period of some eight years that would be frustrating, painful but ultimately rewarding in ways I never expected. Realizing the need to broaden my image from the sophisticated, efficient Uhura, I accepted a juicy role of the tough, sensuous madame Dorinda in the Isaac Hayes adventure film *Truck Turner.* Initially I was offered the part of Turner's girlfriend, but when I read the script, I saw a much meatier role: I knew I had to play Dorinda. Hayes, who starred in and produced the film, said, "But, Nichelle, Dorinda's part is not a starring role."

"Oh, yes, it is," I replied. "All you have to do is say it is."

They agreed, and I got the role. And I worked to make it memorable, even gaining an extra twenty-five pounds, a reminder of the film that stayed with me a little longer than I planned.

I loved Dorinda. She was everything Uhura was not: vicious, wicked, nasty. In fact, when I first read for the part, one of the three men I read for said, "You scared the hell out of me!" Even though the movie's twenty years old, women still stop me on the street and shout, "Dorinda!"

It's a far different greeting from "Live long and prosper," and that is fine with me.

In spite of that great role, the seventies were the advent of Black exploitation films where Blacks were generally portrayed as pimps, whores, dope addicts, or hopeless slum victims, at best. And nude sex scenes for women were a must. I turned down so many offers that by 1974 they stopped asking. I'd had a contract with Epic Records, but my albums weren't selling, and a return to the theater did nothing to revive my flagging career.

In these years I went through my second divorce. When my son starred in Gordon Parks's *The Learning Tree,* I basked in his glory as a proud mother. I moved into a small house in Benedict Canyon in Beverly Hills and tried to regroup. I don't ever recall specifically making a decision to stop performing, but for a period of over five years, I did exactly that. I missed it, and living among the Los Angeles glitterati, I was constantly reminded of the fact that I was no longer working at what I loved.

In spite of appearances at Star Trek conventions, I felt stagnant and creatively daunted. However, I've never been one to content myself with an idle nonexistence. In 1975 I became interested in our space program and established Women in Motion, Inc., through which I undertook a number of government contracts. By 1976 I'd changed directions from performing to writing and producing educational films, programs, and projects for young people, incorporating music as a teaching tool. Among the government agencies and others I contracted for were the U.S. Department of Health, Education and Welfare, the U.S. Department of Housing and Urban Development, the U.S. Department of Energy, the U.S. Department of Transportation, the University of California at Irvine, and the Smithsonian Air and Space Museum. I also had several NASA contracts in addition to the astronaut-recruitment project, which you'll read about later. And I was busier than I'd ever imagined and feeling fulfilled for jobs well done. Yet, something was missing.

I continued to attend the conventions, where demand for *Trek*'s return had reached a fever pitch. As we headed toward 1976—and *Star Trek*'s tenth anniversary—we all began to wonder if Gene's project would ever come to fruition. What transpired in the nearly six years between Gene's beginning work on a new *Star Trek* in 1973 and the premiere of *Star Trek: The Motion Picture* in December 1979 is a heartbreaking, hilarious microcosm of Hollywood at work, one long fumble as the *Star Trek* ball changed hands, even changed games, before it finally touched down.

His first script for a *Star Trek* movie was rejected. In early 1976, the studio then announced that *Star Trek* would return as a made-for-television movie; later that year, it was back to becoming a feature film. While the powers that be flip-flopped, everyone else in the cast, with the exception of Leonard, who was embroiled in legal problems with Paramount, signed on to reprise our roles. Needless to say, fandom couldn't have been more euphoric if they'd been drinking Romulan ale.

The studio might have dawdled forever were it not for a series of seemingly unconnected but fortuitous events. The first occurred that summer, when over 400,000 Trekkers wrote letters urging President Gerald Ford to rechristen the first Space Shuttle from the *Constitution* to the *Enterprise*. On September 17, 1976, the Space Shuttle *Enterprise* made its public debut, rolling out as a band played the *Star Trek* theme and five thousand people and specially invited guests, including Gene and the original *Star Trek* cast, went wild. What a thrill that was. Just a few days later, Paramount took out a newspaper ad that read, "Starship *Enterprise* will be joining the Space Shuttle *Enterprise* in its space travels very soon. Paramount Pictures begins filming an extraordinary motion picture adventure—*Star Trek*."

Contrary to the impression given, *Star Trek*'s return was proceeding at anything but warp pace. The summer of 1977 saw the release of the history-making box-office smash *Star Wars* and another Paramount announcement. Now, it had been decided, there would be a *Star Trek* television series, tentatively titled, *Star Trek: Phase II*. With an eye to starting a fourth television network, Paramount viewed a new *Trek* series as attractive bait for potential affiliates. In the meantime, Leonard had been brought back into the fold, on the condition that he not reprise Spock every week. A new Vulcan character, Xon, was created and cast. Sets were built, scripts put in development, actors signed up.

What was hilarious was that we'd already been compensated for holds they had on us for the television or feature films that had been scuttled, so the delays and changes were not exactly killing us. But they were taking their toll on Gene, a decade older and even more driven to see his vision through. Over the summer, Gene set to work assigning scripts for the *Enterprise*'s second five-year voyage, instructing writers to include several new characters, including Commander Will Decker, the son of Matt Decker, who died in the original series' "The Doomsday Machine," and Ilia, the sensuous Deltan.

It was traditional to kick off new television series with two-hour premieres. Twelve episode scripts were complete, and everyone was set to go. Then about one week before shooting was scheduled to start, Paramount head Michael Eisner decided it should be a motion picture instead. Another contract, another check. It was now late 1977. When my agent called me up to give me the news, he couldn't stop cackling over how much money we'd all made for doing absolutely nothing. I was ecstatic about the decision to move ahead with a motion picture, but knowing *Trek* as I do, I was not holding my breath. In March Leonard finally agreed to participate; later that month

Eisner announced the production of *Star Trek: The Motion Picture* would commence, with Academy Award–winning director Robert Wise at the helm. *Finally*, I thought, *permission to come aboard granted.*

CHAPTER TEN

Well, not so fast. As Paramount, Gene, and a host of writers and agents struggled to launch the fictional *Enterprise* into movie-screen space, I was embarking on my own adventures.

Not long after Dr. von Puttkamer's speech at the Chicago Star Trek convention, Jimmy Doohan, George Takei, and I were invited to tour the Washington headquarters of the National Aeronautics and Space Administration, or NASA. By then Dr. von Puttkamer, who served as senior staff scientist in the Advanced Programs Office at NASA's Office of Space Flight and program manager of space industrialization and space colonization, had become a familiar speaker at Trek conventions. He introduced us to Dr. James Fletcher, then the agency's administrator.

"I must confess to you that I am such a *Star Trek* fan," he said. "I am in awe. I'm nervous just meeting you." As we soon learned, NASA was overflowing with Trekkers. Through Dr. von Puttkamer and many other wonderful people I met at NASA, I learned so much about the space program, and especially its newest manned-flight project, the Space Shuttle.

Unquestionably, the successful launch of the first Space Shuttle was NASA's top priority. A reusable craft that was launched like earlier spacecraft but landed like an airplane rather than parachuting into the sea, the shuttle was crucial to the space program both economically and scientifically. The idea that the craft could be launched several times and its reusable solid rocket boosters retrieved from the ocean (where they fell after liftoff) certainly appealed to taxpayers and critics. More important, however, the Space Shuttle, with its larger crew capacity, large cargo bay for transporting satellites and other payloads, and ability to remain in orbit a week or more, opened infinite possibilities for scientific experimentation and study of space and the Earth. The crucial repair of the crippled Hubble Space Telescope would not have been possible without the Space Shuttle, for example. In space's perfect, gravity-free vacuum we can create materials and chemicals—including life-saving drugs—that would be impossible to manufacture on Earth.

What too many people don't fully realize is how much we benefit from the space program without ever leaving the planet. We get a lot more out of the space program than just Tang and a collection of moon rocks. Every day we avail ourselves of space technology developments, from microwave ovens and the ubiquitous Velcro to cardiac pacemakers and fetal-monitoring instruments. The miniaturization of electronic components, the technology behind everything from watches to automobile-dashboard instruments, also enables weather satellites to forecast potentially devastating natural phenomena. Wind machines for generating electricity, solar panels for heating and cooling homes, precious oil and mineral deposits located from satellites like Landsat, life-saving protective uniforms for firemen, medical instrumentation of all kinds, Mylar and other plastics we take for granted—I could go on and on. My point is that all of these developments represent John and Jane Q. Taxpayer's return on their investment in space. In real dollars, in terms of jobs produced and technological development, that comes to about seven dollars paid back on every dollar spent. If only all our government agencies could meet these standards.

As I toured several sites, I had some amazing, eye-opening experiences, such as flying an eight-hour mission aboard the Kuiper C-141 Astronomy Observatory (with an all-Trekker crew of serious scientists and astronomers thrilled to have Uhura aboard), touring the Marshall Space Flight Center and the Alabama Space Rocket Center. In 1976 I was honored to be invited to the Jet Propulsion Laboratory to witness the touchdown of the Viking lander on Mars and delighted in receiving a copy of the first photograph it transmitted from the planet's surface.

In early 1977, because of my interest in the space program and the work we'd done to promote the program through Women in Motion, Inc., I was appointed to the Board of Directors of the National Space Institute, a civilian organization founded by Wernher von Braun, the pioneering rocket engineer who, among other things, led the development of the Saturn rockets used for the Apollo lunar missions and became a deputy administrator of NASA. That January I gave a speech before the NSI's annual joint board/council meeting in Washington, D.C., entitled "New Opportunities for the Humanization of Space." In it I challenged NASA and everyone else involved in the space program to answer the question I'd heard a thousand times in my travels: "Space? So what's in it for me?" I recounted the criticism of the program I'd heard from women, minorities, and the general public, then offered a range of suggestions for regaining the American people's trust, understanding, and support.

Apparently my speech made an impression, because

soon John Yardley, who headed NASA's Office of Manned Space Flight, invited me to discuss some of the issues I'd raised. NASA was more than halfway into its sixth astronaut recruitment drive, and while the administrators assured me that they had made every effort to attract more women and minorities, they had a big problem: Precious few were applying. This was especially disappointing, since the Space Shuttle mission was the first that would be partially manned by astronauts who were not pilots, theoretically opening the doors to people who might not have been considered or needed for earlier missions.

They were absolutely baffled. "What *I* don't understand is why *you* don't understand it," I responded. "You've had five recruitments prior to this in the years since Apollo and before, and you have never seen fit to acknowledge the qualifications of women and minorities by including them in the astronaut corps. Not one person of color? Not one woman on the entire planet qualifies? We all know that's not so. But you've already sent a message: Don't bother to apply."

"What should we do about it?" John Yardley asked. "We only have four or five months left in this recruiting drive, and, Nichelle, we mean business this time."

"How is this time different?" I asked.

"Before, we had an all-male astronaut corps because we needed test pilots, people with jet training. With the shuttle, though, we need a new kind of astronaut, a scientist astronaut. Now the qualifications are totally different. Size is not a factor, and eyesight is not a factor as long as it can be corrected with glasses."

Dr. Harriett Jenkins, administrator of Equal Employment Opportunity, said, "Nichelle, we've got to find a way to let people know about this, and somehow our message is not being received. How would you correct this?"

Convinced of the sincerity of John Yardley, with whom I had worked several years before on another project, and that of Dr. Jenkins, one of NASA's first Black female administrators, I felt I could be frank.

"Well, of course, time is of the essence. I think you have to get somebody with great visibility and great credibility to do a media blitz, through speeches, articles, public service announcements and commercials, on talk shows, and any other way you can. You also need someone who will get out there and identify qualified people. Let them do an outreach and convince the public that NASA is serious, no matter what the inequities before this. Tell them that this is a new era, a new step. You need to change people's minds, make them understand that you're serious and that this isn't just some public-relations ploy."

"Who do you suggest we use for this?"

"John Denver! He has always been a supporter of the space program. He is highly respected for his humanitarian work. He's a beautiful person; everyone loves him. Bill Cosby! He's the father figure to the nation; people trust him. Coretta Scott King! There's no one finer than she to say, 'This is a new opportunity.' "

I was lost in thought, trying to come up with more names, when John Yardley asked, "How about Lieutenant Uhura?"

I laughed. "I thought we were talking seriously. Besides, you don't want me to do it. The first thing everyone will say is that NASA went and got a Hollywood astronaut, that it's a publicity stunt. No one will listen. They'll laugh at me."

"Not after they hear you speak for five minutes, Nichelle."

I asked for it, didn't I? It's very easy to get up on a soapbox and talk about who should be doing what, to complain and to criticize. Now NASA was offering me, on a silver platter, no less, the chance to help make the changes I believed in.

"Okay, but I have some conditions," I said. "It has to be

more than a media blitz; I want to seek out and identify qualified people. And they must be truly qualified, because I don't want anyone to think for one second that someone unqualified only got here through 'affirmative action.' There cannot be a token woman sitting by the door here. If you want this done in the few months you have left, then you must let me work as a NASA contractor, and let my company handle everything. I don't mind reporting to you, but to make this happen, I have to be free to formulate it, organize it, and carry it out.

"And, finally, this: If I put my name and my reputation on the line for NASA, and I find qualified women and minority people to apply, and a year from now I still see a lily-white, all-male astronaut corps, I will personally file a class-action suit against NASA. I will not be used to attract publicity and then later hear you say, 'Gee, we really tried, but there just weren't any qualified women or minorities out there.' "

All agreed. Of course, when it came time to talk money, the department heads present pleaded poverty. Finally John said, "This project gets done!" He directed his staff, General McNichol, and von Puttkamer to see that it be funded through his office. The next day over lunch he paid me a great compliment: "That was the fastest thinking I ever saw."

In February, Women in Motion, Inc. signed a contract with NASA, and my partner Shirley Bryant Keith, good friend and all-around right-hand Shannon O'Brien, and administrative assistant Janet Holbrook swung into action, suspending all other business to man our headquarters while I traveled across the country. I had only until the end of June—less than six months—to find the astronauts of tomorrow. In January I flew to Houston to undergo a modified version of astronaut training and briefing. In February my office set up my travel itinerary, and I was ready to go.

By this time, I had fallen in love with my mission, so I suppose there was something to the fact that I began my journey on Valentine's Day. Over the next several months, I stopped in every major city in the country, visiting colleges and high schools, speaking and testifying before legislatures, professional organizations, technology-oriented and aerospace corporations, and anyplace else I might find a potential astronaut. I made a series of public service announcements and produced a film with Apollo XII astronaut Alan Bean, to say that "Space is for everyone," underwent real astronaut training, and even had my own authentic NASA astronaut's uniform, which I treasure to this day. News of my involvement in the recruitment drive spread through the media, into national publications such as *Newsweek* and *People,* the major daily newspapers of every town I visited, and national television programs, including *Good Morning America.*

My fears about public distrust of NASA were soon confirmed. Many times my contact at a university or organization warned, "They've heard all this stuff from NASA before, and they're not going to believe it now." I faced down these cynical glares, answered the hostile questions, and while most of my appearances met with interest and enthusiasm, not all did.

Midway through the recruitment drive, I appeared with Gene Roddenberry at the Fourteenth Space Congress. Dr. von Puttkamer chaired a panel Gene and I were on, and it made me very proud to see the respect and admiration Gene and *Star Trek* commanded among the space program's top people. That August Jimmy Doohan and I were NASA's guests to witness the Space Shuttle *Enterprise* make its first desert test landing. And in September, when many of us from the original cast reunited for a Trek convention at New York's Statler-Hilton, the media chronicled my recruitment drive.

In 1978 the Public Broadcasting Service's award-winning science series *Nova* explored the Space Shuttle in "The Final Frontier." Not only did the program show Lieutenant Uhura at her console and Nichelle Nichols speaking with students and making a recruitment film with Alan Bean, but it opened with the twenty-third-century *Enterprise* streaking across the screen and Captain Kirk intoning, "Space . . . the final frontier." In the hearts of those who cared about the space program there existed a bond between Starfleet and NASA. And it continues: Dr. Mae Jemison, the first African-American woman in space, and now a dear friend, even played a guest role on Gene's next *Star Trek* television series, *Star Trek: The Next Generation.* Dr. Jemison, who as a child was inspired by Uhura, opened each of her Space Shuttle flight shifts with a "Hailing frequencies open" that was heard around the globe—and, perhaps, beyond. In *Star Trek III: The Search for Spock,* we on the *Enterprise* encountered a Federation Starship named the U.S.S. *Grissom,* in honor of astronaut Virgil "Gus" Grissom, who in 1967 was killed in the tragic launchpad fire of Apollo I. Most recently, it was revealed that in October 1992 Gene Roddenberry's ashes were carried aboard the Space Shuttle *Columbia* among the personal effects of mission commander James Wetherbee. This was said to have been Gene's last wish. The Star Trek universe is strewn with references—tributes, I would call them—to the accomplishments of our forebears in space. Never mind that NASA is real and Starfleet "imaginary." As Uhura says in a film I later produced for the Smithsonian Air and Space Museum, "The difference between fantasy and fact is that fantasy simply hasn't happened yet."

Those whirlwind months were among the most exciting and personally rewarding of my life, so rich with experience that I could have written a separate book about them alone. Women in Motion, Inc.'s final report to NASA on our recruitment drive, weighing in at over four pounds, was thicker than the Manhattan Yellow Pages. By any measure, the shuttle-astronaut recruitment drive was a success. In the seven months before Women in Motion, Inc. began, NASA had received only 1,600 applications, including fewer than 100 from women and 35 from minority candidates. Of *these,* NASA told me, none of the women or minority applicants qualified. By the end of June 1977, just four months after we assumed our task, 8,400 applications were in, including 1,649 from women (a fifteen-fold increase) and an astounding 1,000 from minorities. Without an active outreach effort, fewer than five percent of those might have applied. Among these applicants were many names destined for history, including Sally Ride, the first American woman to go into space, and Fred Gregory and Guy Bluford, two of the first African-American astronauts, as well as three astronauts whose lives were cut short in the *Challenger* disaster: Judith Resnik, Ronald McNair, and Ellison Onizuka.

Altogether NASA received over 24,000 inquiries regarding the thirty to forty available positions.

Although I closed our final report to NASA with: "Hailing frequencies closed, signed, Project Manager," for NASA, our space program, and our future, I remained standing by, ready to receive.

My work on behalf of the space program continued, and through it I met many wonderful people. One special person in particular was Jim Meechan. I was in Dearborn, Michigan, to speak at the Rockwell International annual shareholders' meeting about the Space Shuttle astronaut recruitment program. Rockwell was NASA's prime contractor for the Space Shuttle, responsible for designing and testing the shuttle's orbiter, including its main engines, thus my presence. But Rockwell's involvement in defense contracting, and in the B-1 bomber in particular, inspired an order of Catholic sisters to mount a large and noisy demonstration outside the hotel where the meeting took place. I didn't know that Rockwell's chairman had requested that Jim Meechan, its Corporate Vice President of Research and Engineering, fly in from California to speak with the sisters, since he was Catholic. He did, but by then the sisters' protest had attracted some louder, more aggressive participants, and Rockwell officials decided it would be better if I didn't appear, since they felt that would attract even more press.

Earl Blount, Rockwell's director of public relations, assured me that Mr. Meechan would be happy to share his limousine with me to the airport and sent his assistant ahead to catch "Big Jim." But when we got down to the lobby, I saw Meechan shaking his head no. Just then his limo pulled up and out jumped his chauffeur, Charles, who greeted me as "Miss Star Trek" and said to his boss, "Say, Mr. Meechan, I see you're moving up in the world." Meechan gripped my elbow and politely commanded, "Get in." By then, I was simmering and decided I'd teach this redneck, corporate paper-pusher a lesson. So for the next forty minutes I delivered the "Value of Space" speech I meant to give back at the shareholders' meeting. Aside from the polite "Uh-huh" and "I see," Mr. Meechan didn't say much else. I finished, then sat back, smugly satisfied with myself.

We were at the Detroit airport before Mr. Meechan uttered his first full sentence: "What do you know about music?"

Stunned, I stammered, "Music is my life. I grew up on music. It's my career, it's—"

He calmly removed a business card from his breast pocket and said simply, "When you get back to L.A., give me a call and we'll talk about music."

The chauffeur stopped at my airline terminal entrance

and opened my door. After a clipped "Thank you and goodbye," I threw my fur jacket over my shoulder and marched into the airport, thinking, *You arrogant bastard!* I tore his card in half and was just about to drop it into a garbage can when I stopped, and for some reason, started to place the two torn pieces back in my bag when I finally read it: C. J. Meechan, Corporate VP—Research & Engineering, Rockwell International, Inc. Sitting on the plane, sipping my drink, I tried to assuage my total mortification, but it was impossible. Somewhere high in the sky, in another first-class seat on another plane Mr. Meechan was surely laughing his head off at me.

Well. I was en route to Portland, Oregon, to work with the Oregon State University Drama Department. Under another NASA contract, I had agreed to write, produce, and direct a space-oriented musical, and the school agreed to stage it. As if my trip hadn't gone roughly enough already, upon arriving in Oregon I learned that there was a scheduling conflict, and due to final exams the drama students would not be available to rehearse and perform. *Great!* I thought. Now I'd have to find and rehearse the players in Los Angeles, then transport everyone back to Oregon to fulfill the contract. I had already allocated most of my budget, and there was nothing left to cover this large, unexpected cost.

Then it hit me: Well, if Mr. Big Jim Meechan, vice president of research, et cetera, is so damned interested in music, let's see if he'll fund this very worthwhile cause, my space musical. My staff and I quickly put together a compelling presentation, and I made an appointment to see Mr. Meechan. Our meeting this time was much friendlier, but after my presentation, Mr. Meechan asked me to submit a proposal. Having just finished the "New York Telephone Book" for NASA, I shuddered. Jim concluded with "but don't make it more than one page." I sighed in relief, and two days later I was handed a $10,000 check. *Wait a minute,* I thought. *That was too easy.* But I was not about to question my good luck. I could get my kids to Oregon and fulfill my NASA contract. Only later did I learn that Oregon State University was Jim's alma mater.

About a month passed when Jim called and asked me to look at a song he had written. I felt obligated, naturally, and thought, *A corporate vice president? How good can this possibly be?* I braced myself to offer some polite compliment, but when my partner Shirley and I saw the lead sheet, we were amazed. The song, "Ancestry," was simply beautiful. And, eerily, it perfectly fit an operetta I was composing about life in a space colony. It was as if Jim knew me. I retitled the operetta *Ancestry,* Jim composed several more songs, and from that day on, Jim and I have been co-composers, business partners, and friends.

By then my business partners had begun departing for various "personal reasons." I knew the problem was really our clients' requests for my (or Uhura's) personal involvement and appearance as a condition of our acquiring contracts. With me always out of town, we were no longer planning and creating together; they felt relegated to running an office and keeping up with my schedule. Suddenly, I was the sole owner of a business with the remainder of my NASA recruitment contract to complete. Shannon O'Brien blessedly continued as office manager, executive secretary, and chief cook and bottle washer. She saw me through the contract completion. By the time that was finished, I knew in my heart that business really was not for me, and shortly thereafter Women in Motion closed.

Despite our easy rapport, I had no idea then that Jim Meechan would change my life forever by pushing me back to my first love, the world of music and performing. When he heard me sing the songs for *Ancestry,* he told me he was determined to put me back onstage where I belonged. I soon learned that when Big Jim Meechan arrives at a decision on something he considers important, it would take a team of Clydesdales and a passel of pit bulls, along with some damned solid logic, to convince him otherwise. Jim took early retirement from Rockwell, and we went to work. Over the past several years, through our company, aR-Way Productions, we have produced several record albums, several musical plays we wrote, and numerous theatrical and singing engagements, including my recent performance as a solo artist for the eightieth-anniversary celebration of the Erie, Pennsylvania, Philharmonic. As I write this section of *Beyond Uhura,* I am in Denver, starring in a wonderful musical, *Nunsense II,* playing Mother Superior, no less, at the Arvada Arts Center. And having a glorious time.

None of this would have been possible were it not for Jim. Through his guidance and management, I've enjoyed the resurgence of a career I'd almost given up on. Ably assisted by Florence Butler and Vicki Johnson-Campbell, he recently led the campaign in which thousands of fans petitioned for my star on the Hollywood Walk of Fame, which was installed on January 9, 1992, just a month after I became the first Black entertainer to place her hands in the cement at the world-famous Grauman's (now Mann's) Chinese Theater in Hollywood. In addition, for the last fifteen years, I have found in Big Jim, his wife and my friend Bunny, and their six children, an extended family. It is quite a sight when the Nichols clan and the Meechans all get together at either of our "plantations." For all these blessings, I consider myself a very lucky lady.

In 1978 or so, during dinner with my friend Dr. Kerry Joëls, education director of the National Air and Space Museum, he suggested I write and create a twenty-minute orientation film to attract young people, especially the disadvantaged, to the museum. I proposed using young non-professional kids from local schools to depict an English class visiting the museum. The star would be a little girl to whom Uhura would appear. The title: *Space: What's in It for Me?* The film ran at the Smithsonian Air and Space Museum for a year and received rave reviews.

The story line held special meaning for me. Among the class visiting the museum would be one little Black girl, whom I named Lishia. The teacher (played by their real-life teacher, who was just wonderful) has given each child a different assignment, and Lishia's is to distinguish the difference between fact and fantasy in space. When she comes across the original model of the Starship *Enterprise* hanging in a place of honor, Uhura materializes before her though unseen to everyone else. As Lishia guides Uhura (and the viewers) through the museum, they talk about space and dreams, and Uhura sings, "Reach for Your Star," one of two songs Jim and I cowrote for the film. Lishia rejoins her class and eagerly tries to tell her teacher that Uhura is there. But when Uhura realizes Lishia and the class might be coming, she says, "Scotty, I think it's time for me to return to my own time zone." Lishia finds only Uhura's earpiece on the floor, and as she holds it, she hears Uhura say, "Remember, Lishia, [singing] always reach for your star . . ."

Around 1980 Jim and I founded a youth organization called Space Cadets of America, what you might think of as Boy Scouts or Girl Scouts with the emphasis on space. We produced, presented, and distributed space educational programs and projects, and visited space-oriented sites, such as the Oregon Museum of Science and Industry and Space Camp. We provided annual educational scholarships. Blessedly—yet unfortunately—the group grew so quickly, I soon found myself in over my head. Between the new *Star Trek* movies and my other professional commitments, there wasn't enough time to dedicate to the group and, with much regret, we disbanded it. Fortunately, the idea was revived by space enthusiasts newsman Hugh Downs and columnist Jack Anderson.

In fall 1984, I happened to be in Washington to receive NASA's Public Service Award when the President was to announce the formation of the Young Astronauts. Jack Anderson invited me to sit on their board of directors and acknowledged that the organization was inspired by the now-defunct Space Cadets, which I very much appreciated. Because of my strong political beliefs, which were diametrically opposed to those of President Reagan, I could not with a clear conscience appear on the same dais with him. In fact, I left before the ceremony began.

Nonetheless, I fully supported Hugh, Jack, and the new organization. It's never too early to nurture a child's natural wonder and curiosity. In 1979 I was voted Friend of Year by the American Society for Aerospace Education for creating educational programs that ran the gamut from space musicals to nursery rhymes. If kids can skip rope to some silly nonsense rhyme they never forget, why not have them remember:

> *"Two hundred fifty million miles to Mars,*
> *Two hundred fifty million miles: That's far!*
> *Two hundred fifty million miles to roam—then*
> *Two hundred fifty million miles back home!"*

Whether speaking to schoolchildren or delivering the commencement speech at a university's graduating class, as I had the honor of doing at Cal State, Northridge, I reinforce the three prerequisites of success my father taught my siblings and me, and, later, my son, Kyle: Education, Dedication, and Application. I encourage young people to believe in their dreams and to pursue them wholeheartedly. Children come to us ready to learn and eager to achieve. We owe it to them and to ourselves to feed their hunger for knowledge and to spur their sense of adventure, to stand behind them even as they venture to places we ourselves may never go, and if it means going where no being has gone before, all the better.

It's not that difficult to spark the imaginations of young minds, to plant the seeds of their dreams. What is difficult is ensuring that our space program is consistently and adequately funded so those dreams can come true. The national space program should be reclassified as an entitlement program, and its fate—our children's future in space—wrested from the hands of politicians, whose shortsighted, politically expedient budget cuts threaten its very existence. This is an obligation we must meet if our children are to continue on the journey humankind began with its first footstep.

It was summer 1978, but within a few hours Uhura, Sulu, Chekov, Scotty, and Mr. Spock would rejoin Captain James Tiberius Kirk on the bridge of the Federation Starship *Enterprise* in the year 2271. Supposedly, a mere two or three years had passed since the *Enterprise* returned to space dock following Kirk's perilous consciousness switch in the episode "Turnabout Intruder." On this side of the time portal, in real Earth time, nine years had flown by. And while each of our paths took us in different directions, for the cast and Gene, through the conventions and the fans' devotion, all roads led us back to *Star Trek*.

Because I so often saw my friends—particularly George, Walter, Jimmy, Gene and Majel, Dee, and sometimes Leonard—at the conventions, and we'd all kept up with one another's lives, for us *Star Trek* never really ended. Over the six years between when the second proposed television series was announced and the summer day when we first stood on the new *Enterprise*'s bridge, a dizzying procession of promises, delays, and disappointments had sapped any sense of anticipation. After all, less than a year before, Paramount had blown the whistle on us when we were one week from blastoff and counting. It didn't seem logical, as Mr. Spock might say, to get one's hopes up too high.

Sitting in our makeup chairs that first day, we all joked, "Who'd have ever thought we'd ever be back here again?"

"It's not exactly the face I had last time," Walter quipped.

But back we were, and happily so. I was too excited at the prospect of working with Academy Award–winning director Bob Wise to give the script much thought. Its intriguing premise—the merger of humankind with technology in a new life-form—was, I thought, fantastic. Unfortunately, as I could see when I read the script and as the movie began to take shape, *Star Trek: The Motion Picture* did not live up to its potential. Still, as with any voyage, we all embarked with the highest of hopes.

We had been working together for several weeks by then, rehearsing, undergoing costume fittings, and posing for promo stills, and suddenly nothing seemed different. It was like Old Home Week. It wasn't until the first day of actual shooting that the realization that we were all here—back in our old stations on the bridge—hit us. We were in full uniform, except for Leonard, who happened to be on the set in the black Vulcan robe-style tunic he wears when Spock first appears on the ship later in the film. When director Bob Wise stepped into the bridge well, we turned our attention to him, waiting for him to talk us through the first scene.

Instead, he froze and turned almost white as he breathlessly said, "Oh! My God!"

"Bob? Are you okay?" everyone seemed to be asking at once.

He didn't answer but kept looking at us as if he'd never seen us before. Finally he blurted, "For the first time, standing here, I just realized: This is historic! It didn't hit me until this moment, but now, seeing all of you here on the bridge, all made up and at your stations. *This* is the command crew of the Starship *Enterprise!* You are all legends!"

It was a chilling moment. No one said a word in reply, but I'm sure I wasn't alone in thinking, *But this is the legendary director Bob Wise calling me a legend.*

Finally George Takei said softly, "Bob, it is *you* who are the legend that *we* stand before."

Well, that did it. I was the only woman on the bridge and, as in my tomboy days, determined not to let them catch the girl being weak and soppy. When a little tear threatened to trickle down my cheeks, I raised my hand to my face and pretended to scratch my nose so no one would see. When I glanced up I saw that all of the guys, those great he-men—Bill, George, Walter, Jimmy, Dee, even Leonard—had tears in their eyes, and were making no attempt to hold them back.

It was a magical moment, broken only by the gasp of the head makeup artist as he witnessed his fine work running down our faces. With that, Bob seemed to snap back to the job at hand. "Let's take five and come back and attack this thing!" he ordered.

"We'll take *twenty-five,* dammit!" an exasperated crew of makeup artists shouted back, leading us to our makeup booths.

The making of any major motion picture is fraught with snafus, delays, and tension. To one degree or another, that was true of all the *Star Trek* films. Of course, the difficulties never detracted from our happier moments, and overall, I treasured these chances to return to the twenty-third century and be with my friends once again.

Still, more often than not, the story behind the making of a film is of what could have been and why it was not. That was especially true of our first film, which began shooting without a full and final script. As everyone else involved soon realized, a movie was much more than a long television series episode. Not surprisingly, some years before, Gene approached the first film with many ideas and characters he had developed back when *Star Trek* was intended to return as a television series. From his original series concept came the beautiful Deltan navigator Ilia (who was played in the film by the stunning Persis Khambatta) and Commander Will Decker (played by Stephen Collins), the son of Commodore Matt Decker, who sacrificed himself to stop the killer planet in the original series episode "The Doomsday Machine."

In that episode, as well as *In Thy Image* (the script for what would have been the television movie), "Robot's Return" (an episode Gene wrote in 1973 for a proposed series called *Genesis II* that was never sold), and a *Star Trek* series episode entitled "The Changeling," machines escape humankind's control as a result of becoming somewhat "human" in their need to seek their creators or discover their purpose. In the series, the changeling was a Nomad information-gathering satellite that had concluded that humans, "carbon units," were inferior. (In that episode Nomad erases Uhura's mind after it deems her "female" thinking illogical and fails to understand the purpose of her singing.) The doomsday machine in the episode of the same title was a weapon of incredible destructive power that had been built, much like our nuclear weapons today, as a so-called peacekeeper. In *Genesis II,* it was a race of human-looking robots returned to Earth to seek their creator. The resulting film combined these concepts, so that at the heart of the giant destructive cloud is "V'Ger," the then-ancient NASA space probe *Voyager VI.* The probe's original mission—to collect all information and return it to its creator—became corrupted when the probe encountered a machine planet whose "inhabitants" gave the probe the power to annihilate anything it did not recognize as "the Creator," including those pesky "carbon units."

Consistent with *Star Trek*'s and Gene's optimistic, humanistic philosophy, however, the movie offered a hopeful ending as the *Enterprise* saves Earth and stops V'Ger. Like his father, Will Decker sacrifices himself. Still (illogically, I suppose) in love with the V'Ger-generated replicate of the dead Ilia, Decker allows V'Ger to believe he is its creator and offers himself up as the recipient of all the information in the universe. In a shower of light and energy, Decker, Ilia, and V'Ger merge to create what Kirk and the crew assume will be a new life-form, perhaps even the next step in human evolution. With his riveting blue eyes and understated demeanor, Stephen Collins was perfectly cast as the first human being to voluntarily meld with a machine. Gene had long been fascinated with this concept. The note of optimism is apparent in the fact that when Uhura relays Starfleet's request for a status report, Kirk chooses to list Decker and Ilia as missing in action rather than dead. Infinite Diversity in Infinite Combinations, indeed. In many ways, this would seem a perfect *Star Trek* story, and while I was not particularly enamored of it, I think it is a brilliant cinematic work, despite its flaws. One other point of note, which may color my objectivity regarding *Star Trek: The Motion Picture,* is that the only prop that made it from the series to the movies was Uhura's earpiece. Talk about pièce de résistance!

In the wake of *Star Wars* and *Close Encounters of the Third Kind,* not to mention Stanley Kubrick's *2001: A Space Odyssey,* moviegoers had developed a far more sophisticated view of science fiction (thanks in no small part to *Star Trek*) and a ravenous appetite for eye-popping special effects. Complex special effects never had much of a place in *Star Trek* for two reasons. First, Gene focused on the human issues rather than the machines, gadgets, and phenomena of space that drove other, in my opinion, lesser science-fiction productions. And second, even had such effects been available then and Gene had wanted them, we could not have afforded them. Even the most impressive special effects work of the late sixties paled in comparison to what the new wizards, armed with computers, lasers, and all manner of cinematic tricks, could now achieve. Through the work of director George Lucas's special effects company Industrial Light and Magic, his *Star Wars* redefined how a science-fiction film should look and sound, setting the standards by which audiences would judge all subsequent films.

Without *Star Wars* to *prove* there existed a large moviegoing audience for space adventure, *Star Trek* might never have made it to the big screen. Ironically—and I am not the first person to make this argument—had *Star Trek* not inspired such a dedicated following whose pent-up demand for more new, intelligent science fiction had reached fever pitch, *Star Wars* might not have been quite so big a hit. So it's doubly ironic that the elaborate, expensive—but ultimately disappointing—special effects *Star Trek: The Motion Picture* served up would prove its undoing, at least critically. You could say that in crafting the script to showcase the high-tech production, Paramount and the writers inadvertently unleashed their own V'Ger, which overshadowed the critical "carbon unit" interactions and dynamics that had always been *Star Trek*'s soul. If not totally destroyed, we were at least diminished. And amid the overly long, reverential shots of the new *Enterprise,* Spock's interminable voyage inside the V'Ger cloud, and a drawn-out climax, the familiar characters were sorely missed.

Despite the passage of time, some things about *Star Trek* did not change. Gene and Paramount still barely tolerated each other, and Gene's relationships with Bill and Leonard remained prickly, to say the least. The biggest change, however, was that Leonard and Bill lobbied for and won script approval. By the time we started shooting, the script had gone through many hands, and throughout the production we struggled with an endless flurry of revisions and rewrites.

There were plenty of little problems, too. Like any good

director, Bob Wise brought to *Star Trek: The Motion Picture* a new, all-encompassing vision of how our "universe" would look and sound, and for the cast that meant unisex. Rather than the dramatic colors used in the series, he opted to have the newly refitted *Enterprise* awash in softer putty and off-white tones. That color scheme extended to our new uniforms, all cast in neutral beiges, browns, and soft blues. Originally, the "bib" portion of our uniforms was white, which provided a crisp contrast to the rest of the suit, which I loved. Wise decided he wanted a more homogeneous look, so most of the uniforms (Kirk's in the first scenes is of the original design for all uniforms and an exception) were made in one color. The first time I saw the "blah" version of the snappy original, I almost started to cry.

Another costuming change called for our boots to be attached to the bottoms of our pants, then covered with matching material to create one unbroken line. They called in a famous Italian bootmaker to fit the stars, but instead of doing his job, he bought some cheap, uncomfortable shoes and simply attached them and covered them. When I looked inside mine, I was shocked to see they were a pair of those tacky shoes you can get custom-dyed to match your prom dress. Not only were our feet killing us, but he had miscalculated and cut the pants too short into the shoes on about three hundred uniforms. It was very hard not to die of embarrassment or laughter, since the crotch seam of the pants now hovered somewhere around the knee. (For some reason, costumes have been a point of contention and an object of derision throughout *Star Trek*. I'd like to go on record here: Except for the "ruffles" on the guys' pants, I liked the costumes from the original series very much. Even the so-called go-go boots.)

I really disliked the bland unisex approach, not simply because it was unattractive, but that it just wasn't Uhura. Bob Wise had made it clear that he did not want to see fingernail polish, jewelry, or any other personal or extraneous adornment. When I showed up on the set with Uhura's long silver nails, jade earrings, and high-heeled boots, he was not pleased, but I argued that it was right for Uhura. When they finally submitted to the court of last resort—Gene—he agreed. "Absolutely," he said. "This is not the military, and that is Uhura expressing her individuality. Besides, she's a special woman."

In the overall scheme of things, it may seem like a small point, but it was this attention to detail, to the consistency of the characters, that Gene always provided. It is what made *Star Trek* endure. From the first movie on, Gene and those of us who cared about *Star Trek* were suddenly up against people who, while freely admitting they'd never watched an episode until they were hired to work on a movie, still insisted they knew more about *Star Trek* than Gene did. Excuse me? The basic attitude toward Gene was an odd combination of begrudging respect for having dreamt up the gravy train they were riding on and condescension. Basically, they were saying, "Yeah, sure, that's fine for the small screen, but this is a *major motion picture.*" Yet when the reviews came out and the film—one of the most expensive of its time—failed to meet the studio's high expectations, the blame landed squarely on Gene.

For me, the experience of the first film can best be summed up in one word: *wormhole.* One of the most trying times came in the many long days we devoted to capturing the wormhole-effect scene. Since we were taking a not yet completely refitted *Enterprise* out on her maiden voyage, not all the technical bugs had been worked out. Despite Scotty's warning, Captain Kirk takes the ship up to warp 1, and the ship's improperly balanced warp drive is no match for a treacherous encounter with a wormhole. As you may know, a wormhole is an unstable tunnel through space in which space and time are dangerously distorted. In our case, the wormhole set the ship rocking, and time seemed to slow as we hurtled through the "tunnel." Red alert, Captain!

In the series, scenes like this called for the most primitive of special effects; namely, a bunch of strong, burly guys to rock the entire bridge off-camera, as the actors dramatically leaned and pitched themselves against consoles and chairs to create the illusion of being thrown. This being big-time moviemaking, however, the old reliable human brawn was replaced by a sophisticated hydraulic lift on which the bridge was mounted. Now the bridge really rocked. For some reason, though, every time we got ready to do the scene, something went wrong. One time a fuse blew; another time a huge lamp crashed to the floor; and, as always, someone missed his line. People fell down repeatedly, fake blood spurted repeatedly, I shouted, "Subspace frequencies jammed, sir! Wormhole effect!" until I was hoarse. Every day we would look at the dailies and cringe; it was awful. The special-effects men of the moment felt strongly they could make it work, so we took our places again, and: "Wormhole effect!"

Eight days later, nursing bruises and broken nails, I'd had it. I was exhausted from waking up every night for two weeks screaming, "Wormhole effect, Captain!" Still, we had to shoot the scene a few more times, and I was watching the clock because I had to leave at six on the dot to catch a plane. I knew Bob Wise always quit shooting at six o'clock, so I felt safe. But every time he called for another shot, I cringed. As the afternoon wore on, I began to get nervous. Walter knew about my plans, and so at a quarter to six, when he heard that Bob was going to stop the shoot in ten minutes—leaving me plenty of time—he rushed over to us and grunted, "Dammit, they just said we had to shoot until at least eight o'clock. Maybe even nine!"

That was it. I snapped, and before I knew it, was ranting and raving all over the set. I was about to communicate a piece of my mind to Mr. Academy Award when an assistant director suddenly called, "That's a wrap!"

I shot Walter a look that was definitely set on stun. He shrugged, grinned, and said, "I was just practicing my dramatic skills on you, Nichelle."

I cracked up with everyone else. That was our dear Walter. You could always depend on him to put the ridiculous into perspective. However, I did want to wring his neck.

"I will get you, Walter," I promised.

My big chance came just a few days later. Everyone had to park by the studio entrance gate and walk to our RV trailer dressing rooms near the soundstage. I had plans to go out one evening after work, so I brought along a change of clothes and told the guard at the gate I would drive over to my dressing room, drop off my clothes, and then bring my car back to the parking lot. He said that was fine, so I drove through. When I got to the soundstage, the security people told me they would park my car and bring back my keys. *How nice,* I thought. But it got even better: Since I arrived before sunup and left after sundown, they offered to park and retrieve my car every day. Some days, when the lot was particularly crowded, my car stayed near the soundstage all day.

Actors being actors, we're always on the lookout for anyone getting special treatment, and it didn't take Walter long to notice my car conveniently parked next to my dressing room. I caught him looking suspiciously, but he didn't say anything for several days, until he couldn't stand it another minute.

"Nichelle, do you have a new parking space assigned to you?"

"Of course," I replied coyly. "Doesn't everyone?"

I'd already made Jimmy and George collaborators in the joke, and George particularly delighted in "informing" Walter that in addition to my new parking space, I was also getting paid more money than they were. The security people played along, too, making sure that whenever Walter stepped outside, he would see them busily cleaning my windows and polishing my fenders. I ended Walter's misery by telling him the truth only when I saw he was ready to assail the front office. Then I reminded him of his little trick on me. He grinned sheepishly and returned to plotting against his usual victim, poor George Takei.

One day we were waiting for a shot to be set up, when George arrived around eleven, after having had a whole day off. "Good morning!" he called chipperly.

Didn't he ever learn? Walter muttered to me, "Look at that son of a bitch," then assumed a downcast look, and whispered, *"George bites again."*

I started looking sad myself, but "managed" to reply, "George, how are you?"

George immediately picked up on Walter's expression and asked, "Walter, what's the matter?"

"Oh, man, it's been awful while you were off."

"What's going on?" George asked in an urgent whisper.

"Bill and Leonard," Walter replied cryptically. Just then Leonard walked by, obviously preoccupied. When he absentmindedly returned George's greeting with a distracted, "Yeah, hi, George," George assumed the worst. As luck would have it, they were in the midst of resetting up a difficult two-shot with Bill and Leonard, and when George then greeted Bill and got the same perfunctory reply, he jumped to the desired, wrong conclusion. Before George could even ask, Walter nodded ominously and said, "Them."

"What?"

"They have been at it like you have never seen," Walter said. Of course, Leonard and Bill never fought on the set. Anytime Leonard got annoyed with Bill, he'd simply step off the set and wait in his trailer until the matter was resolved, which usually happened posthaste. As a matter of fact, I'd never seen Leonard fight with anyone, so the idea that there had been some confrontation had George very worried.

"What happened?" he asked.

Before Walter could answer, Dee happened by and, astutely recognizing a great practical joke in progress, observed, "Well, George, it's been a lulu."

"Walter was just telling George what's been going on," I offered, deliberately keeping it vague.

"Yeah, yeah," Dee replied, nodding. "God, George, you should have been here."

"I don't know how to tell you this," Walter said, "but I don't know how we're ever gonna get this film done. I never saw anything like it."

Meanwhile, Dee was as fascinated by Walter's story as George was, but for a different reason: He just couldn't believe that George was falling for it, again. As it happened, both Bill and Leonard *were* in a snit over something scriptwise having nothing to do with each other, so they "played" their roles in Walter's little drama perfectly. Just then the two returned to the set in deep, heated conversation. Walter's eyes glistened. "They damn near came to blows," he whispered.

"Yeah, I've never seen Leonard so upset," I added. "So angry! And to blow up like that. I mean, Bill's enough to drive anyone crazy—"

"Hear, hear," Dee interjected.

"But this." I shook my head in disbelief.

"Did they come to blows?" George asked breathlessly.

"No, but it was somewhat of a pushing match. He pushed him, and he fell into Nichelle, and knocked her off the thing."

Walter could not be stopped.

"And then he fell into the boom guy, and the boom guy's boom went into one of the overhanging lights—"

"Ugh!" George moaned.

"And the light fell down, and the director was screaming. As a matter of fact, he ran off the set, he was so scared," Walter said.

"I don't want to talk about it," Jimmy put in firmly. "It

was just disgraceful. They were acting like two kids. I say the union oughta be called in on this. And Nichelle: She bruised her knee and burst out crying."

"I did not cry!" I retorted indignantly, then remembering my "role," bent over to hold my knee.

"Oh, my God!" George exclaimed. Just then, Bill and Leonard, who now knew what was up, walked by. Bill cracked up, and Leonard just turned and smiled at George. "You guys!" George screamed. "You're all in on it!"

That will teach him to cheerily call, "Good morning!" to us at eleven A.M.

The film premiered on December 6, 1979, in Washington, D.C. I received the American Society of Aerospace Education's Friend of the Year Award for the film I produced for the Smithsonian Air and Space Museum, where, incidentally, our reception was held. The premiere, which benefited the National Space Club's educational program, brought out stars, politicians, NASA administrators, and, of course, fans. Trekkers not only made *Star Trek*'s return possible, over one hundred of them appeared in the film in the recreation room scene where Kirk briefs the crew on the unknown force threatening Earth.

Reviews of the film were mixed, and some have credited its initial box-office success to pent-up demand from fans starved for anything *Trek*. Hardly a commercial failure, with over $100 million in ticket sales, *Star Trek: The Motion Picture* would have had to earn far more to put Gene back in the studio's good graces. There's no question but that Paramount wanted a sequel. In fact, Gene had already completed a script for our next voyage when he was informed he no longer had an office on the lot.

CHAPTER ELEVEN

Whatever its flaws, *Star Trek: The Motion Picture* proved to the businesspeople at Paramount what Gene and those of us who were attending the Trekker conventions knew firsthand: *Star Trek* lives! Gene set to work on a new script that involved a time-travel story line, but it was deemed unacceptable. Although nearly two years would pass between the first movie's release and the crew's next Starfleet tour of duty, I don't believe there was ever a question but that *Star Trek* deserved and would get at least one more chance. The question was when, and who would take the helm.

Paramount offered the producer's chair to Harve Bennett, whose television production credits included several well-regarded television movies and miniseries, *The Mod Squad,* and two science-fiction series: *The Six Million Dollar Man* and its spinoff, *The Bionic Woman.* The studio made it clear that it wanted a more successful movie made with far less money. Initially Harve had reservations about the offer. For one thing, he'd never watched *Star Trek,* and was on the verge of turning it down until his children convinced him to reconsider. In reviewing episodes from the series, Harve discovered Ricardo Montalban's richly villainous Khan Noonien Singh, the eugenically engineered late twentieth-century dictator who fled Earth aboard the sleeper ship *Botany Bay*. In "Space Seed" Captain Kirk sent Khan and his followers into exile on the presumably habitable Ceti Alpha V rather than punish him for attempting to take over the *Enterprise*. A humanitarian decision, to be sure, but one that comes back to haunt us all in *Star Trek II: The Wrath of Khan*.

Played by Ricardo Montalban, Khan was a fascinating character study of animal cunning, personal charisma, and imperious self-righteousness, and clearly one of *Star Trek*'s most memorable villains. Having Montalban reprise the role over fifteen years later was a great coup, and the fact that he was then so well known as the enigmatic, debonair Mr. Roarke of *Fantasy Island* put a nice twist on it. Once Ricardo arrived on the set, it was clear that time had not tempered Bill's animosity toward him. For my part, I found Ricardo as gracious and entertaining as ever. Whatever competitiveness Bill felt toward him, however, was put to good use in the film, as they battle to the death.

By mid-1981 the basic story line was set and Montalban cast. Nicholas Meyer, who had written both the book and the screenplay for *The Seven Percent Solution* and directed *Time After Time*, was appointed director. As the script began to take shape, the next task was to lure Leonard back. Like the rest of us, he had been disappointed in the first movie and had hinted publicly that he would prefer to leave Spock behind. When he was presented with the idea of playing Spock's death scene, he agreed. To what degree Leonard really believed he would be killing off Spock with that scene, only he can say. But from the moment I heard about it, I thought it was a bad idea and a betrayal of *Star Trek*'s ideals. Some would argue that without Spock there could be no more *Star Trek,* theoretically or in reality. There were other elements of the script some of the cast objected to, and at one time or another, George's and Dee's participation was uncertain. When we began shooting in November 1981, however, two facts were clear: Mr. Spock would die, and this would probably be our last film together.

Everyone involved with the first movie understood what went wrong there and made every effort not to repeat those mistakes. From the first scene of *Star Trek II,* which introduces the Vulcan-Romulan female Saavik during the *Kobayashi Maru* training exercise, the action runs swiftly and smoothly. Wisely, the special effects were relegated to a secondary role while the story unfolded to reveal what had transpired in the lives of the crew over the past fifteen years: Spock is teaching at Starfleet Academy; Kirk is an admiral, who, according to Bones, is stagnating behind a desk. With its many references to ancient literature and events familiar to viewers today, the script tackles the universal experiences of growing old, change, death, and relationships, especially friendship. The continuity of experience is reinforced by the fact that we senior crew members become mentors to the newer cadets once an emergency call transforms the *Enterprise*'s routine training cruise into a dangerous mission.

While Gene had very little to do with this film, his position as *Star Trek*'s creator, nurturer, and protector could not be ignored. One point of contention was the new look and attitude of the crew. Our uniforms, a royal burgundy red, tailored tunic with an epaulet on the right shoulder, conveyed the impression of a military force. While the uniforms looked great on everybody (and the high-water bell-type bottoms were reinstated on the men's pants), mine were particularly uncomfortable. They are made of heavy, thick wool, which is padded and inner-faced and then faced again in the front in a contrasting color of the same weighty fabric. As if that weren't enough, they are double-breasted.

"Hey, these are fine for the men and flat-chested women," I complained vehemently, "but I'm already double-breasted. I feel like the *Titanic!*"

More important, though, portraying Starfleet as a military organization flew in the face of everything *Star Trek* stood for. Gene was especially upset about this, and about the fact that Nicholas Meyer wanted the women in the crew to be addressed as "Sir." (Although, interestingly, in the series pilot, the female Number One was called "Sir.") At one point I forcefully but tactfully reminded Meyer and Harve that Starfleet was the philosophical descendant of NASA, not the Air Force, and managed to convince them to delete some of the "sir" references. By the next film, they were all but gone, yet the uniforms stayed with Gene's final blessing. I suppose the only other thing about *Star Trek II* that still bothers me is the bloodsucking Ceti eel. I still can't stand to see it crawl out of Chekov's ear. Yuck!

One of the joys of working on *Star Trek II* was getting to know Kirstie Alley, who played Saavik. It was her first film and her first starring role. She told us she considered us her idols. Recalling how I felt on my first film, I was impressed by Kirstie in so many ways. She is bright, radiantly beautiful, outspoken, and very funny. We got to know each other quite well, since, being Vulcan, she joined Leonard and me for our predawn makeup calls. She sat in the chair next to mine and playfully hissed at me each morning: "Where are your wrinkles? It's been fifteen years. You should have wrinkles, dammit!"

Before long, however, I got to know another side of her that made me admire her all the more. Despite the fact that early in the filming her parents had been in a terrible car accident, and her father was dying, she never once let her own suffering affect her performance or interfere with her professional responsibilities. Over the years, of course, she's gone on to become a major star, yet she's never changed. Whenever we meet, there are always warm hugs and kisses—followed by sotto voce gossip, of course, and a whispered, "Where are your wrinkles?" She cracks me up, and I love her.

Leonard and I were sitting in the our makeup chairs one day when Harve came in, obviously very upset because some fans had learned that Spock was going to die in the film. The reaction was unanimous disapproval, and some fans vented their anger toward Leonard. To them, his agreeing to "kill off" Spock, as it were, was a betrayal. Unprepared for the vehemence of the fans' response, Leonard was baffled, hurt, and somewhat angry, though he strived to understand how they felt. At the same time, I believe that Leonard was beginning to have second thoughts. Seeing the difference an outstanding script and the right director made opened the possibility that another film might follow. Maybe killing off Spock was not such a great idea after all. By that point, however, most of the movie had been shot, and though several other possible scenarios were explored, none could be integrated satisfactorily. There was simply no choice: Spock had to die.

Like too many other people in whose hands the fate of *Star Trek* has fallen, Harve refused to accept or respect the fans. He could conceive of only one way they could have learned about Spock's demise: through Gene. Harve's smooth, friendly manner masked a propensity for arrogance and cruelty that would grate on more than a few nerves over the next four films. I shook in my chair as I heard him tell Leonard that the leak was Gene's doing.

Having seen pieces of my original costume and scripts in all versions offered for my signature at conventions, I had no qualms about the need for tight security on the lot. What the studio and Harve never understood is that Trekkers are everywhere, and the lure of anything Trek—be it a script page, a memo, an "artifact," or a bit of information—is more precious than dilithium crystals. Paramount, as well as every other major studio in town, was full of people who worked on the television series and/or the first film, and gossip is gossip. When everyone in the cast and crew was pressured to sign letters agreeing to confidentiality, though, it was an insult. Walter adamantly refused to sign his, and I covered mine with my thoughts about trust and McCarthyite loyalty oaths. "I am not now nor have I ever been a squealer on *Star Trek!*" I angrily scribbled across the page.

Even more galling than Harve's presumption that we could not be trusted was his refusal to consider any of the thousands of other ways the story might have leaked. Even though the studio had come up with elaborate systems for identifying script pages (so that later it could trace counterfeit copies to their source), it still sent them out to be copied at a copy service off the lot! From there the scripts passed through the hands of messengers, secretaries, assistants, not to mention the staffs at the special-effects companies and everyone else called in to work on the film. What self-respecting Trekker could be in the same room as a script and not take a peek?

I finally said to Harve, "Listen: When you go home at night, you talk to your children. It is not only every fan's dream to find out these things, it's their mission. They have an extensive telephone network, they have newsletters, and they have proven their power over and over again. If they want this information badly enough, they will get it. They don't need us or Gene."

But Harve did not want to hear about Gene or the fans.

As the shooting wound down and Leonard's/Spock's death scene approached, you could feel the tension in the air. Everyone sensed that this scene would be extraordinarily difficult, and so it seemed that we always found good reasons to put it off. Finally, time caught up to us.

The events leading up to Spock's death came at the picture's end. Khan, mortally wounded aboard the decimated U.S.S. *Reliant,* has started the countdown to launch the Genesis Device, which upon impact on an uninhabitable planet would reassemble matter to create a fully functioning, habitable world. The paradox of Genesis is that in order to create, it must first destroy. With the *Enterprise*'s engines seriously compromised in their battle with Khan, it cannot achieve the warp speed necessary to escape before Genesis detonates. Spock slips unnoticed from his post on the bridge and enters the reactor room to manually repair the engines, thus knowingly exposing himself to a fatal dose of radiation. Spock completes his task with seconds to spare, and the *Enterprise* escapes.

Everyone stood on the set and watched, transfixed, as Bill and Leonard played out Spock's final scene. From within a transparent containment chamber, in a voice hoarsened by radiation burns, the visibly weakened Spock makes his dying pledge to Kirk: "I have been, I always shall be, your friend."

I couldn't help crying. It was an incredibly draining scene for the two of them, and I recall that it was shot in the minimum number of takes. I believe it was the best acting either of them had ever done. When Nicholas Meyer called, "Cut!" you could hear people weeping.

Interestingly, Leonard was not on the set when we filmed the funeral scene, where Spock receives a full Starfleet burial in space, so to speak, in a shiny, coffinlike black photon-torpedo shell. Before it is ejected, Kirk delivers a brief, emotional farewell, and Scotty plays "Amazing Grace" on the bagpipes, which was Jimmy Doohan's wonderful idea. As the camera pans the mourners, Saavik—in opposition to her stoic Vulcan nature—is shown crying. That was Kirstie's idea, a beautiful touch that added to this poignant, powerful scene. After the torpedo streaks toward the Genesis planet, and Kirk, his newly discovered son, David Marcus, and the boy's mother, Carol, behold the newly born planet where Spock is "buried," the film closes with the series theme and Leonard intoning, "Space, the final frontier . . ."

Was Spock truly dead? And if so, how dead? Nicholas Meyer insisted that Spock die. Period. But others had begun having second thoughts, which is why his corpse lands conveniently on the Genesis-revived planet. It is also why just before Spock enters the reactor room, he gives his old philosophical nemesis Dr. McCoy a stunning Vulcan nerve pinch, urgently whispers, "Remember!" then conducts a mind-meld, transporting his essence to Bones. With Spock's *katra*—or soul—handily if irritatingly stored in Bones's subconscious, there were, as Spock so often reminded us, always possibilities.

Another mission? The *Enterprise,* disassembled for storage and space docked in some Los Angeles warehouse, would await its orders, emanating not from Starfleet Command but the box office.

After the release of *Star Trek II: The Wrath of Khan,* the original cast, selected guests, and thousands of fans converged on Houston's Astrodome for what its promoters billed as "The Ultimate Fantasy": all of us together again on the same stage. This was especially meaningful to the fans, who felt that Bill and, to a lesser degree, Leonard had distanced themselves from *Star Trek* by not attending the conventions. Now that we had a new movie to promote—and still smarting from the disappointment of the first—Paramount cooperated fully with the promoters to create an extravaganza no one would ever forget.

Well, nobody ever did forget Houston, except now it is remembered as "The Ultimate Disaster." Basically, everything that could possibly have gone wrong did. The centerpiece of the event was a lovely skit Walter Koenig wrote in which the entire original cast would appear, except for

Leonard, who had a previous commitment elsewhere. *He* would materialize on giant television screens placed throughout the Astrodome. I had agreed to sing two songs from my most recent album as well.

That morning, we arrived at the Astrodome to rehearse my singing segment only to find that there was virtually no sound system. What's more, instead of the twenty-piece band I'd been promised, there were six unhappy rock musicians. They were on their way out, complaining they had not been paid, as were the sound technicians and all the equipment. Thank God Jim Meechan had flown in for this event. Sizing up the situation, he quickly made a deal with the head sound man, rented some equipment, and hired one of the engineers. We hastily set up a rudimentary system. Fortunately, we'd brought along tapes of my music, so I could sing to that, since the musicians refused to play. As it turned out, the system had to be used for the main skit as well. This was the only contracted gig I ever played where I had to fork out five hundred dollars before setting foot onstage, then ended up not getting paid myself!

It wasn't long before we learned that the convention's problems extended far beyond the stage. Thousands of fans had traveled from all over the country, paying for admission in advance, only to arrive and discover that the money had been misappropriated. The Astrodome ticket takers would admit only those fans who held tickets, so when we came out to perform our skit, which included Kirstie Alley, Walter, George, and Jimmy, just a few hundred people sat where over twenty thousand were supposed to be. Even though we were not working under the best circumstances, we all agreed that we owed it to the fans to carry on.

One early event during the convention captures the mood perfectly. Those of us in the cast had taken our seats on the stage of a large ballroom for a press conference. Since this was "The Ultimate Fantasy," the national media was out in force, and fans with special tickets were admitted as well. Because they would be able to ask us questions, too, many stood in line outside the ballroom for hours to claim the best spots inside. We hadn't sat down for more than a few minutes when a man carrying a microphone walked through the room announcing, "Ladies and gentlemen, please don't panic, but there is a fire in the hotel, on the tenth floor. We must evacuate the hotel. Please keep calm and start moving out to the street."

A disappointed moan rose from the crowd. I felt so sorry for them, the least I could do was try to save the press conference.

"Excuse me, sir," I said.

The hotel manager turned to me. "Yes, Miss Nichols?"

"Would you please come back and let us know when the fire reaches the third floor?"

Everyone laughed and applauded, the fire was contained, and we continued without missing a beat.

Harve Bennett was with us at the ill-fated convention when he remarked to my friend Jim that they weren't sure what to do for the next movie, since Spock was dead. Apparently everyone at Paramount was pondering the same question: How the hell do you get a dead Vulcan back? Jim, a trained physicist with years of research on the effects of radiation, told Harve that it was within the realm of scientific possibility for Spock to have survived the radiation that had (seemingly) killed him by projecting the effect of the Genesis Planet's regeneration. Since the series began, Gene had always consulted with scientists and other experts to ensure that there was some scientific basis, if only theoretical, to our twenty-third-century fiction. In fact, my friend Dr. Jesco von Puttkamer from NASA served as a technical consultant for the first film, and dozens of other highly regarded specialists have lent their expertise to the series and the films.

Clearly, Spock had to be revived, but in a manner that

made scientific, logical sense. Harve eagerly invited Jim to his office at Paramount and asked him to read some early drafts of *Star Trek III* and offer his advice. When Harve learned that Jim was a corporate vice president at Rockwell, he also asked if he could arrange for him to visit NASA's Mission Control in Houston. One phone call to his friend and golfing buddy, Mission Control Center Director Dr. Christopher Kraft, and Jim had it set. We accompanied Harve and his family to Mission Control, where we were treated like royalty and given a special VIP tour that included the space control center itself, which is normally off-limits to the public. Chris Kraft received us in his spacious office, and after our meeting, Harve nearly gushed with gratitude thanking Jim for making it possible.

Back in Los Angeles, Jim read a few early script drafts, and at Harve's request, wrote a brief treatise on the effects of radiation and other technical information. Jim posited that, in theory at least, radiation-induced mutations can be good as well as bad, and that in the miraculous, unexplored environment of the Genesis Planet, the "rules" of science, so to speak, might be suspended. There on Genesis, the radiation that killed Spock in his own environment could heal and regenerate him. Jim suggested that Dr. McCoy be the hero of the story, and that Spock's whispered command that he "remember" impel him to lead the mission to Genesis to retrieve his friend.

Harve was very excited about this idea. "That's fantastic," he said. "How can I thank you?"

Jim mentioned that because he was moving into the entertainment business, he would appreciate a credit as technical adviser without pay.

"No problem," Harve replied, and promised to see it was done. Harve later called me, thanking me for "bringing that genius on board."

More meetings and several phone calls followed, during which Jim answered Harve's many questions. Then we never heard from him again. When the film came out, there was no credit, no acknowledgment of Jim's vital input. I was, of course, greatly disappointed. I cannot believe that Harve didn't know how much this meant to me, but perhaps he didn't.

Because critics and fans loved *Star Trek II: The Wrath of Khan,* Paramount prudently brought back Harve Bennett who, for all his faults, is a strong producer. Despite the fine job Nicholas Meyer did on *Star Trek II,* Paramount agreed to let Leonard direct. Although Leonard's previous experience behind the camera consisted of directing episodes of television series, including Bill's then-current police action show, *T. J. Hooker,* the studio was willing to give him the chance. From its point of view, I suppose, what could be more fascinating to fans than to have Leonard directing *The Search for Spock*? Like the rest of the original cast, Leonard had a long history of protecting and nurturing his character. The qualities that made Leonard so wonderful to work with as an actor served him well in the director's chair. What Leonard brought to the task that neither of the previous directors nor our producer, Harve, could was a respect for and loyalty to Gene's vision of *Star Trek.* He and Gene shared a strong philosophical bond. This is not to say that whatever problems plagued their personal relationship were resolved; they were not. To his great and enduring credit, however, Leonard rose above whatever he felt about Gene personally to ensure that *Star Trek* stayed on course.

Everyone seemed pleased with the idea of Leonard directing, except Bill. Despite the fact that Leonard was our coworker and friend of many years, becoming the director made him the boss. Bill, who jealously protected his position in the captain's chair both onscreen and off, admitted that this was not an easy time for him. However, in the wake of *Star Trek II*'s extraordinary success, Bill, Leonard, their lawyers, and the studio got together and drew up contracts giving the two "favored nations" status. What that means is that Bill and Leonard enjoy parity in everything, and that whatever one gets, the other does, too. In one way, this arrangement benefited us all, since the high fees the pair commanded almost guaranteed they would participate in any future films, and everyone involved would be spared months of anticipation, wondering if either or both would return each time out. This agreement also had some far-reaching repercussions that no one could have foreseen.

Whenever I'm asked which are my favorite *Star Trek* films, I always reply, "The even-numbered ones." While *The Search for Spock* was a very good film, it was impossible not to know that we would find Spock, in some form, and that he would rejoin the crew. The question of how offered countless possibilities, granted, but the end result was a foregone conclusion. In essence, it was an expository film. Of the three movies until then, *Star Trek III* was by far the darkest and the most violent. Picking up with Spock's death and burial, the story opened with Saavik (now played by Robin Curtis instead of Kirstie Alley) and Kirk's son, David, investigating an unexpected life reading on the Genesis Planet. Just as Kirk had cheated to defeat the *Kobayashi Maru* test as a cadet, his son David has "cheated" on his Genesis project by adding to its life-forming matrix a dangerous, unpredictable material called protomatter. The inclusion of protomatter in the new life on Genesis has several unexpected results: one is that it rejuvenates the dead Spock, whom David and Saavik discover as a young, apparently "mindless" child. Another is that the planet (its early verdant beauty shot in San Francisco's Golden Gate Park, by the way) evolves at a highly accelerated rate, so that by the time the Klingons arrive to steal the Genesis secret, the planet has become a heaving, quaking, unstable mass.

On Earth, the presence of Spock's *katra* in Bones's subconscious has led to his being hospitalized. When Spock's father, Sarek, discovers that Spock's *katra* is not with Kirk, as he assumed it would be, he urges Kirk and crew to head for Genesis with Bones so that Spock's rapidly developing physical body and his *katra* can again be reunited on Vulcan by *fal-tor-pan.* To accomplish this the crew must hijack the *Enterprise,* since the Genesis Planet is off limits. Before we can find Spock, however, David is brutally murdered by the Klingons, and Kirk decides to feign a surrender of *Enterprise,* only to beam down his own crew and program the ship to self-destruct after the Klingons board her.

Interestingly, I don't think very many people missed David, least of all Bill, who wasn't that fond of Merritt Butrick, the actor who played him. (Sadly, Merritt died some years later of AIDS.) Before the second movie, we didn't even know Kirk had a son, and from what little we do see of David, he serves as a symbol of what Kirk has sacrificed for his career. We feel Kirk's loss not because we feel that we have lost David, too, but because we care about Kirk.

The fiery destruction of the *Enterprise,* however, was something else. The single enduring constant in the *Trek* universe, the vessel of our voyages, and our home, the ship claimed a special place in most hearts. The decision to blow it up was a dramatic and controversial move, one that Gene opposed vehemently. "I felt it wasn't really that necessary," he said. After all, the *Enterprise* was designed so that the saucer section could be removed from the ship's main body. It could have been destroyed and replaced, Gene argued, leaving most of the ship intact. Once fans got wind that the *Enterprise* was doomed, they mounted a campaign to save it, but Leonard and Harve, among others, would not budge on this. They felt, perhaps correctly, that without the ship being truly and irrevocably destroyed, the sense of sacrifice would be diminished. That may be so, because the scene of Kirk and the crew watching helplessly as the burning *Enterprise* streaks across Genesis's horizon is every bit as dramatic a moment as Kirk's powerful response to learning that the Klingons randomly murdered his son. Even now *I* find it very painful to watch as explosions rip apart the ship, so I understand why fans would be upset and why they have such a proprietary sense about *Star Trek*.

At the time, Leonard said, "The major theme . . . is friendship." Not only was Leonard a wonderful, capable director, but he brought out the crew's dynamics and recaptured the humor that graced the original series and would feature prominently in the next movie, *Star Trek IV: The Voyage Home*. The early scenes of us together at Kirk's apartment, commiserating over the loss of Spock, McCoy's deteriorating mental state, and our uncertain futures in Starfleet, and then each of us carrying out our assignments to facilitate the hijacking of the ship were done beautifully.

I especially enjoyed doing the scene where a young, cocky cadet—unaware that Uhura's unexpected presence during his duty shift is part of Kirk's scheme—remarks disdainfully, "You amaze me: a twenty-year space veteran, yet you chose the worst duty station in town . . . the hind end of space." While the cadet muses over the great adventures he's sure await him, Kirk, Bones, and Sulu march in and head for the transporter. To his amazement, Uhura illegally beams them aboard the *Enterprise,* then forces him into a closet at phaser point. It is a wonderful, funny scene, and throughout the film, Leonard gave each of us a chance to shine.

The scene in which Sulu helps Kirk abduct McCoy from a psychiatric hospital is also a favorite. Shortly after a suspicious security guard remarks, "Don't get smart, Tiny," George proceeds to disable him and his console. As he makes his escape with Kirk and McCoy, Sulu stops and warns sternly: "Don't call me 'Tiny'!"

As always, when we were together, there was a lot of

laughing and joking. Despite the hard work and long hours, being on a set with your friends brings out the kid in everyone. Well, almost everyone. The whole shooting of *Star Trek III* was a little surreal to begin with. Since Leonard had to direct Spock's scenes, he had to go back and forth between acting on the set and directing behind the camera, often in full costume. With all due respect to Leonard, how seriously can you take a director with pointed ears? One day, several of us, including Jimmy, Mark Lenard (who plays Spock's father, Sarek), and me, were standing around talking. We knew that Leonard was on the set nearby trying to establish a particularly difficult shot. Normally Leonard is unflappable, but the strain of acting and directing was beginning to show, and he was determined to keep the project on time and within budget.

We tried to keep our voices down, but then Dee arrived and told a stupid but hilarious joke about short men, full of double entendres. I know that most people think that anyone they see onscreen is very tall, so it comes as a shock for some when they see that actors are often shorter than they expect. In fact, upon meeting me, people often exclaim, "I thought you were six feet tall!" I always respond, "Well, Uhura *is!*" When we would film a shot that included George and Walter, I'd catch the two of them clowning around, each up on tiptoes, playfully trying to upstage each other by being "taller." Sometimes I'd join in, and we'd all laugh.

Anyway, George sauntered by and asked what was so funny. Dee repeated the joke. When George didn't get it immediately, Dee explained the punch line, which prompted one of George's bellowing, ruptured-goose laughs. By then we were all cracking up—at the joke, at George not getting the joke, at George's laughter—when who should come by but Walter. George told Walter the joke, then inadvertently insulted him by explaining the punch line. "I got it the first time," Walter said, bristling, before launching into an apparently serious tirade about how everyone picks on "the vertically impaired" and how wrong it is. By then the rest of us were out of control, howling, and George laughing loud enough to shake the rafters, oblivious of the work going on around the corner.

Suddenly: "CUT!!"

We stopped, looked at one another, and knew we were in trouble. Leonard, ears and all, came flying around the wall, cursing and screaming at us. It seems he had finally captured that crucial scene, but our laughter ruined the audio track and they had to reshoot. Like a bunch of guilty schoolkids, we took one look at our furious Vulcan director and scattered. All except Walter, of course, whom we left standing there mumbling to himself, "I don't see what's so funny about short men . . ." while George was reduced to tears, desperately trying to stop laughing.

Although most fans still preferred *Star Trek II: The Wrath of Khan,* the overall response to *Star Trek III* was very positive. I was happy to see that for several reasons, not the least of which was that it proved to the studio that *Star Trek*'s "rules" could not be broken nor its characters compromised. Closing the film with us on Vulcan, with a Klingon bird of prey our only means of transport home, left it all nicely open for the next adventure. Leonard, Harve, and the creative team would spend the better part of the next two years charting our intergalactic itinerary for the next movie. We were all highly aware that the next film would be released to coincide with the original series' twentieth anniversary. It was still the top-rated syndicated television program in history (according to our old nemesis, the A. C. Nielsen Company), and the conventions continued on, stronger than ever. The three vastly popular *Star Trek* movies introduced us to younger people and those who'd never seen or paid much attention to the series before. As they often told us, the older fans enjoyed watching us grow older. In the entertainment world, where nothing lasts forever, *Star Trek* only grew stronger with each passing year. In press interviews each of us joked about the possibility of sitting on the bridge in our wheelchairs, with Uhura communicating across the universe with the help of a hearing aid, and everyone else (but me, of course) grown old and gray. I suppose the sole exception to that would be Mr. Spock; after all, Vulcans usually live a couple of hundred years.

Music remained the one constant in my life. In the late seventies my friend Wade Crookham told me about a remarkable voice teacher who had saved the voices of several very well-known singers. I began studying with him, and although I loved the Maestro, as his students call him, I couldn't get through a lesson without wanting to kill him at least once. I would look at him, my eyes flashing rage, and he would just smile. "You don't tell me what you can't do," he often said. "You just do what God gives you the talent to do, and I'll take care of the rest." By the time I became his pupil, he was well into his eighties, a short but powerful and lovely man. His name is Giuseppe Balestrieri. Sound familiar?

Ever since I first heard his name, I wondered whether or not he was perhaps related to Frankie Balistrieri, but I couldn't bring myself to ask. By then, Frankie had become more than notorious and was, in fact, just a few years away from being convicted of conspiracy and sentenced to thirteen years in federal prison. I had been studying with the Maestro for over two months when I finally asked him.

"You said you're from the Midwest," I said one day.

"Yes," he replied. "Milwaukee. And someday I plan to move back there."

"I have something to ask you. Do you know Frankie Balistrieri?"

Maestro froze for a few seconds, then asked, "How do you know Frankie Balistrieri?"

"Well, it's a long story," I began.

When I finished he said, somewhat reluctantly, "Well, yes, we are related, but we have nothing to do with them. We even changed the spelling of our name, so that people wouldn't associate us with them. But, in fact, I am related to him by blood, though somewhat distantly."

I appreciated Maestro's honesty but respected his privacy enough to never raise the subject again; it obviously troubled him, as he and his brothers are highly respected professional people in music, medicine, and law in the Milwaukee area. But to think of these two men and the roles they each played in my career, I couldn't help but wonder who was working the loom when my fate was being woven.

Music is not only my love, but a doorway through which so many wonderful people have entered my life. One of those people was a young musician named Andy Chapin.

Because of career considerations, it was not possible for me to continue with a direct participation in the space program as I had during the Space Shuttle astronaut recruitment drive. Still, I was and remain a strong advocate of our national space program, and use every personal appearance and interview to remind people of the importance of space exploration. Interestingly, it was my interest in space that led me to Jim Meechan, whose interest in music led him to me. And so it goes.

I was thrilled to be invited by NASA to witness the landing of the Space Shuttle *Columbia* upon completion of her first orbital flight. Of course, Jim was there with his Rockwell team. The two-day mission had been a great success, and the sight of the great craft landing on the salt flats at Edwards Air Force Base was simply breathtaking. There we met Andy, then in his late twenties, and learned he had also been especially invited to the event because of his interest in the space program. We hit it off right away, and soon Andy revealed that he had written a piece of music in honor of the occasion. Interestingly, Jim had composed a poem, "Ode to the Space Shuttle," and when we sat down to combine them, the words and music fit together so perfectly you would think the two of them had sat together on a piano bench and worked it all out. We recorded it and included it on *Uhura Sings,* and Jim produced a very moving video for it, incorporating footage of the shuttle's first launch, flight, and landing. When I stopped to think that these two men didn't even know each other when they each wrote their respective parts, it was positively eerie.

Andy became one of our closest friends, and he and Jim shared a father-son relationship that enriched both their lives. Andy was a highly respected keyboardist who had played with such top rock groups as Steppenwolf and the Association before going out on his own. He wrote fantastic music and was one of the most dynamic keyboardists I'd ever heard. We did a lot of studio and live performance work with Andy and had a number of future projects lined up, but nothing imminent. So when Andy was offered the chance to join Rick Nelson's band sometime around early 1984, he took it. Because Nelson toured over two hundred dates a year, Andy was constantly in and out of town. He really missed being with his wife and small son, Ian. He called one day in late December 1985 to let us know he was going to quit the band after this next short tour—just Orlando; Guntersville, Alabama; and finally Dallas for New Year's Eve—and to wish us happy holidays.

I was preparing to celebrate the New Year with champagne and friends when Jim came over with the news that Andy had died in the plane crash that killed Rick, the rest of his band, and his fiancée. I was deeply saddened by his loss, but Jim was devastated beyond words. On New Year's Day he memorialized his friend in a song, "Andy." We then called together about twenty-five of Andy's friends, among them many top musical talents from the Los Angeles area, and in one recording session recorded the song, using over a dozen singers, four keyboard players, several guitars, flutes, percussion, and horns. Andy's brother played the bagpipes as well. He was a lovely person, and we still miss him so much. Bless you, sweetheart, wherever you are.

Andy loved the space program and the shuttle, so the next launch held a special meaning, coming as it did less than four weeks after Andy's death. My grief over Andy was somewhat assuaged by the fact that the next shuttle would carry three astronauts who were recruited during my drive: Judith Resnik, Ellison Onizuka, and Ronald McNair. Through the years, I've had occasion to speak with many of the astronauts, and some, like Ron and Judy, I got to know quite well. In fact, it was Judy who presented me with NASA's Public Service Award in 1984.

After several postponements, the Space Shuttle *Challenger* was set to launch on January 28. I was out on my morning run when I realized what time it was. Racing up my driveway, I was about to open my front door when Jim beat me to it.

"Something terrible has happened," he said. I knew from the look on his face what it was.

No one will ever forget that day. Tens of millions of us—including the families and friends of the seven astronauts on board—watched in horror as just over a minute into what to all appearances was a routine launch, the shuttle exploded nine miles above the Earth. I sat before the television, watching in disbelief the replay as the ship seemed to disappear amid twisted white ribbons of smoke.

Like most Americans, I was stunned by the *Challenger* disaster. With the exception of a few close calls and the horrible launchpad fire that killed astronauts Gus Grissom, Edward White (the first American to walk in space), and Roger Chaffee in 1967, NASA had become synonymous in our minds with success and safety. Of course, no one entering the space program had any delusions about what was at stake. Space travel and exploration are inherently dangerous pursuits. After all, the astronauts riding the Space Shuttle were sitting atop two 149-foot-long solid rocket boosters, and a massive exterior tank containing liquid hydrogen and liquid oxygen, which feed the main engines. With these giant "firecrackers" expending their millions of pounds of force in a matter of minutes, every Space Shuttle launch was anything but a "routine operation."

In the wake of the *Challenger* accident, most people wondered why there wasn't some kind of emergency-escape system in place. I have been told by some of the dedicated professionals who designed, tested, and built the Space Shuttle that escape systems were studied in great detail, but no viable approach was conceived with this system's configuration. In terms of safety precautions, they say, the Space Shuttle, like a current commercial airliner, depends on its numerous systems and subsystems working as designed. If a rocket-powered or "parachutable" cabin had been provided in the Space Shuttle (which, the experts say, was theoretically possible), the cabin's added weight and complexity would have seriously impeded the Space Shuttle's basic purpose—carrying cargo. The fact that twenty-five missions had been accomplished without a serious problem was a near miracle in itself, and a testament to the care and expertise of NASA and the veteran contractors who formed the Space Shuttle team.

About two years before the *Challenger* disaster, some major mistakes were made in the management of our civilian space program. Some aerospace contractors who had not participated as prime members of NASA's manned space-flight programs began lobbying for their piece of the pie. They were joined by a majority contingent in Congress, who were naturally looking for ways to redistribute tax dollars and bring jobs to their respective districts. Ironically, the very fact that the Space Shuttle program had been so successful contributed to the disaster. Critics eager to open participation in the program to other contractors misinterpreted NASA's sterling safety record as an indication of how easy the program was to manage instead of recognizing it as a testament to the value of experience. The media, which had generally lost interest in the space program, jumped on the cost-saving bandwagon. In the resulting cost-reduction frenzy, the NASA-contractor team directly responsible for carrying off the first twenty-some safe, successful launches was replaced. A few expert voices of caution went unheeded; the die was cast.

It sickened me to observe Professor Feynman's simple but convincing demonstration before the congressional investigative committee, when he showed that the O-ring—the crucial barrier containing the solid rocket's inferno—became brittle and cracked after exposure to freezing temperatures. Everybody knew that a massive Florida freeze had struck the Space Shuttle stack for days before the *Challenger* launch. An experienced team would not have allowed a launch under those circumstances. Unfortunately, the new team did not recognize the imminent danger the freezing weather presented. It's interesting to note that since this disaster forced a return to the precautions that had always been adhered to before, there have been no further problems. Of course, given the nature of space exploration, the odds are that, yes, one day, there may be another disaster. But I pray to God that if such an event were to happen, it would be the result of an unforeseen, unpredictable event—not the product of bureaucratic ineptitude and misdirected cost cutting. The brave and talented people we ask to serve as astronauts deserve better than that.

For weeks following the *Challenger* disaster, I was in a state of mourning so deep I couldn't bring myself to talk about it. Jim, who was also a personal friend of some of the astronauts, understood how I felt perhaps better than anyone else. Aware of my work with NASA, interviewers often asked about my response to the *Challenger* accident, and I always made it a point to stress that while the tragedy raised issues of management, quality control, and safety, it would be a horrible betrayal of those seven astronauts to abandon the dream they died for. Fittingly, our next film, *Star Trek IV: The Voyage Home,* was dedicated to the brave women and men of the *Challenger* crew.

Star Trek IV premiered in November 1986, twenty years after the series first hit the air, and soon proved the most successful film to date. Many factors contributed to that success, but having Leonard direct a story he conceived surely helped. It was great to work with him again and wonderful to be reunited with so many actors from the series who were making their first appearance in a *Trek* film: Majel Barrett (Commander, formerly Nurse, Christine Chapel) and Grace Lee Whitney (Commander, formerly Yeoman, Janice Rand) returned. And, of course, Mark Lenard reprised his role as Sarek.

Leonard and the writers' first challenge was to figure out how to get the *Enterprise* crew, now aboard a Klingon bird of prey, home to Starfleet headquarters. Any good Trekker knows that Kirk and company had run afoul of so many regulations in their quest to save Spock, nothing short of their saving the Earth could spare them the inevitable court martial. It's easy to decide your fictional heroes will save the world, but how, and from what? Leonard solved the problem brilliantly by having the crew save the twenty-third-century Earth from destruction by an alien probe seeking communication with a humpback whale. By then the whales have long been extinct, so the crew must travel in time back to 1986, where we find two whales and then transport them back into the future, thereby satisfying the probe and saving the world. The time-travel aspect of the story provided great opportunities to inject humor into what was otherwise a cautionary tale about the wages of environmental ruin.

Months before we set foot in front of a camera, there ensued a series of delays. One that threatened the very future of *Star Trek* movies was Bill, whose negotiations for a markedly higher salary dragged on for about eight months. Faced with the possibility that Bill might not return at all, Harve Bennett gave his blessing to an idea that was entitled *Starfleet Academy*. This proposed film, which would haunt us for the next couple of years and make Gene furious, examined the lives of Kirk, Spock, and Bones during their academy days. The basic concept was not without merit. There is a long history of fictional writings, some by professional writers, some written by fans, that delve into all of the characters' pasts. Over the course of the movies, especially in *Star Trek V*, personal historical details were added, which I felt only enriched the characters and, belatedly, fulfilled Gene's original premise for the series.

Certainly by *Star Trek III*, Harve Bennett had proved that the films need not be the financial boondoggles the first was. But history was repeating itself. Though Harve was, technically speaking, the boss on the movies, he was no match for Leonard and Bill. Working separately or in concert, they became a force to be reckoned with, particularly after the parity issue was settled between them. From the studio's point of view, the beauty of *Starfleet Academy* was not how it would add to *Trek* lore, but how it would eliminate the original cast and, most important, the large paychecks Bill and Leonard commanded. It was doubtful that the *Enterprise* would ever leave space dock again without Kirk in the captain's chair. Or if it did, there might be a younger (i.e., less expensive, more cooperative) captain and first officer at the helm. *Star Trek IV* was saved when the studio and Bill finally came to terms.

The Wrath of Khan, The Search for Spock, and *The Voyage Home* were not conceived as parts of a trilogy, yet it worked out that way with all of the action taking place in less than an Earth year. While it was true that we had found Spock and helped reintegrate his body with his *katra,* he was not quite himself, and if anything, a little more human than before. This, coupled with the humor inherent in any time-travel story, provided some of the movie's funniest moments. Everyone loved the scene on the bus, where Kirk tries to explain to Spock the correct and effective uses of profanity, which Spock proceeds to bungle throughout the film.

As always, Leonard felt strongly that the familial interaction among the crew members deserved center stage. Soon after the cloaked (and therefore invisible) bird of prey lands in Golden Gate Park, we split up into teams. Kirk and Spock search for the whales, Scotty and Bones try to find an "ancient" material suitable for building a tank for the whales, Sulu procures a helicopter for moving the stuff, and Chekov and Uhura recover the nuclear-fission byproducts needed to regenerate the dilithium crystals for the trip back around the sun.

Filming in San Francisco was such a pleasure. Naturally, we had to have special permits to film on the streets, and these were subject to strict regulations regarding when and where we could shoot. The area we were shooting was roped off, and hundreds of cheering, happy *Trek* fans had converged on the scene. One part of the script called for Uhura and Chekov to stand on a streetcorner and ask passersby the way to Alameda. San Franciscans, who have probably seen everything, barely noticed us, and Leonard shot the scene à la *Candid Camera,* so that some of the people you see us asking for directions to where they keep, as Chekov says, "the nuclear wessels" were not actors but people who just happened by. Now, because of union requirements anyone who speaks in a feature film must be a union member.

Most of the bystanders were delighted to be there and

thrilled to be invited to join the living scenery of the crowd. One woman who showed up caught everyone's eye. She was absolutely stunning, with long brown hair, lovely skin, and a chic beige and white outfit. To top it off, she brought along her little Yorkie, whose brown-and-white coat matched her suit perfectly. It was almost too good to be true. And the moment Leonard laid eyes on her, he decided she had to be in the film.

She asked what all the commotion was about and someone replied, *"Star Trek."*

"Oh, is that the television series?" she asked innocently. When the assistant director asked if she wanted to walk through a scene, she seemed surprised and flattered, just like a normal person who stumbled onto a set.

The problem was that she wasn't an average person but an actress, something we began to suspect after she botched the scene repeatedly by "forgetting" not to talk to me and Walter. After the first time, Leonard patiently explained to her, "Do not say anything to them. Just look at them and walk through. They'll be asking all these stupid questions, but you just ignore them like they might bite you."

"Okay," she replied.

We had only fifteen minutes to finish the scene before lunch. Leonard called, "Action!" and Walter and I began asking everyone, "Where is Alameda?"

Leonard's discovery walked up and answered, "I'm so sorry, but I really don't know."

"Cut!" Taking her aside but within earshot of us, Leonard repeated his instructions. "It's very important—it's imperative—that you not say a word."

"Okay. But I don't understand why."

"Just please don't!"

So we tried it again, and she did it again, but this time offered the lame excuse that it seemed rude to her not to speak with us. It was time for lunch, and the crew had to break down to get ready to shoot down the street later. Walter was livid, Leonard was furious, and everyone was muttering under their breaths about this woman.

"We'll get the shot without her," Leonard said hopefully.

"I'm sorry, Leonard, but we can't," the assistant director said. "Not only that, but the permit says we've got to be off the streets of San Francisco by four. We're talking money!"

Down in the church basement where the lunch was catered, we all sat down mulling over what a bad day we'd had so far. The script contained a beautiful scene in which Sulu encounters a little boy who turns out to be his great-grandfather several times over. The young Japanese actor, who had given a brilliant audition, simply refused to act once he got on the set. His brother, who was dying for the chance, was not very good, and so that scene was lost. Now because of this woman and her Yorkie we were about to resign another important scene to the cutting-room floor.

The more I thought about it, the funnier it got. If Leonard had not found her so attractive, none of this would have happened. In a way, he asked for it. I was laughing over lunch when Walter snapped, "I don't care what you think, Nichelle, it is not funny! We've got to cut the goddamn scene, and what the hell are we going to do now? That was a great scene!"

Just then the woman and her dog entered. From across the room where Leonard was seated with his people, I could see him practically vibrating with rage, which is highly unlike him. When I went to his table, he said, "Nichelle, I'm sorry, but we're going to have to cut that scene, and I don't know what we can put in its place."

I was still laughing; then Leonard said, "It is not funny, Nichelle."

"Oh, yes, it is," I replied. "You've just been snookered, and you don't know how to get out of it."

"What are you talking about?" he demanded.

"She's an actress who's trying to get into the union," I replied.

"Yes, we have actors. So how does that help?"

"Well, you do, but none of them has hair down to her waist or has a Yorkie. She's unique, so it's Taft-Hartley," I answered, citing an obscure exception to the screen actors' union rules. "You called for a tall, slender woman with a Yorkie. At this moment, in this place, there were no other actors available to fill that call. She joins the union, and for four hundred dollars, you save the shot."

"That could work!" he exclaimed. "That could work! Unique, right. The director asked for a tall, slender woman with a Yorkie." Leonard smiled. "Nichelle, I could kiss you!"

We had a wonderful time filming in San Francisco, but it passed too quickly, and George, myself, and some other cast members found ourselves sitting on a plane bound for Los Angeles. We were leaving from a small airport in Monterey, so when the flight attendant announced that our takeoff would be delayed for over half an hour while workmen repaired the air conditioner, George and I decided to deplane. We were assured that once the work was completed, announcements would be made in the terminal.

We got off, leaving everything we had on board except my pocketbook, and found a bar not fifty feet from the gate, where we sat and had a beer. We were so close, in fact, that we could see the plane through a nearby window. George and I were chatting when suddenly we looked up and saw the plane's door was closed.

We ran to the counter, and George, in his most even, gentlemanly manner, explained that we had to get on the plane. When the airline employee proved less than cooperative, George demanded, "You have to stop them! You don't understand. Our possessions are there. Advise them not to move the plane until we board."

"Sir," I said, trying a softer approach, "we are the actors from *Star Trek,* and we *must* be on that plane."

A second airline employee, who recognized us and tried to help, remarked, "I think the plane can be stopped." But the man at the counter was immovable, and George and I watched in disbelief as the plane began to back away from the gate.

"I demand that you bring the plane back now!" George shouted, his face reddening. "I will have your head!"

As the plane started taxiing down the runway, I resigned myself to our fate. We were stuck, stranded, and there was nothing we could do.

"George, please calm down," I said gently.

"But Nichelle!" By then George was spluttering so, all he could do was point at the plane and watch as it ascended into the clouds.

Of course, we eventually got a flight out, but the next time I saw Dee, I demanded, "You knew we were inside the terminal, and you knew we were supposed to get back on the plane. Why the hell didn't you tell them and make them stop and wait for us?"

Dee smiled and replied, "But, Nichelle, how could we? The thought of you and George stranded there, watching the plane take off without you—it was just too much fun! We couldn't resist. We laughed all the way to Los Angeles."

They say there are two sides to every story, so I wasn't surprised to hear that George had been telling the same story but with a few differences. For example, in his version, it is he who remains cool and collected while, as he said, "Nichelle threw her fur on the floor." Maybe someday I'll mention to George that it was summertime.

That's not the only one of George's "stories" I've had to correct. Once, at an early convention, the organizers came and asked us if we could take a minute before we went onstage to meet a special fan. Apparently Sulu and Uhura were his favorite characters, and he was only about eleven or twelve, so of course we said sure. He was a wonderful Chinese boy, and it was such a kick to see how happy he was, especially after George asked, "Would you like to go onstage with us?"

This boy was so excited, I thought he was going to explode. They announced us, and George and I took our places with the boy in tow. After the welcoming applause died down, George said to the crowd, "It's been wonderful to see you all again. Thank you so much for coming to see us today. You know, Nichelle and I have not seen many of you for several years, and a lot has happened since then. Nichelle and I are very proud to introduce you to our son, our love child."

I couldn't believe my ears! And judging from the gasp that rose from the crowd, neither could anyone else. The boy seemed happy, if a bit confused, and afterward everyone had a good laugh, because obviously it was a joke, right? You would be surprised how many people, to this day, still ask me about my "affair" with George and our "son."

By the time *Star Trek IV: The Voyage Home* was ready for release, the original series had been in syndication for seventeen years. Though the show claimed more viewers than ever, there was no getting around the fact that the seventy-nine episodes that comprised "classic *Trek*" could not continue to be shown forever. The fans still loved it, but, having witnessed the spectacular success of the film, someone in the studio accounting department must have wondered how else Paramount might profit from *Star Trek*.

One day in October 1986, about six weeks before *Star Trek IV* was set to be released, I got a series of phone calls from journalists the world over, each one asking, "How do you feel about the new *Star Trek* TV show?"

I was caught totally off-guard, because not only were they calling on my private line—to which I believed no one had the number—but a television show? What television show? There had been talk for the past two years about bringing back the original cast in a new television series or in a miniseries, but nothing was final, as far as I knew. I tap-danced my way around the questions before I said, "Well, I think you really should get all of your information directly from Paramount, don't you?"

"Yes, but how do you feel about it? What is your reaction?"

I really didn't know until a few hours later when someone I knew at Paramount surreptitiously called to say, "You don't know this, but there's going to be a press announcement this afternoon from the studio about the new *Star Trek* TV series with an entirely new cast. It's going to be called *The Next Generation.* I just thought you should know before you hear it from someone else."

"Oh! That's what this is all about," I replied.

"What do you mean?"

"I've been getting calls from England, Germany, Japan—everywhere in the world—all morning."

"Oh, I'm so sorry. I was hoping to get to you before they did, but we just found out about it ourselves."

I thanked my friend, who shall remain nameless, and hung up the phone, absolutely furious at Gene. What was he thinking, putting me—and probably everyone else from the old cast—on the spot like that? What he chose to tell others about his business was his business, and I could understand why he might not have felt particularly open with some other people, but we were friends outside the business.

"Dammit, Gene, I cannot believe that you left me in the dark like that," I said to him not long after. "It was embarrassing and humiliating to be asked about something everyone just assumed I would know."

"Yes, I see your point," he replied calmly. "But it was part of the deal: We had to keep it under wraps and not tell anybody."

"Gene, I am not just anybody, and you *know* it," I snapped.

"No, Nichelle, you're not. But if you had been coming around more and keeping up with me, you would have known."

Gene's words hit me like a slap in the face. What did he mean? We saw each other socially, we met for lunch sometimes. As a friend, he knew he could always count on me. I might have said these things, but the only words I could form in the heat of the moment were "You bastard!"

Gene didn't even flinch. He shrugged and gave me a boyish grin, as if to say, "Well, you knew I could be," but I could also see that he was hurt. It finally dawned on me that after all these years, I still meant something special to him. This is not to say that he was in love with me, or that there was any chance that we would resume our romantic relationship. It was something deeper and more complex than that. He had found a great, wonderful love with Majel, and while he had gotten over me, he'd never quite resolved the fact that I had left him voluntarily, without being asked, without being pushed. Time and again over the years, he asked, "How could you do it?"

Exactly what this was all about, I don't think I can ever say for sure. He resented something about me and something about how our relationship evolved. Was it because I was not, in his mind, there for him? Did he resent me for having the strength to keep my distance all these years? Did he ever really forgive me for leaving? Was this why he'd prevented me from leaving *Star Trek* to join *Mannix?* For a man as warm, generous, and fair-minded as Gene usually was, he could be painfully petty.

Still, I was happy for Gene. There aren't many people who get a second chance like that one. For the first time,

Gene finally had full creative control, a healthy budget, and the freedom that comes from selling a show straight into syndication. At last he got to produce a show that had a true ensemble cast. Although fans didn't warm to the series immediately, eventually it became quite popular.

About a year later I remarked to Gene, "You're sitting here with a very schizophrenic situation: You've got two children. The older one got kidnapped from you, but he came back and still loves you. In the meantime, though, you got a new kid, whom you love better than the poor little one that got taken away."

"You always had a way with words," he said, smiling. And he knew I was right. I can't blame Gene for feeling ambivalent at times toward the first series. It had been his blessing and his curse, something he would always be remembered for but could never escape and never fully control.

One month after the new series was announced, *Star Trek IV: The Voyage Home* was released to critical acclaim and great box office success. Everyone in the cast agreed it was near perfect. In the final scene, the entire crew, with the exception of Kirk, is acquitted of the charges, and his "punishment" amounts to a reassignment to a new ship bearing the name *Enterprise.* As a result of his demotion, he would return in the next film not as an admiral but a captain. Behind the scenes, however, Bill was awaiting promotion, from star to director.

CHAPTER TWELVE

While working on *Star Trek V: The Final Frontier,* I discovered something about Bill Shatner: He was a wonderful director to work for. Supportive, encouraging, inspiring—Bill turned out to be among the finest, most respectful directors I've ever worked with. Even Jimmy Doohan, whose dislike of Bill is quite well known, admitted that he was terrific in the director's chair. Ironically, Bill became more of a human being than he'd ever been as an actor. I realized that what drove all of us crazy about him when he was acting was that he was directing. For whatever reason, Bill needs to control the action and be the center of attention. It was not so much his needing those things that made him so impossible as an actor as what he had to do to get them. His authority in the director's chair secure and unquestioned, Bill joined the team, however briefly.

To say that most of us in the cast were dreading standing before a camera with Bill on the other side of it would be an understatement. After twenty years of enduring his overbearing behavior on the set, our apprehension about starting work on *Star Trek V* was not unfounded. While making the first four movies, Bill's behavior toward his fellow actors became so disruptive that the moment he stopped a scene and began demanding changes in the scene, the script, the staging—whatever—everyone went into a sort of freeze frame. Because the directors were unwilling or unable to tell Bill no, their discussions often dragged on, thwarting the flow of the scene and breaking our concentration as actors.

While Bill had done some directing in television, it's highly doubtful that he would have been chosen to take this particular captain's chair were it not for the parity agreement with Leonard. By then Leonard had not only directed the two previous *Star Trek* films but also written the story for *Star Trek IV*. Long before that movie was in the can, Bill conceived the basic premise for his motion picture directorial debut. We of the *Enterprise* saved the Earth countless times and proved a remarkable ability to find things throughout the universe, from a regenerated Vulcan to a pair of whales. Certainly there were infinite mysteries remaining to be discovered and plumbed, yet Bill chose to embark on the most ambitious adventure yet: a search for God.

Intriguing as the premise sounded on paper, it posed a lot of problems, not the least of them being that few people believe you can find God—even in the future, even in science fiction—the same way you might track down a cache of dilithium crystals. You simply cannot "find" God, and if you do, how do you depict God in a way that audiences will recognize and respond to? These would be challenges for any director of any film, but the idea was particularly unworkable within the *Star Trek* framework. Beginning back with the series, when Gene Roddenberry refused to include a chaplain among the *Enterprise* crew, and again, during the making of the second movie, when he opposed a burial service for Spock that struck him as being too Christian-oriented, he always steered *Star Trek* away from any direct religious inferences or messages. Bill's twist on the story was to make what was initially presumed to be God turn out to be the Devil or some other evil force, but to Gene—and quite a few others, even including our producer, Harve Bennett—this was a well-worn approach, painfully lacking any of the fresh twists *Star Trek* fans had come to expect.

After Gene voiced his criticism of the idea, Harve and Leonard, with others, recast the script, changing key details so that the story became less a search for God than the search for truth. Briefly, the plot revolved around a spiritual zealot Vulcan named Sybok, who turns out to be Spock's half brother from Sarek's previous marriage. Sybok, who has rejected the philosophy of logic, seeks to lead his followers to God, who he believes exists in some physical form at the center of the galaxy in a place called Sha Ka Ree. Sybok assumes control of the *Enterprise* by using a form of the Vulcan mind-meld to deliver each person from the emotional pain he or she cannot otherwise escape.

Here was another troublesome aspect of the script, but this time the criticism came from several of the actors. Both Leonard and Dee felt that their respective characters would not side with Sybok against Kirk, no matter what. In the end, even though each relives his most painful experience—for Spock, it is seeing his father's rejection of him; for Bones, it is performing euthanasia to relieve his dying father's suffering—they each remain true to Kirk.

Once the shooting script was in hand, there were additional delays, as Leonard finished directing *The Good Mother*, and a Writers' Guild strike brought Hollywood to a halt. For a number of reasons, the film quickly ran overbudget, and so cuts had to be made in the special effects. This was especially unfortunate, since after the FX debacle of our first movie, the *Star Trek* movies had all been visually stunning, with believable, breathtaking effects. Unfortunately for Bill, with *Star Trek V* we took a giant step backward. Certain scenes, such as the one where Scotty and Uhura seem about to make love, never quite meshed with the rest of the film. And some unforgettable moments—like Kirk demanding to know why "God" needs a starship—proved memorable for the wrong reasons.

The film opens with the *Enterprise* crew being suddenly called to duty and dispatched to Nimbus III, the so-called Planet of Galactic Peace, where the messianic Sybok has taken Klingon, Romulan, and United Federation of Planets consuls hostage. Kirk, Spock, McCoy, and other crew members attempt a nighttime rescue of the hostages, but when faced with a hostile group loyal to Sybok, Kirk instructs Uhura to create a diversion. Producer Harve Bennett explained that Uhura would attract Sybok's men's attention by performing a sensuous nighttime dance on a mountaintop.

"I want this to really look nude," he said, "so we don't mind if you want a body double to actually do the dance."

"Over my dead body!" I replied. "Harve, I'm in great shape. I'd rather not be totally nude, though, so let's use a G-string."

"Okay. Now the other thing is that Uhura will be singing, sort of a siren's song. We're not sure what it will be yet, but at last the world is going to get to hear that beautiful voice of yours."

"I have the perfect song, and if you like it, it's yours," I replied excitedly. For the past year or so I'd been performing my one-woman show called "Reflections," in which I portrayed a series of great Black women performers, among them dancer Katherine Dunham (sound familiar?). For that Afro-Cuban dance number, Jim wrote a song appropriately titled "Hauntingly," a beautiful native love song that melds Swahili phrases and an almost eerie primal melody. Harve said he would listen to the song and consider it, but, he warned, "I can't promise you anything." Of course, I knew the decision was not his alone, and while I hoped he would choose "Hauntingly," I would understand if he did not.

Nimbus III was really Death Valley, where the temperatures hit a scorching 100 degrees plus during the day but plunge to near freezing at night. Between shots for the dance, I was huddled in a heavy battle jacket, but once Bill called "Action!" there I was, practically nude, doing the dance to "Hauntingly" over and over again. My teeth chattered, the sand beneath my bare feet shifted, and the whole scene seemed doomed. The crew kept me laughing, making flattering and suggestive comments about my legs, and Bill could not have been nicer as we shot it from one angle, then another, then another, then another. We were all in the same cold, sandy boat together, and although most of what we filmed that night proved unusable, we'd had a great time.

Back in L.A. we shot the same scene again, but in a studio, where I stood on a scaffold covered with sand. Why no one thought that the new imported sand wouldn't shift like the sand in the desert escapes me, but we had a lot of the same problems shooting it, only it wasn't nearly as cold and Bill could get the two moons of Nimbus III into the shots. The music and my singing would be dubbed in later.

Each day's filming—the dailies—were rushed to processing, and Bill, Harve, and others, including Gene, viewed them every day. After watching one set, Gene phoned me and said urgently, "Nichelle, we have to have lunch."

"Okay, but, Gene, we haven't had lunch together in so long, it's not even funny."

"I know, I know, but you have to meet me for lunch, at the Paramount commissary."

A few days later we were having a wonderful lunch together. I was thinking about how often we saw each other and spoke, but how we so rarely got the chance to have a private heart-to-heart and how much I missed his brilliant mind and easy smile.

"I have to ask you something," he said, his eyes twinkling devilishly. "I saw the dailies of you doing that dance."

"Yes?" I asked, certain he was about to say that he hated the scene.

"Are those really your legs?"

"Gene! Of course, they're my legs!"

"I know they're your legs twenty-five years ago, but still? Now? You still have those legs?"

"Gene, I certainly do!" It was as if a quarter century fell away. "Is that what this lunch is really all about?" I asked in mock suspicion.

"Oh, yeah," he replied. "Nichelle, you make an old man feel so good!"

We both laughed, and I thought how lucky I was to have a friend like Gene. We talked about old times for a while, and then Gene fixed me with a very serious look and said, "You know, someday you'll tell our story." It was the first time he'd ever said that to me, but it would not be the last.

Throughout the months of shooting, editing, and postproduction, Harve Bennett led me to believe that they would be using "Hauntingly" in the desert scene, and if not, that I would sing whatever song was chosen. Finally Harve took me aside and said that as much as he and Bill liked "Hauntingly," they had to defer all decisions on music to Jerry Goldsmith. I was disappointed but not surprised; that's the way things go in this business. There were no hard feelings.

Several weeks later, I was called back to do looping, which is where an actor rerecords her voice to a previously filmed scene where, perhaps, background noise obscured it originally, or the director wants a different effect. It usually takes three or four days to loop each part, and since I hadn't recorded my singing yet, I assumed it would be soon after the looping session. Since the time we finished shooting, I'd appeared at probably a dozen fan conventions. All the fans knew that I sang, so they would be thrilled to learn that Uhura would be singing in the new film. I was careful not to say anything about this, however, until I checked with Harve to confirm that he still planned to have me sing. Several times I asked, and each time he answered yes.

The first person I saw at the studio when I arrived to start looping was Bill.

"Hi, baby!" he said, smiling. "You know, it's really too bad about the music, because you would have done just as good a job."

Bill knew immediately from the look of surprise on my face that this was news to me. Back when they had rejected "Hauntingly," Bill too had assured me that, "Whatever song you do sing, you'll do it beautifully." It took only a few seconds before I realized that Bill had just let the cat out of the bag. When Harve came in, he was very upset, but only because he got caught with his pants down, so to speak. *Star Trek V* was Harve's fourth film with us. I'll admit he was a very good producer in that he got the movies made on time and within the budget. But personally he did little to endear himself to the cast.

"Gee, Nichelle, I should have called you," he said lamely. "But I told you—"

I was crushed and felt that he had not been straight with me. Fighting back my tears, I said, "No! You have embarrassed me in front of the fans. I trusted you, and I will never forgive you, Harve. Never."

Neither Bill nor Harve knew what to say, which was just as well for their sakes. The first time I saw the finished film, in which the singer from a rock group called Hiroshima sings my part, I thought I would die. To this day, many people still believe they are hearing my voice.

Regardless of the problems in making a motion picture,

you always hope that with a little editing wizardry or an unexpected shift in audience tastes, it will come out a winner. That was not to be the case for *Star Trek V: The Final Frontier,* and we were all disappointed when it failed to hold its own at the box office against a group of record-breaking blockbusters that included *Batman.* Harve was among a number of people who felt that *Star Trek: The Next Generation* was draining our audience, but that was absurd, as would be proven with our next movie. To Bill's credit, he was very open in the press about what went wrong and accepted his share of the blame.

In the year between *Star Trek V*'s opening and when we first got word that there might be a sixth film, Harve again attempted to revive the *Starfleet Academy* concept without the original cast. Again Gene resisted it vehemently. When he first informed Harve that *Starfleet Academy* would be made only over his dead body, Harve replied with words to the effect of, "Well, that's okay, too." I'm not sure what Harve thought he would accomplish by alienating Gene, Leonard, me, the rest of the cast, and the fans. The latter proved to be Harve's undoing, as they deluged Paramount with letters opposing the proposed "prequel." Ironically, Harve defended *Starfleet Academy*—and the presumably all-new cast it would introduce—as a means of expanding the *Trek* "franchise," while at the same time laying blame for the fifth movie's sluggish box-office sales at the feet of *The Next Generation.* If he saw Gene's second *Trek* series as competition for the classic cast, what did he consider the new, third cast he proposed? Clearly, he would have been content to keep doing *Star Trek* without us.

Harve was not alone in feeling that Gene and our cast had too much to say. We each commented on the scripts; if something about our characters or our lines struck us as wrong or in violation of the well-established *Star Trek* parameters, we said so. Harve once said of his experience with us, "I had a life, it's not like I hadn't done anything else before *Star Trek*. The *Star Trek* curse is something that the poor supporting cast has to live with, but I don't." I think you can understand why when Harve left, and *Star Trek VI: The Undiscovered Country*—produced by and based on a story by Leonard—became such a resounding success in 1991, we were especially pleased.

As we approached the original series' twenty-fifth anniversary, I think everyone became acutely aware of how much time had passed. Both Jimmy and Gene had suffered near-fatal heart attacks in the eighties. But nothing seemed to diminish the fans' love for *Star Trek*. The conventions kept getting bigger and bigger, and we discovered Trekkers in some of the most unexpected places.

Like Buckingham Palace. When George called to relay Prince Andrew and the Duchess of York's invitation, I accepted with glee. Andrew and Fergie were holding a large benefit for her favorite charity, the Children's Hospital, and our presence was requested for a polo match, high tea, and skeet-shooting. George and I arrived to discover that we were the only Americans in attendance; all the other guests were British film and theater stars. Andrew, the epitome of charm, and Fergie, so gracious yet down to earth, had us under their spell.

I will never forget this day as long as I live, and George will never forgive me for it, either. Andrew and Fergie arranged a space-age skeet-shoot in our honor. It was really something, using laser beams rather than buckshot to "hit" the clay pigeons. It was a sunny June day but so windy that my large, wide-brimmed straw hat threatened to take flight at any moment. I don't think I took my hand off it for more than a few seconds at a time.

Andrew and Fergie decided that the laser skeet-shoot could be a competition, with men lined up on one side of the field, and women on the other. Cradling a rifle under my right arm, hanging on to my hat with my left hand, my beautiful silk dress flapping every which way in the breeze,

I was quite a sight. But out of respect to my royal host and hostess, I resolved to do the best I could in the most proper manner possible. Of course, I would never dream of removing my hat so that I could hold the rifle with both hands like everyone else did. And I was determined to shoot. So there I was, and when my turn came I swung my rifle skyward, braced it against my hip, took aim, and scored once. George led the company in laughing at my dumb good luck, but they weren't laughing long. With every shot, the electronic scoreboard lit up like a pinball machine.

Dumb luck, royal fortune, or true talent, I cannot say. But the fact is I whipped the pants off of everyone, including George, who vowed never to forgive me for stealing what we now refer to as "the royal skeet scene." Through high tea, George, a true Anglophile, was in his glory. His British accent so perfect, his little finger ever so precisely crooked, George was the most gracious loser. It was a wonderful, unforgettable day.

Elsewhere in the world, other fans were keeping the *Star Trek* legacy very much alive. I have always enjoyed a nice rapport with the fans, and they comprise an invaluable network of information. It probably began in the eighties, when a few people delicately inquired if it were true what Gene had said about me. And what was that? I would ask. That you and he . . . After so many years of jealously guarding that secret, I simply laughed and replied, "Oh, that Gene . . ." and let it go.

The first hint I had that he felt differently about it came when I presented him with an award at a Lockheed function in his honor in San Francisco. My appearance was supposed to be a surprise. Gene and I boarded the same plane earlier that day, but I convinced him I was on my way to meet a new rich boyfriend.

Later, after I gave him his award and the applause died down, he stunned everyone by remarking, "Nichelle's always surprising me. That's why I've always loved her."

As always, I smiled at the joke, certain he would go right into his acceptance speech. Instead, he said, "All these years, she's been a woman who is not only a great actress but a great lady. And what most people don't know is that if she had played her cards right, she might have been Mrs. Gene Roddenberry."

I wrote it off to a moment of indiscretion, but through the eighties, the subject kept coming up. One day over lunch, I said, "Gene, have you been telling people about us?"

I could see a trace of hurt in his eyes, when he looked up and replied, "I'm not ashamed of it, are you?"

"I'm not ashamed, Gene, but—"

"It was one of the most beautiful experiences of my life," he continued. "I don't have a problem with it."

"Well, that's all fine, Gene. But I think discretion is the better part of valor. You are married to Majel, and you have a young son now."

"He knows about it."

That took me aback, and I realized that Gene did not fully appreciate my concerns. In his eyes, everything he was saying was true, so how could it be wrong? If other people were troubled by it, that was their problem. Perhaps I was being old-fashioned, but I didn't agree.

Several years later, not long before Gene died, we were all on a *Star Trek* cruise to Bermuda: Gene and Majel, of course, and several cast members from both the original series and *The Next Generation.* About twenty of us had gathered in Gene's stateroom to talk and have some drinks. By then Gene was in a wheelchair, and some people who worked closely with him were aware that because of his failing health and the medication he was taking, he was prone to moments of confusion. I think that is what some assumed was happening when he asked me to sit on the arm of his wheelchair and took my hand.

As soon as Majel heard him say, "If she had played her cards right . . ." she laughed and headed for the door.

"That's it. I'm out of here. I've heard this one before! Meet you at the bar for champagne, Nichelle."

"She was so beautiful," Gene said as I sat beside him, "and then she left me." He talked for several minutes about our love affair as I sat there not sure whether to laugh or run. My attorney, Doug Conway, a good friend, Allen Crowe, Marina Sirtis (who plays Deanna Troi on *The Next Generation*), her fiancé, and others stood with their mouths practically hanging open, while I wished someone could beam me up. Then Gene reached for me and kissed me.

At my first chance, I stood up, smiled, and quipped, "Well, I think I've heard this one, too!"

As my friends Doug and Allen walked me back to my stateroom, they gasped, "Is that true, what Gene just said? You've never whispered a word in all these years!" No, I hadn't, yet here was Gene, telling everyone. Excusing myself, I headed for the ship's bar, where I found Majel.

"Is he through?" she asked, half-joking.

"He loves you, Majel. He really loves you," I said, as we broke open a bottle of champagne.

"I know," she replied.

"So do I," I answered.

As Spock says to his protégée Valeris early on in *Star Trek VI: The Undiscovered Country,* "All things end." We began shooting *Star Trek VI* with the full understanding that it probably would be our last screen voyage together. That's what Paramount said, that's how the script was written, and maybe it was time, after all. Still smarting from the *Star Trek V* debacle, we were relieved to have Leonard back in charge. He brought in Nicholas Meyer, who so brilliantly directed *The Wrath of Khan,* to write and direct, and for the first time since *Star Trek: The Motion Picture* Gene was involved on an almost daily basis.

The resulting film proved once again—for anyone who didn't get it before—that *Star Trek* wasn't a magical trademark you could slap on any science-fiction script and make it fly.

Just as the original series addressed current-day issues in a "safe" futuristic setting, *Star Trek VI* examined how we respond to and redefine ourselves in the face of change. Inspired by such recent real-life events as the fall of the Berlin Wall and a teetering Soviet government (which collapsed shortly after the film was released), Leonard explored the repercussions of a Klingon-led peace initiative. He placed upon Captain Kirk, who'd spent his career containing Klingons and whose son was murdered by them, the burden of delivering Chancellor Gorkon and his party safely to Earth. Because the plot has so many fantastic twists, I won't reveal it here. Suffice it to say that the film provided a fitting and satisfying end to the voyages of the Starship *Enterprise.* Of course, it soon became evident that things were going so well, some last-minute changes were added to leave the door open for a possible seventh movie.

Despite all *Star Trek VI*'s many admirable strengths and its faithfulness to the original premise, the script and the production were not without their problems. The first was explaining what became of the *Enterprise* crew once we returned to Starfleet Headquarters after we escaped Sha Ka Ree. Originally we were all to have retired from active service, although we each volunteered to return under specific conditions. Given our high status in Starfleet, that would only be an emergency of galactic proportions. Supposedly, we each would be notified by Kirk, who would personally contact each of us, bearing a special symbol or secret password. Nicholas Meyer tried to solve the problem of what happened to us in the six years between the incidents depicted in the last two films by writing up an opening prologue.

It was only logical that the men and women of the *Enter-*

prise—acknowledged as among the best the universe had to offer—would have continued leading meaningful, productive lives. After living with these characters so many years, I often speculated that several of the crewmen would be captaining their own ships, Bones teaching medicine, and Uhura heading Starfleet Command of all communications on Earth. So I was appalled to read Meyer's first draft in which we were depicted as a bunch of down-and-out losers. He had Bones out vegetating in the countryside, Chekov idly playing chess somewhere, and a bored Uhura hosting a trashy space-age radio talk show that appeared to be based on Howard Stern's.

"Absolutely not!" I said. "To put forth the idea that heroes like these can just disintegrate sends a horrible message. They should be leaders, teachers, counselors, mentors. At least make me an intergalactic Oprah Winfrey!" Gene and the rest of the cast agreed, so that when we make our first appearance, at a classified, emergency Starfleet briefing, it's clear that we are each being called away from other important duties.

One of the film's crucial themes was how we deal with prejudice. Although everyone in the Federation long hoped for an end to Klingon aggression, when it threatens to become reality they are forced to face their attitudes and the fact that absent an enemy, their lifelong purpose becomes obsolete. Given that, it was necessary to show how even members of Starfleet were not immune to some degree of bigotry. As Trekkers know, there is a lot not to like about Klingons; namely their aggressive nature and war-based culture. Through the two centuries of hostility between the Klingon Empire and the Federation, they proved themselves duplicitous, treacherous, and fearsome. Still, I believe that the way the crew's prejudice against the Klingons was presented in the film was wrong.

The most egregious example occurs in a conversation between two young crewmen moments after the Klingon delegation leaves the room. One remarks that "they all look alike," and his buddy mentions how bad they smell, adding "only top-of-the-line models can even talk." I admit that I was perhaps more sensitive to these lines because they so closely echoed the ugly remarks made throughout history about Blacks and other nonwhite ethnic groups. That connection was made uncomfortably clear in a scene immediately preceding that one. There the crew learns that Gorkon and his party have accepted Kirk's invitation to dine aboard the *Enterprise,* and Uhura was to have said, "Guess who's coming to dinner." That line, the title of a controversial 1967 film about a white woman bringing her Black fiancé to meet her parents, upset me terribly. I refused to say it and insisted it be stricken from the script altogether. Instead, it was given to Chekov.

These scenes were offensive not only because of their real-world racist implications, but the whole premise of *Star Trek* was founded on humankind's evolution toward tolerance. If Starfleet accepted only the best and brightest, would it make sense that officers dispatched to "seek out new civilizations" be so small-minded and bigoted?

I immediately wrote a letter outlining my concerns, and when Gene got his copy, he called to say, "I just read your letter, Nichelle, and I couldn't have spotted everything better myself." Despite our objections, and much to my personal disappointment and the detriment of the film's integrity, some of those lines remained. But the denigrating prologue was cut, and our characters appeared as still-important members of Starfleet. I was relieved and pleased to have achieved *that* much.

Before we began filming, a great deal of preparation went into writing a speech for Uhura to deliver in Klingon. Of course, with her being a top linguist, it should have been a snap, especially since the professional linguist who developed a Klingon language wrote it and taped it for me to learn phonetically. Ever since *Star Trek IV,* there had been a lot of pressure to retain some humor wherever possible, so midway through, Uhura's perfect, dramatic speech was scrapped. In its place is a scene where the *Enterprise* is hailed and questioned by a Klingon vessel, leaving it up to Uhura to convince them that the crew is Klingon and on a mission of mercy. Meyer envisioned Uhura at her console, surrounded by piles of musty old books, desperately paging to find the correct words. At first I protested: Books in the twenty-third century? On the Starship *Enterprise?* Maybe something on CD ROM, perhaps. Even microfilm! But Meyer, who knew me well enough by then, replied wearily, "Nichelle, just don't question me on *this.*"

I stopped myself, and stifled a chuckle. It was the last movie, after all. Forget the fact, which Trekkers would not permit us to do anyway, that Kirk had known enough Klingon in the third film to get himself beamed aboard a bird of prey. Or that the Klingons had so thoroughly mastered English that throughout our dinner, Christopher Plummer's General Chang spouts Shakespeare (which he insists is best appreciated in the original Klingon) at the drop of a gravity boot. It pleased me no end that it was Uhura—not the chief engineer nor the science officer—who figured out how to detect and destroy the elusive, invisible bird of prey. "That thing's gotta have a tailpipe, doesn't it?" Uhura reasoned. And indeed, it did, and so Uhura saved not only the *Enterprise* but any hope of intergalactic peace.

If this was to be, as Kirk says in the final scene, the "final cruise under my command," we certainly went out in style. Perhaps because we'd all been through "the last time" so many times before, the sense of finality never took hold. We went right from the set to a group interview for *Good Morning America* and a wonderful party, with lots of hugs and kisses. It was impossible to imagine anything that could truly bring the *Star Trek* we knew, nurtured, and loved to an end. And then one day that October Gene died.

Star Trek VI was dedicated, "For Gene Roddenberry," but in fact everything we ever did was for Gene. And while there are some among us who would argue, no one, nothing, in Gene's universe ever was or ever will be as important as he.

Although people know me best as Uhura, I've always considered acting the "other" thing I do. While months, sometimes years, passed without my setting foot before a camera, music filled every day of my life. Jim and I conceived a one-woman show for me after the University of California at San Bernardino invited me to present a show in honor of the great singer Ethel Waters. Since it was part of the school's Black History Month festivities, I chose to celebrate Waters's contribution to music by "becoming" several Black singing legends, including Pearl Bailey, Lena Horne, Mahalia Jackson, Eartha Kitt, and, of course, Waters. I had used a similar presentation to showcase my three-and-a-half-octave range in the solo act I did after *Porgy and Bess* and loved the challenge of combining my singing, dancing, and acting.

The show's success inspired me to expand it into a two-act musical-theater piece; a musical history, if you will, of Black women from the Roaring Twenties to the present. Not only did I include such obvious and well-known figures as Ma Rainey, Bessie Smith, and Josephine Baker, but the little-known Florence Mills, who was the first Black woman to star on Broadway and has been lost to memory largely because she was never filmed or recorded. The mid-century period was represented by Sarah Vaughan, Billie Holiday, Ella Fitzgerald, Lena, Pearl, Mahalia, dancer Katherine Dunham, and Leontyne Price, the first Black woman to sing at the Metropolitan Opera. Blues, jazz, ballads, gospel, and opera. But was it enough? No way!

I dreamed all this up in the car ride home from San Bernardino, the crowd's thunderous applause still ringing in my ears. When I announced my plans to Jim, I thought he was going to drive off the road as he exclaimed, "You're crazy!"

"I know. And the other thing I would like is a lot of original music to complement the classics, which I know you can write. And then to tie it all together: a title song for the show."

A few days later, we got around to thinking up a good title and settled on "Reflections," and after I rattled off the specifications for the song, Jim replied, "That's ridiculous! You want a love song that anyone can sing, that has some connection to all of these legends, and uses the word *reflections.* Name me one damned word that fits your spec that rhymes with *reflections.* Just one!"

"Well," I stammered, "how about connections? Dejections? Erections?"

We both burst out laughing, and Jim promised to give it a try. I was not the least bit surprised when he showed up a week later with the most beautiful song I could have imagined.

In early 1991, before we began filming the last *Star Trek* movie, I had a six-week run at the prestigious Westwood Playhouse. With less than a month's notice before opening night, we rehearsed tirelessly. Kyle came to help with the sound, lighting, and sets, while Jim wore all the hats of producer, director, writer, psychiatrist, and roadie. It was an exhausting, exhilarating effort, but on opening night I was rewarded with five standing ovations and rave reviews from both old friends in the press as well as those who came expecting to hear, "Hailing frequencies open, Captain." We were especially thrilled when many critics mistook the original songs Jim wrote for each singer for songs she had actually sung. One writer from Chicago boasted in his column of having heard Mahalia Jackson perform "I Wanna Be Rich—In the Eyes of God" shortly before her death. Little did he know that she couldn't have, since Jim didn't write the song until almost two decades after she had passed on. I can't imagine a finer tribute to Jim's impeccable songwriting talent than that. The great reviews confirmed my feeling that I was back where I belonged.

Through all of this, I never really left space behind. In the fall of 1992 I agreed to host thirteen episodes of *Inside Space* for the USA Network's fledgling SciFi Channel. For several months, I traveled back and forth between my home and New York City, and it was a hectic but ultimately rewarding time.

My favorite episode featured Dr. Mae Jemison, whom I interviewed after her historic Space Shuttle flight aboard *Discovery*. She and I both call Chicago home, so we decided I'd conduct the interview there. For a day, we were chauffeured about in a long white limousine, going to the different places where Mae's welcome-home celebrations were being staged. Mae and I had a great time, and audiences were nearly hysterical upon seeing Uhura onstage with their local astronaut heroine.

One of the week's highlights took place at an 18,000-seat auditorium, packed to capacity with seniors from the entire Chicago Unified School District and press from around the world. Naturally, the seniors from Mae's own high school were out in full force. Because she had been a cheerleader, the current cheerleading team greeted her, and when they challenged her to join them in the school fight song, Mae—in her astronaut jumpsuit, no less—rose to the occasion and, with pom-poms in hand, really showed those kids a thing or two. It was truly a sight to behold.

In the course of our interview, Mae related to me how seeing Uhura on *Star Trek* when she was younger was a factor in her decision to become an astronaut. You can't imagine how proud I was, and am, to have the privilege of knowing this wonderful, talented woman. I am especially happy to count her as a dear friend. There are many rewards in the business I'm in that cannot be measured in monetary returns or headlines. My continuing and abiding friendship with Mae Jemison is one of these.

For everything we do to make it otherwise, life is never a simple journey. We think we're plotting a course from point A to point B, when in fact practically every step we take is a detour, a digression, a side trip. Having grown to a certain age, seen my wonderful son into adulthood, and watched as my sisters and brothers and their children carve out their own lives, I never cease to be surprised at how often and how clearly my parents' influence figured. Without their example and their guidance, how different my life might have been.

My father always was, always will be, my hero, but my mother and I traveled a hard, rocky road before we became truly good friends. We had entered an unspoken truce when Daddy died, but I couldn't help longing for the mother she never was to me. All these years, probably as far back as that damn vaccination, she and I knew we loved each other, yet in my young life we weren't really *friends*. Even then, however, I relied on her wisdom and her strength. She was the Rock, the Duchess, the head of our family. Her strong arms were always there to pick me up.

In the early eighties, she was living with me and, frankly, driving me a little crazy, constantly finding fault with everything I did. One day after a routine argument had taken an ugly turn and we reconciled, she finally began to open up.

I can't really say why it happened then and not ten, thirty, forty years before, but it happened, and that's all that matters. Until then I knew so little of her life or the hardships she endured. Virtually everything I've written about my mother's early life here I learned only in the last decade of her life. My mother had so many friends, of all ages, that one time I remarked, "I wish you and I were friends. You love them more than you love me."

"Well, they have a greater need than you do," she replied.

"Is that why you never showed any affection for me?"

"Why should I have? Your father was giving you all the affection. You didn't need me."

I sat there stunned. *Of course, I needed you!* I wanted to shout. Mother told me about her early life, and how it pained her to have Daddy thwart her every dream while he lavished so much attention and encouragement on me. She was, she confessed, somewhat jealous and resentful of me. "My problem with you is that you were too damn smart for your own good. And if you'd just come out a little lighter . . .

"You know," she said finally, "you were just too much like me, and I didn't know what to do about it." Being a mother myself, I was astounded by her candor and courage. And from that day on, we began anew. We began to *talk*. We talked for hours, for days into months until we found each other. At last, I truly had a mother; at last, we became friends.

I treasure all my memories of her, but those from the last few years are special. Wherever she was, whether gambling with George Takei's mother on a cruise to Alaska, serving gourmet chitterlings to party guests, or counseling any of a number of her friends—young and old—Lishia Nichols was a *dame magnifique*. People were drawn to her, and she was, as we often joked in the family, just like E. F. Hutton: When she spoke, everyone listened. I was so very, very proud of her.

In the late eighties, Mother began to have health problems. For the most part, they stemmed from her aging; she was nearing her mid-eighties then. But toward the last year, it seemed it was one thing after another, and after a few hospital visits, she moved into a twenty-four-hour-care facility. She suffered from heart failure, pulmonary congestion, and diabetes and often forgot to take her medication, so we had no choice. Fortunately we were able to place her in one of the finest homes available, and it was nearby, so all of us—including some great-grandchildren—saw her daily. Diane's son Brett was with his Gramma every day; their bond was remarkable. Diane, Marian, and I took turns visiting Mother, bathing her, combing her hair, and keeping her in fresh, pretty clothes.

For the first months in the nursing home, Mother coped pretty well, but as her health deteriorated and she realized that she would never go home to live again, she grew extremely depressed. You go through your entire life knowing somewhere in the back of your mind that no matter what happens, your mother is only a phone call away. And whether you're twenty-two or fifty-two, whatever your problem, she'll either have the answer or at least a loving word. The day she said, "You know, I don't think I'll ever be able to live alone again," my heart broke. The realization that Mother might not always be around shook me in ways I didn't expect.

By Thanksgiving of 1992 Mother was quite ill, but we made arrangements for her to spend the holiday at my sister Marian's lovely home in San Dimas, California. It was a beautiful day, and though very weak, Mother basked in the love of her children, and especially her grandchildren and their kids. When we saw how that one visit helped her rally, we decided to make Christmas Eve at my home in Woodland Hills a special event. It gave her something to look forward to, and her depression seemed to lift as the holiday approached.

We picked her up around noon on Christmas Eve, and she looked so lovely. Later that evening she surprised us by taking a sip of champagne before we drove her back home to Pasadena. The next day was Christmas, and all her great-grandchildren and grandchildren and their parents came to see her. When Kyle and I arrived later that afternoon, she proudly showed us all the gifts she'd received. All the doctors and nurses came by to wish her well.

After they served her dinner, which was around seven or so, Kyle and I lingered for a while. Kyle and his Rama still had their special relationship, which was so beautiful to see. We were getting ready to go, and for the first time I could remember, Mother didn't ask us not to. She was lying in her bed, and she muttered a soft, almost childlike "Oh."

Smiling, she said, "You two just go on home, because I have had the most beautiful two days of Christmas. It doesn't get any better than this. Now, you two go home, now, because I'm tired." We talked a little more, and she asked if I'd seen the beautiful walking suit I'd given her, then she began to doze off.

"I love you, Nichelle," she said softly.

"I love you, Mommy," I replied, gently stroking her hair.

"I know you do. And I love you, too," to Kyle.

"Grandma," Kyle said, "you kinda like this gettin' up and getting around and going out and doin' things, right?"

"Oh yes," she replied, "you know the Duchess. She loves attention."

"Well, Grandma, if you like this, we're going to do this more often. Can I come and take you out next week?"

She smiled at my son and said, "I'd love it." And with that, we left.

My sister Ruth was involved in a car accident, so Diane, Marian, and I planned to fly to Las Vegas the twenty-seventh to be with her for her operation. My other sister, Billie, was coming in from Chicago as well. Our sister Olga had passed away some years before. I called Mother that afternoon after Christmas, and when I asked how she was, she said, "I don't know, but I feel terrible. I'll be okay, though. Don't worry about it." She asked me to let Ruth know she loved her and was praying for her, then she said, "I love you." Sometime around midnight she died peacefully in her sleep.

Because everyone at the nursing home had come to love

Mother so, they bent the rules for us and delayed notifying the morgue so they could keep her in her room, where the whole family congregated. By the time we arrived, she had been bathed and dressed in a gown, so that when I entered the room, I could have sworn she was sleeping. Her beautiful long gray hair fell over the pillow, and I marveled at how death had eased all the strain; her face, still as smooth as a baby's, looked so peaceful. I touched her hand; it was still warm. For some time I felt certain that she would open her eyes and say, "Oh, you're here." I had never seen a dead person before, so I don't know what I thought I expected. But I knew from looking at her face that my father had kept his promise: He surely had come for her at the end.

Many things changed after Mother died. From the tributes her children and grandchildren paid at her funeral, the stream of friends of all ages from every stage of her life, the cards and letters, the flowers, the kind words, I began to fully realize what an incredible woman she was. Even today, I still catch myself picking up the phone to ask her about a recipe or talk about what was on the news last night. I discovered that my sisters Diane and Marian were experiencing the same sensations. I sense her and my father around me always, and even now that brings me great comfort.

One day around the time Mother died, I was surprised to receive a phone call from Bill Shatner. After exchanging pleasantries, he got to the point: He was writing his memoirs about *Star Trek*'s early years and needed help in jogging his memory. I told him I would think about it and get back to him. The idea of Bill, of all people, writing about *Star Trek* struck me as odd. Except for when we were making or promoting a movie, until recently, Bill went out of his way to dissociate himself from Captain Kirk and the fans. He seemed to feel that had his career not been hijacked by the *Enterprise,* he might have become a leading man in films or done something more "serious." I can assure you that Bill is not the only cast member who at times has regarded his or her tour of duty in Starfleet as a mixed blessing. We've all suffered from typecasting, for example. At the same time, we all respect and appreciate *Star Trek* and are grateful to the fans who are responsible for keeping *Trek* and Gene's dream alive.

Bill, never that fond of Gene, has always bristled at the fact that he is and will always be known as Captain Kirk. As a result, he has been contemptuous of the fans for years, and they know it. That is why when he appeared on *Saturday Night Live* a few years before and played himself in the now-infamous *Star Trek* convention skit, the fans rose up in arms. It was obviously written to poke fun at the most extreme, obsessive fans, but when Bill exhorted the Spock-eared fans to "get a life" and "move out of your parents' basement," it struck an all-too-familiar chord with Trekkers. They knew when Bill said those lines, he wasn't kidding. That's how he had regarded them for a long time.

Between the call and the day we met, I spoke with several other cast members, all of whom received similar calls and none of whom was exactly thrilled at the prospect of meeting with Bill. While we were all very much devoted to preserving *Star Trek,* I think I can fairly say that we were reluctant to open up to him. I resisted saying yes or no to Bill for a couple of months. Finally, he said, "Listen. I wouldn't put in anything that would hurt you. This really isn't about you or anything. It's just that there were things that happened during the run that I can't remember."

In the end, everyone except Jimmy spoke with Bill. Without harboring any illusions that Bill was interested in leaving my home with anything more than material for his book, I suppose that between Gene's death and the end of *Star Trek* I was seeking some kind of closure, some understanding of what went on all those years.

Contrary to what Bill subsequently wrote in his first book, I did not "conspire" with other cast members to use these interviews to "confront" him. That is just one of many, many distortions and inaccuracies he presented, which I'll address later. The point is, when he arrived early one evening (not in the morning, as his book claims), I welcomed him warmly. He had never been to my house in Woodland Hills, and he admired the property and the beautiful landscaping you could see from my living room. We chatted over herb tea and hors d'oeuvres, then we started talking about *Star Trek* in earnest. In the days before Bill's visit, I'd thought about those years, and I recalled a couple of incidents—such as his "rescuing" me after I passed out on the set, our heart-to-heart conversation about his divorce—I thought he'd enjoy.

Throughout my life, I've always been writing something—songs, lyrics, poems, essays, speeches, reports. After Gene died, then my mother, I often found myself compelled to commit my memories and feelings to paper. With the encouragement of my family and friends, I began writing my autobiography, and at the time Bill and I met, my proposal was being considered by a major publisher. I had obtained an agent and set to work. As Bill set up his tape recorder and opened his notebook, I said, "Now, Bill, you should know that I am writing my own book. I am happy to help you jog your memory, but I must insist on two things: one, you may not quote me directly from these conversations; and, two, if you use any of these stories, I have to review your manuscript to see that the story is told accurately."

Bill, whose memory of his days on the series was the proverbial blank slate, agreed. We started talking, but I was immediately troubled by Bill's rather rabid interest in me and Gene. Feeling that this subject was quite personal, and knowing that Gene and Bill did not have a good relationship, I deflected Bill's attempts to lead the conversation in that direction. Before long, I realized that when Bill confessed that his memory was fuzzy, he wasn't kidding. As I recounted incidents, Bill would occasionally exclaim, "Yes, that's right!" and laugh at one thing or another, like when I referred to the studio and network brass as "suits." But overall, anything that occurred during that time that didn't directly concern Bill and Bill alone was a big blur. *Well, that was just Bill,* I thought.

After about two hours, as the conversation wound down, Bill started packing up to leave. I was thinking to myself what a nice time we'd had, how his charm still sparkled, and how the passage of time had dulled some of the hurt and disappointment. And then, in his self-satisfied way, he said, "Well, we really were one big happy family then, weren't we?"

Totally taken by surprise, I couldn't answer. Sensing my hesitation, Bill pressed. "Well, weren't we?"

"Well, no, Bill," I answered. "Not really."

"I know that for some reason Jimmy and Walter have some feelings about me, but what about you?"

Over the course of twenty-eight years, I'd witnessed Bill change from my hero to an insensitive, hurtful egotist and had seen his callousness affect everyone around him, including myself. Yet I never uttered a negative word about him. In fact, I so zealously protected the good image of Captain Kirk and our Star Trek family that some of the guys in the cast called me "Pollyanna." Now that Bill was going to present our private fiction to the world as gospel truth, I couldn't hold back. What it is crucial for you to understand, however, is that I said these things to Bill assuming he would honor his promise to me and not print them.

"Bill, I've always loved you," I said. "But you know you can be a rather difficult person to work with."

His eyes widened ever so slightly in surprise, then he said, "Please, tell me . . . I really want to know." He turned on his tape recorder, and now I realize I should have asked that he turn it off right then.

"Well, sometimes you really pissed me off royally, Bill!" I answered, laughing.

"Oh, how? I was not even aware of it."

"That's just it, Bill. You were not even aware of much of the hurt you caused. *We* were a family, but we never felt you were a member of that family."

"Well, we all joked and laughed."

"No, Bill, you joked and laughed, and everyone else just went along."

"I don't know what you mean."

"Bill, you cut people's lines, you took away their time. You really don't understand why Jimmy Doohan refuses to talk to you? Why I initially didn't want to talk to you? And why Walter is loath to talk to you? Is George going to talk to you?"

"Yes, of course. In fact, he and I had a very nice conversation—"

"Yes, Bill, because George is a diplomat. Did you know George was a politician?"

"I learned the most incredible things about George!" Bill exclaimed, and I thought, *After all these years, how did you miss the fact that George had been a delegate to the Democratic Convention, or that he was politically active?*

"Exactly, Bill! I'd known that since the series—over twenty-five years ago. Walter, Jimmy, Dee, even Leonard knew that. We knew one another, but you didn't know us. And we didn't know you."

I think I would have let it go there, except Bill retorted, "Oh?" Then with a dismissive laugh, he added, "Specifically, how did I piss *you* off?"

Gee, I thought, *Where do I begin? The cut lines? The scrapped scenes? The last-minute rewrites? The tantrums?*

"Bill, what you did was insensitive. You were looking out for your career, but we were looking out for ours, too.

When you cut lines and took away our scenes, you hurt us as people and as actors. That you don't remember that, or you don't think it's very important only makes it worse."

Bill nodded, and it seemed that he understood. In a way, I felt we'd connected, that I'd gotten through to him. We kissed goodbyes, and he thanked me and left. When months passed without a word from Bill, I assumed he didn't use any of the material I'd given him, and when I received an invitation to spend Thanksgiving at his Malibu beach house, I believed that perhaps something I'd said that day made an impression. Maybe he wanted to join the family after all.

The week before Thanksgiving I started getting phone calls from friends asking if I was going to Bill's. Yes, I said, but how did you know? Oh, they'd seen Bill on a late-night talk show and that's what he said. I didn't understand why my going to Bill's was important enough for him to mention on national television until my friend Allen Crowe told me that Arsenio Hall kicked off the interview with a line to the effect, "So, Nichelle Nichols really hates your guts, huh?" to which Bill replied that he hoped not, since I was coming to his place that Thursday for dinner.

Bill's secretary had been calling every day to confirm that I would attend, which struck me as odd, since it was a buffet rather than a sit-down dinner. Then my phone rang incessantly as reporters called to ask, "What do you think of Bill Shatner's book?" I hadn't yet read the autographed, limited-edition copy Bill sent me, but I gathered from the line of questioning that there must be something in there I wasn't going to like. Still, I took Bill at his word, and, knowing how the media relishes blowing things out of proportion, I said, yes, I did tell Bill he made me angry, and yes, the interracial kiss did in fact take place, and, no, not exactly as Bill recounted it in *TV Guide. So he got two things wrong,* I thought. *So what?*

When I arrived at Bill's house with a friend I was surprised that no one else from the cast was there. I don't recall ever having been invited to his home without at least some of the other cast members. He greeted me, and I asked, "How's that book doing?"

"It's selling like hotcakes," he replied. "But I can't go anyplace without people asking me about *you.*"

Having not read the book, I missed his meaning entirely. "Yes, I understand all the world knows I'm at your dinner today."

"Yeah. Well, I thought it was time to put this fucking thing to rest."

This what? Looking back now, I realized that Bill was as self-centered and unaware as ever. The public response to his version of our conversation—which, you'll recall, he'd promised not to publish—took him by surprise. When I finally sat down to read his book, it dawned on me that the only reason Bill invited me to his beach house on Thanksgiving was so he'd be able to say to future interviewers, "Hey, look, how bad could it be? Nichelle spent Thanksgiving with me."

I was more than upset by Bill's book. No wonder he didn't offer to let me review my comments, as he'd promised. I gather he didn't want me to know his book contained pages of my allegedly direct quotations, virtually all taken out of context. His attitude toward Gene and the rest of the cast—with the exception of Leonard—was patronizing, and his take on a number of events, particularly the interracial kiss, was just plain wrong. I did not, as Bill claims, raise a big fuss. And we did kiss. I could go on point by point, but suffice it to say this is my rebuttal to his distortions and outright lies.

One passage that angered me above the others was that in which Bill discusses my relationship with Gene—a topic I never discussed with Bill ever! I was very distressed to see that Bill wrote that I described Gene's "appetite" as "voracious," presenting it in such a way as to imply that I was speaking of Gene sexually. This "quote" had appeared all over the press around the time I sold my book. My proposal had been circulated to a select number of top editors under a heavy veil of confidentiality. Someone, somewhere blatantly, deliberately violated that confidentiality. A sentence from my proposal that stated that Gene had "a voracious appetite for *life*"—not sex—suddenly showed up everywhere misleadingly edited to imply something far juicier.

For gossip columnists and tabloids to pick up and run with something like this is distressing but no surprise. Being a celebrity, however, Bill knows how the media operates. Given my reticence to discuss Gene with him, the decades of discretion, and the "quotation" 's suggestive tone, I feel that Bill owed me the courtesy of at least asking me if it was true. Of course, it was not, and to see such nonsense in his book hurt me deeply.

Around that time, there was a lot of talk going around the studio about a seventh *Star Trek* movie. Originally, the plan was to include the classic cast with that of *The Next Generation,* whose series ceased production in early 1994. Several preliminary scripts were circulated, and although I never got to see one, several friends who did assured me that our parts were very small. Then Paramount decided to use only Bill, Leonard, and Dee of the original cast members. When the film finally got under way, Walter and Jimmy, with Bill, were included after Dee and Leonard turned it down flat. George and I weren't asked.

I was in the middle of writing this section when Walter Koenig phoned. "I know that you are working on your book, Nichelle, and I thought that you might like to know this." He then proceeded to recount an incident that occurred on the set of the seventh *Star Trek* movie, then in production. Apparently, it wasn't until Whoopi Goldberg got on the set that she learned that Uhura had no part in the film. Whoopi, who has always graciously acknowledged the inspiration she derived from Uhura, Gene, *Star Trek,* and myself as a Black actress, was livid. According to Walter, she said, "Where the hell is Nichelle? The fans have been waiting for years to see Nichelle and me and Uhura and Guinan on the screen together."

God bless that beautiful woman. She makes me proud to call her my friend.

Anything might happen, of course, and I can't say with certainty that I would refuse another chance to beam aboard the *Enterprise,* even with Captain Kirk at the helm. However, as for Bill personally, I say, with some regret and much hurt, "This communication channel is now closed. Uhura out."

I was asleep, dreaming on my living-room couch, when I was jolted awake by a loud rumbling crash and the sickening sensation that I'd been tied to a roller coaster bound for the center of the Earth. There was a momentary flash of light before everything went black, and the very floor, the ceiling, the walls, the couch began lurching and rolling and the Earth itself seemed to scream in its fury.

This is it, I thought. *The big one. I'm going to die.*

In the first blessed seconds of stillness, I made my peace with God, fearing the beast would rise up yet again and I'd never get another chance. It did not disappoint. "The Lord is my shepherd . . ." The hot-water heater crashed against its pipes, the furnace rumbled as if it were about to explode. "I shall not want . . ." Shards of crystal, china, and glass rained down, as slowly the shaking abated. "Surely goodness and mercy shall follow me all the days of my life," I whispered to whoever was listening, trying to see anything through the darkness and the ruin. "And I shall dwell in the house of the Lord . . ." The floor seemed to vibrate, some beams creaked sharply. But it was over. "Forever. Amen."

I was alone. I reached and, miraculously, found my eyeglasses. Out of the corner of my eye I saw a faint glow, and as I moved toward it I realized it was my mother's Princess phone. The quake had knocked the receiver from the cradle, and I picked it up, pressed the buttons, and almost cried with relief to hear a dial tone. As I soon learned, the quake severed every other phone line in the house. Only my mother's, which I couldn't bring myself to have disconnected after she died, remained. The whole phone system was in such chaos that, while I could dial out, I couldn't reach anyone. There was an aftershock that convinced me to sit still and wait. That little light made me feel so safe, though. I knew Mom was with me.

Later, when Jim arrived to see if I'd survived, we surveyed the damage with a flashlight. It was incredible. The large television in the living room had crashed to the floor, missing my sleeping head by inches. Peas, olives, pickles, rice, sugar, oil, honey, and milk from the refrigerator and the cabinets covered the floor in a devil's gourmet delight, seasoned with broken glass and shards of dishware. In the music room, the grand piano had crossed the room, and every piece of equipment, every tape, every piece of sheet music lay scattered in heaps all over the floor. Under the wall that had once been covered with *Star Trek* memorabilia, little Spocks, Sulus, Uhuras, starships and starfields were smashed into a scale model of Dr. McCoy's worst transporter malfunction nightmare. Where were those damn force-field shields when we needed them?

Satisfied I was in one piece, Jim hurried back to his family. Armed with a portable light, a radio, and a large bottle of water, I started dialing. I couldn't reach anyone in or around the quake area, but—miracle of miracles—I did get through to my son, Kyle, in Santa Fe, New Mexico, at six A.M. Having survived a number of "no big deal" quakes, he couldn't quite grasp the gravity of the situation. Still, always his mother, I didn't break down, but when I told him there was no gas, no water, no power, and a lot of damage, he understood and promised to try to call the rest of the family so they would know I was all right.

I ventured down the hallway to scavenge for breakfast. On one side of the floor sat a can of pâté, under the table a nice piece of cheese, and somewhere else a hunk of fresh bread and some crackers. Recalling the "earthquake kit" my second husband and I assembled twenty years ago, I knew I had to find one crucial item: a bottle of Piper-Heidsieck champagne. Lo and behold, there it was. And not far away, one single unbroken crystal flute from the set Mother had given me for my second wedding. I collected my precious cache and made my way back to the den.

The sun started to rise, and I found myself studying the champagne bubbles as they floated up to the surface. Exhausted, shaken, overwhelmed by what the next few minutes, not to mention days, would bring, I sat quietly. It wasn't the first time I'd braced myself for death, and it certainly would not be the last. I had no place to go, and, for the present, really nothing to do but sip my champagne and savor the pâté. As my mind was racing through the worst aftershocks—which would continue for weeks to come, as Earth reminded us not so gently who we really are in the grand scheme of things—the past, present, and future collided, literally and figuratively.

Yet there I was, feeling as I have so many times before: This is just the beginning, all over again. And how far I've come—beyond Uhura.

EPILOGUE

I am a firm believer in the old adage that life comes full circle. My favorite corollary of this piece of wisdom—repeated everywhere throughout the world, from ancient China to Chicago—is *What goes around, comes around.* My personal approach on this is a little bit different, however. I believe that, rather than moving in a circle and returning to the same starting point again and again, we travel the course of an infinite spiral akin to our basic physical structure—the helix of the DNA molecule. When we return to a starting point, we are at a different level, hopefully a higher one.

In this book, I have relived and related some of the more interesting experiences of my life. However, I hope *Beyond Uhura* promises something more, something consistent with my belief in the continuing upward spiral of life. Now, in the spirit of continuing the continuum, I have created a fictional character of the future: a very different, adventurous, and positive intergalactic role model. I named her Saturna, after my ruling planet.

Born in the late twenty-first century, Saturna is the offspring of a Fazisian father, Tetrock, and an Earthling mother, Nyota Domonique. Each one being an expedition leader from their respective planets, the couple meet and fall in love on Saturn's largest moon, Titan. Their scientific experiments and Saturna's conception violate the laws of both their home planets, and so Saturna's very existence becomes the dangerous secret of a Fazisian elder named Krecis, who nurtures and raises her.

Saturna's adventures begin in my first novel, *Saturn's Child,* which will be published by Putnam's in the near future and written in conjunction with noted science-fiction author Margaret Bonano. If I do say so myself (immodestly!), Saturna promises to be the most exciting female character introduced to the world of science fiction since Robert Heinlein's Friday (who, speaking of circles and spirals, Heinlein told me was inspired by Uhura).

She will be visiting your quadrant before you can say Deoxyribonucleic Acid! Watch for her as she carries into the twenty-first century the continuum initiated in *Beyond Uhura.*

And now if you'll excuse me—it's time to beam out! Thanks for being a part of this journey!

INDEX